THE EFFECT OF CHILDREN ON PARENTS
Anne-Marie Ambert, PhD

SOME ADVANCE REVIEWS

"Anne-Marie Ambert's book nicely summarizes what is known and—equally important—what is not known about the effects of children on parents. The book's strength lies in the questions that it asks and the diversity of materials from which it draws. Provides a much-needed balance to the parent-child research literature. Recommended reading for anyone seriously interested in understanding parent-child interaction."

Ralph LaRossa, PhD
Professor of Sociology
Georgia State University
Atlanta, GA

"This book will make a valuable contribution to our understanding of the ways in which children influence the lives of their parents. Dr. Ambert's book is well-researched and scholarly, yet written in a style that should make the material easily understood by nearly everyone. The proposed model for studying the effects of children on parents is one that should be useful to researchers and could eventually build a body of information on this important topic."

Lawrence Ganong, PhD
Professor, Human Development and Family Studies
University of Missouri-Columbia

The Effect of Children on Parents

HAWORTH Marriage & the Family
Terry S. Trepper, PhD
Senior Editor

New, Recent, and Forthcoming Titles:

Christiantown, USA by Richard Stellway

Marriage and Family Therapy: A Sociocognitive Approach by Nathan Hurvitz and Roger A. Straus

Culture and Family: Problems and Therapy by Wen-Shing Tseng and Jing Hsu

Adolescents and Their Families: An Introduction to Assessment and Intervention by Mark Worden

Parents Whose Parents Were Divorced by R. Thomas Berner

The Effect of Children on Parents by Anne-Marie Ambert

Multigenerational Family Therapy by David S. Freeman

101 Family Therapy Interventions edited by Thorana Nelson and Terry S. Trepper

Therapy with Treatment Resistant Families: A Consultation-Crisis Intervention Model by William George McCown and Judith Johnson

The Effect of Children on Parents

Anne-Marie Ambert, PhD

The Haworth Press
New York • London • Sydney

© 1992 by The Haworth Press, Inc. All rights reserved. No part of this work may be reproduced or utilized in any form or by any means, electronic or mechanical, including photocopying, microfilm and recording, or by any information storage and retrieval system, without permission in writing from the publisher. Printed in the United States of America.

The Haworth Press, Inc., 10 Alice Street, Binghamton, NY 13904-1580
EUROSPAN/Haworth, 3 Henrietta Street, London WC2E 8LU England
ASTAM/Haworth, 162-168 Parramatta Road, Stanmore, Sydney, N.S.W. 2048 Australia

Library of Congress Cataloging-in-Publication Data

Ambert, Anne-Marie.
    The effect of children on parents / Anne-Marie Ambert.
      p. cm.
    Includes bibliographical references and indexes.
    ISBN 1-56024-117-9 (acid-free paper). — ISBN 1-56024-118-7 (pbk.)
    1. Parenthood—Psychological aspects. 2. Parent and child. I. Title.
HQ755.8.A47 1991
306.874—dc20

                  91-8366
                  CIP

CONTENTS

ABOUT THE AUTHOR

Anne-Marie Ambert, PhD, Professor in the Department of Sociology at York University, Toronto, has been on the faculty at York University for over two decades and previously taught at three different American universities. She has authored six books and published widely on child development, family relations, and mental health in journals such as the *Journal of Marriage and the Family, The Canadian Review of Sociology and Anthropology, The Journal of Divorce, The Journal of Adolescence, The Journal of Youth and Adolescence, The Journal of Personal and Social Relations,* and *The American Journal of Psychiatry.* Her areas of research expertise are family studies and women's studies. Dr. Ambert received her PhD in sociology at Cornell University after securing several degrees in related areas at the Université de Montréal.

Senior Editor's Comments

Having recently become a parent (my little boy is ten months old as of this writing), I was very excited to read Anne-Marie Ambert's book, *The Effect of Children on Parents*, as most research has focused on parents' impact on children rather than on the influence that children exert on their parents. As a new parent, I have become increasingly aware that, indeed, this little person has had a profound effect on me, my relationship with my wife, and on our family as a whole. Reading Dr. Ambert's book has helped me put many of my own experiences in perspective, and has challenged my thinking on the interactional nature of parent-child relationships.

The Effect of Children on Parents is a carefully researched, well-written book that makes an important contribution in the field of parent-child interactions. Because the area is ground-breaking, and there is no "traditional" outline from which to proceed, Dr. Ambert had to decide which topics to include. Her choice turned out to be comprehensive and still allowed for some interesting "special" areas to be presented. For example, her chapters on the effects of children on divorced parents, the effects of chronically ill children on parents, and children's active role in mother's premenstrual syndrome indicate the scope and breadth of this work. She even includes a fascinating chapter that explores the "mother-blaming" phenomenon by examining the recent biography of Ernest Hemingway by Kenneth S. Lynn, where much of Hemingway's adult personality quirks are directly or indirectly blamed on Grace Hemingway's parenting.

Anne-Marie Ambert is highly qualified to write such a comprehensive book as this. A professor of sociology at York University, her career has shown her to be highly prolific and amazingly broad in her interests. She is the author of numerous books, including *Sex Structure* (1976, Longman of Canada); *Divorce in Canada* (1980,

Academic Press of Canada); and *Ex-Spouses and New Spouses: A Study of Relationships* (1989, JAI Press). She also has authored or coauthored over 30 chapters in books and articles for professional journals in areas as diverse as minority issues, divorce, and the effects of children on parents.

This book will be essential reading for students and researchers in the areas of family studies, sociology, and developmental psychology. Scholars will find this work particularly useful in generating new research in a heretofore neglected area. Family therapists will find it an essential resource on parent-child interaction, this time seen from the children's-effects-on-parents framework. I trust that readers will find *The Effect of Children on Parents* as enlightening, thought-provoking, and fascinating as I did.

Terry S. Trepper, PhD
Senior Editor
Haworth Series on Marriage and the Family

Acknowledgements

I am especially indebted to Maureen Baker for giving me a first chance to test my ideas in the field of child effect. Indeed, the outline of the first three chapters of this book originated in a chapter I wrote for *Families, Changing Trends in Canada*, 2nd ed., edited by Maureen Baker (Toronto: McGraw-Hill Ryerson, 1990).

I gratefully acknowledge invaluable comments on various drafts of chapters from Evelyn Kallen, Ralph LaRossa, John Peters, Barry Thorne, Livy Visano, plus two anonymous reviewers.

As I am entering the second and last leg of my career as a researcher, it is only fitting that I have come full circle in terms of areas of interest. After devoting two decades to women's studies and to the field of divorce/remarriage, I am returning to the sociology of childhood. Children were actually the focus of my dissertation — a very long time ago, it seems. I have undoubtedly been greatly influenced by my two main supervisors, Robin Williams, Jr. and Urie Bronfenbrenner.

I am grateful for the assistance provided by York University's Secretarial Services under Pat Cates' supervision. Grace Baxter and Susan Rainey are especially thanked. Leslie Lerner also helped greatly with the library work.

Terry Trepper's encouragement, as the Marriage and Family Series Editor for The Haworth Press, is gratefully acknowledged. Working with James Ice, Pamela O'Connell, Administrative Assistant, and Patricia Malone, Assistant Editor was a pleasure. I am also indebted to the copy editor, Elizabeth Myers, who provided countless stylistic improvements.

Marion Dodie's study (Chapter 10) was in part carried out under the auspices of a grant from the Social Sciences and Humanities Research Council of Canada. I am also indebted to the same granting agency for Chapter 8.

To conclude on a positive child effect note, my daughter Stèphanie drafted the Author Index last year, at age twelve. She was highly impressed by the extensiveness of my personal network: She believed that all my references were personal friends! Stèphanie completed the task this year with devotion, sacrilegious levity, and for a fee. . . .

The Effect of Children
on Parents

Mom,

Happy Mother's Day
from the kid
who taught you

patience,

understanding,

forbearance,

self-control...

...and all kinds
of other stuff
you wouldn't have needed
if you hadn't
had ME!

Introduction

I'm sorry if I am late in turning in this paper but my daughter had the chicken pox, ran a high fever, and I found it impossible to concentrate on my school work.
(*Married woman student, in a letter attached to her assignment*)

What has been the happiest moment since I've turned twenty-five is bound to be the birth of my son. I cannot describe how much joy and how much life he has added to our lives. An added bonus was that he is the first male grandchild my parents have and this has contributed a lot to my parents' respect for me, something that had been lacking in my life up to this point.
(*Married male student, in his autobiography*)

I had three children when I was between the ages of nineteen and twenty-three and I can definitely say that having children is not what it was cracked up to be. I wasn't prepared for it (motherhood) even though I am sure I was as prepared as any other woman my age. But children aren't always what you want them to be and mine turned my life upside down.
(*Mature, married woman student, in her autobiography*)

What effect I had on my parents' lives? I never thought about this until now. I can see how they affected me and I think I've covered this in the other question. . . . I was always a model child, especially as far as boys go and I honestly think that when my parents compared me with other children they were always relieved that I was turning out so well, was doing so well in school. I am certain that I messed up their plans once in a while but on the whole they were thrilled with me. I had a positive effect on them.
(*Male student, about twenty-one years old, in his autobiography*)

I don't have anything against her but I simply don't care to see her. She is not my wife any more. It's very difficult to want to be truly divorced . . . yet having to see her on a regular basis because of the children . . . it is impossible to wipe the slate clean with children.
(*Divorced father, in Ambert, 1989:31*)

No, if I had to do it over again, I wouldn't have children. I guess mine are fine, well sort of. But being a parent is a downgraded occupation in our society, plus the fact that you get no breaks from the system: everything conspires against you, against your attempts to raise children decently. I sincerely feel that this society is against parents. And then we get blamed.
(*Employed, married mother of two, age thirty-four, during an interview*)

I have presented, as an introduction, a few quotes from average people, rather than from persons who have problems or whose children present particularly difficult problems, so as to make these quotes more representative of what people in general might have to say about child effect in their own lives. Through these examples we slowly begin the process of immersing ourselves into the topic of the effects (positive and negative) that children have on their parents.

I have been asked what inspired me to write on this topic. My children? While I frankly doubt that a book on child effect would have been written by a nonparent, the actual impetus arose slowly, beginning in the years 1978-79, as I was interviewing custodial parents for a study on divorce. I was appalled, on too many occasions, by the manner in which my respondents' children were treating their mothers. (Some of this material is described in Chapter 8.) Then, there were other children who were obviously so loving.

At the human level, the stark contrast between the two sets of children opened my eyes to a reality I had never before encountered (at the time, I had a newborn and a preschooler). Suddenly, I could *see* how these children were affecting their parents. I could *see* how distressed, confused, frustrated and even fearful some mothers were, and how others were thankful for their children's emotional support. This experience of entering into strangers' lives and being in a position to view their familial scenarios unraveling, as if on strips of film which could be juxtaposed over each other, was the beginning of this book — although I certainly was not aware of it at the time.

Then, of course, as I was writing this book, I was frequently asked what it was "really" about. After explaining that I was focusing on the effect that children have, or may have, on their parents. I received a wide range of reactions. "About time!" was a frequent one. "I always thought that we have to think about what *we* do to our children. Now, that's an interesting way of looking at it." Or, in the same vein, "We're so often taught that we can make or break our children that it never had occurred to me that they could affect us adults as well." "You mean, it's acceptable to ask such a question? If our children became delinquent, isn't it *our* fault as parents? Haven't we gone wrong somewhere?" When I answered, "Not necessarily. It could be a matter of peer group," the reply was, "So, perhaps we have to think more about what other children do to our children than what we do to them."

Overall, it was revealing that the lay, but educated, public still sees parents as the prime, and often only, influence on their children. Even if they perceive that peers can be very important, they still feel that, if their adolescents suffer from the effect of the detrimental influence of their peer group, the negative consequences are still the parents' fault. Moreover, people, *especially men*, were generally surprised that we *could* think in terms of child effect. It is difficult to tell whether they had previously wished that this be so or whether the thought had actually never occurred to them. But what I can say is that parents were always delighted to learn of this "new" way of looking at things, as can be judged by the beaming smiles and the remarks which followed. It was as if I had provided them with a new vantage point from which to examine their lives.

At another level, it is also revealing to observe the reactions of students who take my honors seminar on Child Effect. These students, mainly women, are sociology, psychology, and education majors in their senior year. Thus, they already have acquired quite a substantial background in the fields related to our topic of interest.

Yet, for most, it is obviously a very difficult enterprise to think in terms of *child effect*. Unavoidably, their discussions turn to parental effect and, especially, parental causality and responsibility in child development. Even some exam questions specifically focusing on child effect are answered strictly in terms of parental causality. These students have been educated to think strictly in terms of what parents do to children.

Education and psychology majors who are doing a practicum often show great irritation with the "unprofessional" way in which parents treat their children who may have emotional problems or may be developmentally delayed. The students talk, often patronizingly, of how parents undermine their efforts and the children's treatment programs. Then we ask them, but how are these parents affected by the fact that their child has to be in a special program? For that matter, how does your attitude toward the parents affect them? What kind of support does society offer to these parents who have special-needs children? Silence frequently follows.

So basically, both for the general public and the specialized student population, the topic of child effect is one that does not belong to the daily vernacular. How children affect their parents, what kinds of children most affect their parents, and what characteristics in parents make them especially vulnerable to child effect are questions which are not commonly raised, even among professionals. Especially absent is the notion that society's response or support plays an important role in determining how children will affect their parents and whether they will do so negatively or positively. Finally, the circularity of parent-child, child-parent effects is an even less widely known or accepted phenomenon.

On the scholarly level, most textbooks on child development, family, and especially juvenile delinquency, as we will soon see, do not even raise the topic of child effect or, if they do, it is only perfunctorily so. This is doubly unfortunate because, at the theoretical level, the topics of child effect, circularity of effect, and even children as producers of their own development have been already elaborated, as reviewed in the following chapter. Thus, textbooks generally lag behind the more recent advances in the sociology of the family and in child development. This means that students as well as many professionals are being educated within an outdated perspective. Moreover, empirical research has also failed on the whole (although there are numerous exceptions) to follow through with these more recent advances in thinking about parents and children. Basically, while the topics of reciprocity of effect and child effect were brought in two decades ago, the general literature merely pays lip service to them. Child effect has yet to be integrated into mainstream research, although many theoretically-oriented scholars believe it to be a well-accepted notion.

Until now, professionals who service children and adolescents have not generally considered it to their advantage to focus on child effect, as their ideology leads them to question parents' qualifications. The child-saving industry finds families an easy target for "treatment" and for control whenever children experience problems. If child effect was taken into consideration, many professional activities would have to be altered and, in many cases, retraining might be required. Basically, clinicians in a variety of fields are still firmly entrenched within the unidirectional causality path of parents "causing" children's problems, perhaps with the exception of a group utilizing a system perspective. But, even here, the family as a system is often seen as a web of one-sided causality patterns, flowing from parents to children.

This book thus offers a review of what is already "known" but generally ignored in the area of child effect. Above all, it offers additional perspectives in this field. It is also meant to suggest avenues for research, present new ideas, and restate recently advanced ideas that have been accepted only at a very superficial level. The study of child effect as presented herein is designed to complement, not negate, the more traditional perspective of parental causality.

It is usually the tradition to end an Introduction by outlining the contents of a book. I have chosen, however, to detail the organization of this book in the first chapter which follows — that is, after we have become better acquainted with our topic.

Chapter 1

The Neglected Perspective: Children's Effect on Parents

THE QUESTIONS

What types of children are most likely to affect their parents, whether positively or negatively? In turn, what are the characteristics of parents who are most susceptible to being affected by their children? And, most importantly, what role does society play in minimizing negative child effect and fostering positive child effect?

These questions form the core of the inquiry which will be pursued throughout this book. This approach to parent-child interaction is offered because it represents a perspective which has been neglected in the vast sociology and psychology literature on parents and children. The focus of that literature has predominantly been on the process of socialization and on parental causality in parent-child interaction as well as child development. Analyses of the family unit have been informed by the concepts of socialization and child rearing. This perspective has often resulted in a narrow interpretation of family dynamics with an emphasis on the effect that parents have on their children. Interactive effects have consequently been neglected, and so has the matter of child effect.

Questions asked in the literature usually have been couched in terms of the effect that parents have on the well-being and the development of their children (Dunn and Plomin, 1990). Even more specifically, researchers have focused on the background and characteristics of parents of problem children. "In other words, what is it that is *wrong* in such children's *parents* which has contributed or even caused these children's problems?" (Ambert, 1990:149). As well, comparisons have been made between parents of well ad-

6

justed children and parents of problem children in order to see what parental aberrations, lack of skills, or the reverse produce such different children. (For review, see Peterson and Rollins, 1987.)

Such studies are individually valid: parents generally are the major influence on very young children's development and, often, one of the major influences on their adolescent children (Caspi and Elder, 1988a, 1988b). However, as a monolithic group covering most of what has been achieved in the areas of socialization, child development, and parent-child relations, these unidirectional studies represent a *scientific bias*. First, these studies obliterate from our view the matter of the effect which children have on their parents — the focus of this book. Second, the sum of these studies unwittingly generates the erroneous belief that parents are unavoidably the main and, often, *the only* influence on their children's development. And third, this research slant negates reciprocal effects between parents and children.

As we will see later on in this chapter, there fortunately exists a healthy trend, at least in some theoretical and empirical quarters, counteracting this selective perspective. Nevertheless, although these developments toward child effect and reciprocity of effect between parent and child are now solidly entrenched (Bradbury and Fincham, 1990), the literature *in general* has failed to follow suit in a substantial manner. It is thus important to keep in mind the hiatus between these enlightened developments and research publications at large. A cultural lag definitely exists between certain researchers at the forefront of paradigmatic developments and research in general, including most university textbooks on the family, child development, adolescence, and juvenile delinquency. It is consequently relevant that we examine the perspective which still predominates in the area of parent and child interaction in general, as well as in some of its sub-areas in particular.

OVERVIEW

This perspective flows in part from a well-established and popular tradition in clinical research which has determined that the first five years, or even the first two years, of an individual's life are decisive in molding the personality and, consequently, the life trajectory. This theoretical perspective, or even category of theoretical perspectives, especially of Freudian, psychoanalytical origins, posits that a child's early experiences mark him or her for life. Children's personality is set in those few early years and later adult personality will not escape from this original mold. Concepts such as interactional continuity and cumulative continuity have been used to describe how certain interactional repertoires perpetuate themselves through the life span. In other words, the child will repeat as an adult the parent-child interactions that went on in the early years.

This line of inquiry has already been recognized as far too simplistic as it negates the potential for human growth after age five (Rutter, 1981, 1987a). It is true that we possess little information as to the permanency of personality (Brim and Kagan, 1980). But it is probably fair to assume that, while certain personality traits may be enduring (example: shyness and aggressiveness, Caspi et al., 1988, Caspi and Elder, 1988b), others may be more flexible. Moreover, people's attitudes, values and coping styles can change as they age and as they encounter new situations. Adults can unlearn detrimental as well as positive patterns of human interaction learned through their parents as young children and through their peers as adolescents.

There is, indeed, in the relatively new field of adult development, an emerging scientific body of research pointing to childhood as only *one of the* stages in a person's life. Childhood is not necessarily the irreversible mold that earlier causality models have led us to visualize. Human beings can continue to develop once they have emerged into adulthood. The life span perspective focuses on development as a life-long process (Hetherington and Baltes, 1988; Lerner, 1988). This approach, which ideally attempts to integrate all stages of a person's life-span, is becoming more prominent in the literature, including the typical "child development" literature. Moreover, historical and sociological factors are slowly, albeit perhaps reluctantly, being integrated into developmentalists' frameworks (Featherman and Lerner, 1986).

For example, many children who are abused, whether psychologically, physically or both, mature to become model parents. This nonlinear development is certainly not as direct as the simplistic causality models imply: indeed, events in adolescence and young adulthood also contribute to personality development and habit formation. Moreover, in spite of whatever abuse certain children have suffered, many such children do not themselves have any constitutional inclination toward aggressiveness and abuse. Indeed, children's traits, whether inherited or developed, have to be considered as they may affect their responses both to healthy and detrimental situations.

In contrast to child abuse, there are many children who have enjoyed an ideal relationship with their parents, even have lived an idyllic childhood, including receiving genuine love, yet grow to become maladjusted adults. Severe stressors during adolescence and even adulthood can erase the benefits of a happy and well-adjusted early personality and home life. In other words, childhood is not necessarily the marker stage it was once depicted to be. Positive childhood experiences, however, certainly provide a sound basis upon which to build as life unfolds. Contrarily, negative experiences are handicapping because they have to be surmounted, thus requiring greater readjustment in individuals, and forming a more stressful basis for life. Moreover, not everyone can recover from a detrimental early life. Thus, early experiences certainly mark *many* individuals for life, but the exceptions are so numerous that this statement becomes vacuous and leaves much room for consideration of complementary explanations.

One also has to consider that an infant is born with a set of characteristics (called traits, temperament, or personality, depending on the theoretical leanings of each researcher), and it is the *interaction* between these personal characteristics and the treatment received from the parents at first, and later from other agents of socialization, that will ultimately shape a child. And it is these same characteristics that will determine how affected a child will be by a negative environment (alcoholic parents, poverty amidst affluence, a delinquent sibling) as well as by a positive environment (loving parents, a good education). For instance, an autistic child will react less positively to a loving parent and the child's early deficit may not be substantially compensated for by an ideal environment. On the other side, a child with a jovial, easy-going nature may be less affected by parental mistreatment than a fussy and nervous baby.

In addition to the scientific bias of studying only one side of an equation, this unidirectional and unidimensional causality model may have misled entire generations of parents into believing that they could control their children's future and shape its contours (Contratto, 1983). Adolescents, as well as generations of specialists who have made it their profession to service them, that is, teachers, social workers, psychiatrists and psychologists, have only too willingly swallowed this one-sided perspective which actually has made their lives easier because parents are an "obvious" target, easy to reach, easy to blame and control.

An entire book industry arose with the sole purpose of exploiting this parental vulnerability. Bottomley (1983:28) refers to the rise of the "helping professions" in the late nineteenth and early twentieth centuries as "an appropriation of parental functions, with a medical model of family health and social health." These helping professions, along with advertising, exposed families "to more subtle forms of control." Parents have been and still are confronted and intimidated by child-rearing fads which are often serially contradictory and are packaged for them by an assortment of experts who make a handsome living out of parental vulnerabilities. Needless to say, the collective parental guilt over their own presumed failures has been immeasurable. Mothers have probably been more affected than fathers in this respect. Even today, the publishing industry still capitalizes on parental vulnerability (as the fashion industry does on another set of vulnerabilities). A perusal of a regular bookstore reveals not only an entire section of expert books on parenting and child development, but slick magazines: *Parents*, *Parenting*, *Today's Parents*, and even *Working Mothers* (but not Working Fathers, although there is, at time of writing, a magazine called *Dad*).

When the process of child socialization breaks down or fails, the blame is immediately placed on parents. This is especially so when the failure results in adolescent pregnancy, teenage sexual promiscuity, substance abuse, school dropout, and delinquency, to mention only some of the problems that have high social visibility and have been widely studied within this traditional perspective. What unavoidably follows is that parents' personal traits, background, parenting skills, and marital relationships are the "causes" generally targeted for study, blame, "treatment," and policing. In contrast to more recent and enlightened perspectives on the family's environment (Bronfenbrenner and Weiss, 1983; Weissbourd, 1983; Weissbourd and Kagan, 1989; Zigler and Black, 1989), such a line of thinking implies that parental background and behavior are unavoidably responsible for the children's and even adolescents' problems. Even the research on chronically ill and handicapped children often adopts a clinically-oriented and critical position vis-à-vis parents. It is only recently that studies on the effect of these problems on the parents themselves have been initiated (for reviews: Philp and Duckworth, 1982).

While, again, there is no doubt that many parents are at least partly responsible for their children's misfortunes and misbehavior, as well as good behavior, there are many other parents who are not. As we will see later on, children are not passive and do contribute something to their own development and, especially as they age, to their behavior. Moreover, other social groups and institutions impact on children. Thus, while there is little doubt that parents are the prime influence on the average child's early development, this is possibly so only until that child enters the school system, including nursery and even day care. It should be pointed out here that we possess little knowledge on the comparative impact of parents, day care, and kindergarten on children. It is possible that even very young children are more affected by their day-care workers than by their parents, at least in certain areas of development. Consequently, as children acquire additional primary caretakers, and do so at an early age, it is only reasonable to postulate that parental effect will be lessened, especially if the values of the other caretakers differ from those of the parents. For many children, however, parents, especially mothers, remain the major influence in their lives until they enter young adulthood.

In view of the multiplicity of influences which, in our society, reach children (especially adolescents) and often compete with parental influence, it does not happen automatically that parents can remain highly influential in their children's lives. In order for this to occur, I suggest that a set of converging circumstances has to exist. That is, there has to be a conducive mix of parental and child characteristics (in terms of personality, health, and resources), as well as perhaps conducive socioeconomic circumstances. In other words, if parents are to remain strongly influential in their adolescents' lives in urbanized (compared to agricultural) regions of the United States and Canada, converging circumstances have to exist. An example would be a child whose peers' values are similar to those of her parents, who attends a school where there is little difference between parental and school goals, and who either watches few "negative" television programs or is untouched by such viewing.

In our all-encompassing and rapidly evolving technological world, it is certainly naive to assume that parents can be totally in control of their children's development. Our society offers numerous competing influences that can lessen parental effect. Consequently, it is reasonable to study how other social forces (peers, mass media, advertising, popular culture, politics, religion) affect children and, in turn, how these forces compel children to affect their parents. This multicausality model is certainly more complex to analyze than the unidirectional parent-child model. But it is a causality path which avoids the pitfalls of simplistic theories that may be scientifically erroneous and immoral considering the human costs they exact when people, especially professionals, follow them to the letter. This model does propel us into studying the effect that children have on their parents' lives, especially from an effect reciprocity perspective, as detailed in Chapter 3. Thus, the focus of this book is on *how parents are affected by their children as a legitimate topic of inquiry*.

CHILDREN AND PARENTS: THE TRADITIONAL LITERATURE

The blame for the unidirectional view of parents and children rests in part on the concept of socialization which dominates Western sociology of the family, especially that of American inspiration. It should be added, however, that, until now, relatively few sociologists have focused on the sociology of childhood (Adler et al., 1986, 1988, 1990; Ambert, 1986; Furstenberg, 1985). Consequently, the area has been the domain of developmental psychologists who, until recently, have focused strictly on the effect of parents on children, often with a total disregard for the social context of parents and children. Moreover, the focus of that developmental literature has been limited to dyadic interactions, in particular the mother-child dyad and its influence on the child (Lewis, 1984).

As construed, the concepts of socialization and even child development deprive children of the possibility of being considered as social actors in their own right (Peters, 1985). Instead, the various agents of socialization predominate in the analysis, whether actors such as parents or organizations/institutions such as schools and even the various media. Within this context, the child is merely a *recipient* and is a future product. It logically follows that parents cannot be recipients at the same time as agents. With this perspective, parents "receive" the child, yes, but cannot receive *from* the child. The psychologization of children (as human "becomings" rather than human "actuals") is preventing us from focusing on the fact that children "have important *sociological* attributes" (Qvortrup, 1985:130) and perform social functions. Thorne (1987) discusses this in terms of attributing agency to children.

The concept of socialization, as construed in mainstream sociological theory and strongly influenced by a Freudian perspective (Wentworth, 1980:23), precludes interaction and reciprocity between parent and child. This view of socialization has also been reinforced by functionalist sociologists, especially of Parsonian inspiration, with the resultant equation of socialization with internalization (Parsons, 1951, Parsons and Bales, 1955), and the confusion between the two concepts (Long and Hadden, 1985).

In this tightly constructed view of family functioning, the child as a social actor would have represented a serious dysfunction. Within this perspective, parents more or less produce their children. In contrast, more recent research clearly indicates that children are in great part, at the very least participants in their own development, and even co-producers in this enterprise (Scarr and McCartney, 1983). Already, in 1980, a review of the 1970s literature on parent-child relationships pointed to a redirection of the research in this area to include mutual parent-child effect as well as child effect (Walters and Walters, 1980). The contents of the review, however, clearly indicate that most research still proceeded within a traditional perspective, despite early warnings concerning the influence of children on parents (Walters and Sinnett, 1971).

The increased role of children as consumers in technological societies presents a particular dilemma in terms of traditional socialization theory. Children now constitute a substantial market in terms of both consumer goods (toys, games, electronic equipment, fashion) and of culture (videos, for example). As consumers, children *make decisions* for themselves and, very often, against the will or desire of their parents. For instance, few parents relish some of their teenagers' costly hairstyles, leather outfits, and baubles clicking from wrist to elbow. Not only do parents often pay for their children's decisions, but many older children, when placed in a period of overheated economy, *earn* the money to purchase these items by working part-time in fast-food outlets and as sitters.

This double role of Western children clearly places the role of parents as agents of socialization in an interesting theoretical limbo, not to mention practical question mark. The children have already been socialized by the media and by their peers. Children socialize children. Children are members of a culture of their own (Opie and Opie, 1959). Neither parents nor teachers, for better or worse, play a prominent role in this phenomenon. Actually, children have always socialized other children, especially in the context of large families and in less technological societies. But the newness of the phenomenon here resides in that it is one of consumerism rather than familism.

Children are constructed as persons in need of protection (Ennew, 1986) as women have been. The construction conforms to reality for the small child and, one might add, for any older child in a society that is economically and morally exploitative. This reality, however, shields our view of another one: parents may also need protection. Not only protection against rampant consumerism, political brainwashing in totalitarian societies, but peer group influence in some cases, and their feedback on child effect. In other words, as it becomes obvious that children *are* social actors and do contribute to their own development, it also follows that they reconstruct family life and their parents' life style.

Children can be victims of abusive parents, of disturbed, immoral, or simply uncaring and even ignorant parents. But, if one accepts the reality of the child as a social actor (rather than an idealistic *tabula rasa* that is, at the core, good or even angelic), one also has to accept the fact that the actor can impact negatively as well as positively on other actors, including parents.

As Alanen (1990) points out, the triangle of childhood, family and socialization "takes place within accepted notions of the other two, so that we can rarely even imagine novel relations between the three components." One "novel" relation — novel in the sense that it is only being perceived, as well as in the sense that it may not have previously existed in Western societies to its current extent — is that the direction of the socialization process is a two-way street between parents and children. As we will see in Chapters 3 and 4, however, certain types of children are more powerful actors in this respect while certain types of parents are more receptive (for the positive aspects) and more vulnerable (for the negative aspects).

The concept of socialization with its tandem of parents as agents and protectors has led to a distortion of certain realities. One of these realities is that, with the increasing labor force participation of women, extradyadic influences on children are becoming more prevalent (Feinman and Lewis, 1984). These distortions have also led to serious omissions in sociological and psychological inquiry. These distortions and omissions will be detailed through the book.

The critique of the research and theorizing on the family herein presented in abbreviated form may lead us to wonder whether *adults*, as social constructors of theories, may have a vested psychological and social interest, albeit subconscious, in avoiding the reality and the issue of child effect. Is it not possible that, as feminist Firestone once asked, we are "living out some private dream" on behalf of children when we discuss them so sentimentally (1970:94)? The parallel between the powerless position women have been depicted as having in past sociology in general and the current powerless and actor-less position of children is quite evident. It is possible that adults who perceive themselves as powerful, especially men (*pater familias*), are not comfortable with the idea of children as co-producers in their own development and as children affecting parents in ways usually not recognized. The issue definitely diminishes *adult power*.

This may be one of the reasons why many researchers pay lip service to child effect ("*of course* it exists!") and then proceed to completely forget about it in their own research. Others say, "Well, it is not a new idea, really.'' But, if it is not, why is it not integrated into mainstream research in fields as diverse as child development, family sociology, and juvenile delinquency?

In addition, the concept of child effect and of children as social actors may also be threatening to the child-saving industry. One of the methods of most of the agents is to rein in on *parents*. Children as effective social actors (and even planners) make the task rather complicated and perhaps less lucrative. It could certainly, if not ruin, at least recycle certain careers! As David Goode has cogently put it, our research material on children often reveals more about the observers than about the children (Goode, 1986:84).

CHILDREN AND PARENTS: EMERGING THEORIES

Because child care has been and is a feminine activity, it has been placed in the domain of the private. It is only when dollar signs are attached to child bearing and rearing that it transpires into the political domain. Motherwork is actually "an integral part of social reproduction" (Rosenberg, 1987:182) and, as such, is part of the public arena. Unfortunately, our society's refusal to recognize the political value of women's contribution has attributed low prestige and esteem for research in general on parent-child interaction. Similarly, it is possible that the emergence of the study of child effect is related to the greater role which women now play in academic sociology and psychology. Women may be more aware of child effect and of children as social actors because of their own child-caring activities.

In part, one may attribute the emergence of this area of study to feminist influences. The restructuring of male and female roles has spotlighted the inadequacies of the patriarchal system in meeting the needs not only of children, but of mothers as well (Rich, 1976). As most feminist-oriented researchers are women, often mothers themselves, the *structure* of their role as mothers in our societies has highlighted the fact that children have an enormous impact on the lives of their primary caretakers. Moreover, feminist writers are trying to debunk the myth of mothers as all-powerful agents in the lives of their children (Chodorow and Contratto, 1982). More recent writings of feminist inspiration attempt to reconcile the needs of children with those of mothers within a great diversity of family structures (for a review, see Dornbusch and Strober, 1988; and especially Cohen and Katzenstein, 1988). Nevertheless, we owe the literature of feminist inspiration a collective debt because of its insistent "Rethinking the Family" (Thorne, 1982).

Among the more enlightened authors, Bell and Harper preface their book *Child Effects on Adults* (1977) by underlining that the extent to which children influence their parents, as well as other caretakers, is often overlooked in the literature (Harper, 1975). Peterson and Rollins (1987), Walters and Walters (1980), and Maccoby and Martin (1983) look at socialization from the perspective of parent-child reciprocity. Bruner (1977), Stern (1977), and White (1975) also include such elements in their work. Siegal (1985) discusses the importance of the perceptions children have of their parents in the quality of parent-child relations. McLanahan and Davis (1989) examined child effect on adults' well-being and found that, between 1957 and 1976, the perceived benefit of children has declined. Clarke-Stewart (1973, 1978) found that child and mother took turns in "causing" the one to be attached to the other and that, when the father was involved, the direction of the influence became even more intricate. Elder et al. (1984) "allow for the possibility that children can be important influences in the lives of their parents" and, consequently, "view the developmental trajectory of children and parents" within a joint context. Peterson and Rollins (1987) offer a balanced review of the literature on socialization, including bidirectional effects.

Belsky et al. (1984), Lerner (1982), and Lerner and Busch-Rossnagel (1981) add to the discussion by presenting children as "producers of their own development"; they direct our attention to the circular interactions between child effect, and parental effect. For example, a collicky and moody infant who persistently fails to be comforted or to respond positively when her father holds her unwittingly discourages him from further attempts at soothing her. The father may even refrain from interacting with the baby and avoid her. Then, the father's response to the child's stimuli (frowns, cries) may inadvertently reinforce in the child an adverse pattern of interaction, or, at the very least, of avoidance.

Thus, in this way, even a small infant can lead a parent toward a pattern of response which in time will contribute positively or negatively to the child's development. Korner (1971) found that even neonates initiated four out of five of the mother-infant interactions observed. Although these authors are predominantly interested in the effect that a child has on its *own development*, their perspective can be used as a stepping stone to the focus of this book. Indeed, if children are seen as active social actors (participants) contributing to their own development, it is only one logical step to see these children as actors *upon their parents*.

Even the research on child abuse acknowledges that child characteristics can contribute to this unfortunate syndrome (Belsky, 1980). For example, fussy children or babies who cry a great deal are more likely to be targeted than are placid infants who do not arouse their parents' negative behavior. Thomas and Chess (1977) posit that negative interactions with parents can result from a child's difficult temperament (see also Webster-Stratton and Eyberg, 1982). One of the results of a study by Rutter (1978) on families with a mentally ill parent was that children with more adverse temperament were twice as likely to receive criticism from their parents as more easily adaptable children. Rutter (1982) points out that children with different temperaments elicit different responses and behaviors from those who interact with them. Tyler and Kogan (1977) have shown how mothers whose disabled children respond negatively to them often suffer from "affect turn-off." In other words, these mothers become discouraged and refrain from initiating contact with their children or become less responsive to them because they feel rejected or come to believe that they are inconsequential in their children's lives.

In 1978 an article in Psychology Today heralded for the public the new era in child effect. Unfortunately, the article did not produce the impetus it should have; perhaps it was too early and the public was not ready for it. In "Bringing up Mother," Segal and Yahraes summarized whatever little literature existed on the topic and discussed the fact that "parents are the product of the children born to them." They referred to the work of Bell, Sameroff, Thomas and Chess, whom we encounter in this book. They questioned whether it is valid, for instance, to conclude that children who exhibit an overly dependent personality do so because their parents treat them restrictively. Might it not be plausible, they asked, to conclude that parents treat them restrictively *because* the children are dependent? Such questions will be raised again in this book, especially in the chapters on delinquency and on emotional problems.

Until now, the small but burgeoning literature on child effect *has dealt almost exclusively with infants and preschoolers,* as well as with disabled children (Blacher, 1984), rather than older children or anti-social children (Bell, 1968, 1971, 1974; Lewis and Rosenblum, 1974). This is due to the fact that it is easier to study young children and their mothers (fathers are still rarely studied in this context — another result of ideological bias) than to study older children and adolescents. By the time children are six years old, mothers are less available for research as they have returned to paid employment. Similarly, the children may be more difficult to study because of all the other external influences which compete for their time and attention. There is no question about the fact that the dyad of mother/baby or mother/small child has had great appeal for researchers throughout the decades. This explains, in part, the paucity of studies on older children in the area of child effect in particular and parent/child interaction in general.

There is also a relatively small but important literature which focuses on the child as socialization agent for parents (Brim, 1968; Peters, 1985). For instance, in Peters' studies, a great proportion of the parents of young university students admitted to having been influenced (socialized) by them, in terms of both attitudes and behaviors. The areas discussed ranged from politics to sports to personal appearance and grooming. Thus, the role of children as agents of socialization is probably underestimated in the literature. This lacuna, once again, produces an image of children as passive rather than as actors.

In the 1980s, research of feminist inspiration initiated a critique of the clinical literature focusing on parents as the causative agent in their children's emotional and adjustment problems. In this vein, Chess and Thomas (1982), Caplan and Hall-McCorquodale (1985a; 1985b) have analyzed mother-blaming in clinical journals and criticized the maternal causality model which predominates (Chodorow, 1978; Konstantareas et al., 1983). Chodorow and Contratto

(1982) have criticized the works of such women authors as Friday (*My Mother/My Self*) and Dinnerstein (*The Mermaid and the Minotaur*), which imply that mothers are all-powerful in determining the lives of their children and that these children suffer for the rest of their lives because of the most minute offenses committed by their mothers (also, Caplan, 1988).

Similarly, Saraceno (1984) points out that social "policies which concern women always assign them responsibility for the children." Day care for children is associated with working *mothers*, not working fathers. Admittedly, such critical studies are still few (e.g., Spiegel, 1982), but there are more researchers than before who are recognizing the merit of a bidirectional interpretation of data (Schneider, 1987:11). Thorne (1987:98) has pointed out one additional pitfall of the mother-blaming ideology: "it distorts children's experience of the world, denying their intentionality and capacity for action within circumstances that extend beyond ties with mothers." Umberson (1989) has cogently demonstrated that it is important to consider the *content* of parent-child interaction in its potential effect on parents' well-being. All of these critiques indicate "a timely climate which allows for a reorientation of this unidirectional and often biased research on the relationship between parents and children" (Ambert, 1990:151).

Another bias in the research denounced by those who alerted us about mother-blaming is that the role of the father is completely overlooked, although the disciplines of psychology and sociology are finally beginning to address this issue (Lamb, 1987; Lamb et al., 1985; Radin and Goldsmith, 1985; Radin and Russell, 1983). The accompanying problem is that child effect, if studied at all, is studied mainly on mothers (on mothers of handicapped or chronically ill children, for instance), and rarely on fathers. Similarly, fathers are always studied as part of the social support of mothers in their parenting role, while the reverse rarely occurs. That is, mothers are rarely studied as giving support to the fathers in *their* parenting efforts. For instance, Dickie and Carnahan Gerber (1980) have found that fathers' participation in parenting depends, in part, on the extent to which mothers allow and encourage participation. But we do not know what types of fathers are more likely to yield to maternal encouragement and participate in child rearing more.

Thus, in short, there is little that we know from the literature both in terms of father effect and child effect on the father.

It is important to reemphasize that the bidirectional or reciprocity of effect literature reviewed above may lead to a false conclusion; that is, that the traditional parent-child unidirectional model is no longer used. From this, one could also argue that this book is outdated because the cause of bidirectionality and of child effect in particular has already been fought and won (Holden, 1990). Unfortunately, the above review of the literature covers just about all that has been accomplished in this field. And, when one considers how vast this field is, this does not amount to very much in terms of quantity. The fact is that most of the empirical literature is still being carried out within the traditional perspective, as a perusal of scholarly journals and, especially, textbooks will reveal only too clearly. Thus, unfortunately, the advances made by the scholars reviewed herein have yet to be followed through by the majority of researchers. This gap will become especially evident in the chapter on juvenile delinquency.

CHILDREN AND PARENTS IN HISTORICAL PERSPECTIVE

Historically, it is quite possible that it is only during our current decades that the effects of children on parents could be studied for the simple reason that, in the past, children were probably less negatively influential on their parents' lives than they currently are, with the exception of birthing for mothers. I use the term less "negatively influential" here to mean that children were then more *useful* to their parents, were less costly, and contributed to reinforce the parents' lifestyle rather than alter it as has since become the case. Children were essential *resources* to their parents, whether as sitters for younger siblings, as farm, cottage industry, and factory workers, or, overall, to raise the family's income. Thus, although children were then powerful actors within the family context, they were generally acting to *reinforce* family life and to affect parents positively in terms of the requirements of these decades. Lower-class children, often heavily immersed in factory and street activities, grew up quickly and became independent from their parents earlier, thus decreasing the potential for child effect.

Studies of Canadian, American and European material from the past century and early on in this century clearly indicate that children's earnings constituted a substantial proportion of a family's income (Haines, 1985; Hareven, 1977; Nasow, 1985; Nett, 1981; Parr, 1980). Especially in the working class, parents counted on the wages earned by their older children while the younger ones helped with household chores. Gillis (1981) found that, as late as 1914, 10 percent of English families in many communities had no other source of income but their children's wages. Moreover, farm children were always heavily involved in farm work (Parr, 1980) and often still are to this day. Under those circumstances, the family was a more complete and totalitarian institution or unit than it is today. Parents could use their children for the survival of the family and for their own benefit, whether rightly or wrongly, although this situation certainly varied by social class and urbanization level.

As was well-illustrated by the Levines (1985), a prominent value in agrarian societies is a lifelong loyalty of children to their parents: ". . . agrarian parents feel entitled to expect obedience from their offspring when they are children, loyalty from them when they are young adults, and increasing respect and support as they grow older" (1985:31). In many of these societies, by the time children are six, they work side by side with their parents. Because these societies are kinship dominated, children are a source of security, help, and prestige (Goldscheider, 1971) and, consequently, large numbers of children are desired (Freedman, 1968). Boocock (1976:422) has pointed out that a society organized around home productivity is most efficient for the care of small children because this allows for their care on a full-time basis. Moreover, agrarian societies provide greater kin involvement in child rearing; this stands in sharp contrast to the mother-child isolation in North America (Minturn and Lambert, 1964) where most productive economic activities are carried out away from home.

As Westernized, formal education becomes implanted in a society, children become less available to help their parents, and the formal education they receive often contributes to reorienting the children towards a more urban locale and a lower familial commitment. In North America, education of children as opposed to their economic contribution to the family's immediate economic needs took precedence among the middle-classes by the mid-nineteenth century. Zelizer refers to this phenomenon as the "construction of the economically worthless child" (1985:5). Children had, until then, been "objects of utility." Children, says Zelizer (p. 11), became sacred (the "sacralization" of children) as objects of sentimental value. Thus, the new ideology as well as the new economic realities shifted the family members' economic position.

Today, especially in urbanized areas, children need to use their parents' resources to survive and constitute a financial liability rather than a source of income. In this sense, children's influence has been altered toward a cost factor. Moreover, as children became less useful financially and costly to raise, there was a concurrent fertility decline. Consequently, each individual child became vested with greater parental affection, devotion, and resources. In smaller families, each child came to represent more to his or her parents emotionally. This, in turn, opened the door for *parental* emotional dependency on children.

Marvin Koller wrote, in 1974, that most parents today are proud to say that their children's well-being takes precedence over their own. Koller is referring not to infants but to adolescents. These families can be called filiocentric. "When such is the case, parents and elders follow the lead of their children and grandchildren" (p. 13). He adds that, in many ways, the "United States can be singled out as the prototype of a society that, for the first time in human history, is essentially and forthrightly youth-oriented or youth-dominated." For their part, Philippe Ariès (1962) and Lawrence Stone (1977), among other social historians, have discussed at great length the shifts which have occurred in the definition and meaning of childhood. Nevertheless, studies show that parents still place a high value on children and believe that the advantages far outweigh the disadvantages (Blake and del Pinal, 1981; McLanahan and Davis, 1989). It should be pointed out, however, that such results are attained from survey-type research in which multiple choice questions are presented. Qualitative studies would add a great deal to this dimension.

There is a growing recognition that "the roles of self-denying

adults and irresponsible child are frustrating for both parties"
(Skolnik, 1978:331). There is also recognition of the fact that
adults' instrumental needs (such as careers) and the increasing cost
of raising children may depreciate the emotional benefits that parents gain by having children (McLanahan and Davis, 1989; Packard, 1983:23). One should add here that the difficulties in raising
adolescents in a consumerist and, in some circles, drug-oriented
peer group culture can further decrease the benefits to parents. Zelizer concludes her book with a realistic note: "But, perhaps, within
the household, with proper guidance, new attitudes, and safeguards
to prevent their exploitation, children may well become invaluably
useful participants in a cooperative family unit" (1985:228; see,
also, Ennew, 1986; and Mandell, 1988). In his study of children of
the Great Depression, Elder (1974) found that children from poor
families who worked to help out developed qualities of independence, maturity in financial matters, and dependability.

At the same time as the role and status of children and adolescents in particular were evolving, so were children's rights. As
Sommerville (1982) points out, children became objects of state
protection and regulation (Feshback and Feshback, 1978; Takanishi,
1978). Not only was child labor regulated and even proscribed, but
parental obligations were encoded in the legal system (Meyer et al.,
1988) so that parental duties became more subject to public scrutiny. Moreover, in recent decades, certain proponents of children's
rights, called child liberators, have moved one step ahead: the protection (and the increase) of children's rights (to sex, for example)
which only adults now enjoy as opposed to the protection of children. This development has provoked much discussion (Baumrind,
1980; Rogers and Wrightsman, 1978; Stier, 1978). Nevertheless,
whatever the merits of the proposals and of the discussions, what is
important for us here is the fact that this debate could only take
place within a given sociohistorical context. Parallel to developments in the economic situation of children vis-à-vis their parents,
other developments in the legal (and educational) spheres of parents
vis-à-vis their children substantially altered the familial landscape,
including the potential of child effect, as parental effect was being
curtailed.

Moreover, in this technological era, parents generally share their children's attention span with a variety of media, especially television, which even infants view. Television advertising aimed at children, particularly preceding the Christmas season, presents an excellent example of the impact that this medium exercises on parents via their children. We can all recall instances in which, after seeing a game advertised, one of our small children begged us until we finally gave in and bought the desired toy, even if we could not afford it.

Additionally, the values that the media portray may be antithetical to those of parents, thus potentially diminishing parental influence, or, at the very least, diluting it. Allan Bloom, a prominent critic of our education system, even contends, rightly or wrongly, that rock music, universally listened to in North America by children, has resulted in "nothing less than parents' loss of control over their children's moral education at a time when no one else is seriously concerned with it" (1987:76). Neil Postman, in *The Disappearance of Childhood* (1982), cogently describes television as a medium which not only "adultifies" children but "childifies" adults. In short, parents no longer are in a position to exert as much moral influence on their children as before, once again leaving the door open wider for child effect.

Another historical element which has contributed to enhancing child effect is the invention of adolescence as a distinct social entity and the consequent influence of the peer group. We have become so conditioned to the notion that adolescence is a necessary (and often necessarily rebellious) stage in human development that we often lose sight of the fact that it is not a universal phenomenon (Benedict, 1938) but a particular cultural construction of the past century, with a particular focus on North American ideals.

Although the status of adolescents began a shift from the mid-seventeenth century in England, where, according to Musgrove (1964), adolescence was "invented," Kett (1977) sees the period between 1890 and 1920 as the crucial time when youth between fourteen and eighteen years old were labelled adolescents as economic conditions changed. (See also Demos, 1970.) In spite of these developments, preteen and teenage subcultures from a consumerist point of view are certainly a new phenomenon which arose after the Second World War in North America. As peer groups became more autonomous and salient, they also exerted more influence on children's lives. And there are indications that children become peer-oriented at an earlier age than was the case even two decades ago. All of these indicators point to an increased influence of the peer group on children with a consequent reduction of parental influence and a concurrent increase of child effect.

Adolescent behavior learned through contacts with one's peers frequently goes against the grain of parental values and expectations. Such behavior is very powerful in terms of guiding adolescents' activities, coping patterns, personality, and, as a result, parent-child interaction. For example, adolescents who abuse drugs or alcohol as a result of peer pressure may negatively affect their *parents'* lives — because of the very problems they create for their own lives.

In addition, with mandatory schooling, the educational system has at least the potential of influencing children longer and far earlier than in the past. Because of universal education, industrialization, and children's rights, children no longer work alongside their parents at a young age in our society. This structural change further deflects parental influence as well as children's usefulness. Finally, greater egalitarianism in domestic relations, with a focus on children's rights, may be another element allowing for a greater influence of children on family life. The sum of these sociohistorical developments points to heightened child independence from parents and less parental influence on children than in the past; in turn, these developments allow for the possibility of greater child effect.

Basically, what we see is that both child development and child effect on parents are areas of study which could greatly benefit from a cross-cultural as well as a cohort perspective. Different cohorts of parents will be more or less affected by different cohorts of children. In other words, even within one society, as each generation of children succeeds another, parents will be affected differentially. The "nature" of children and of parents as well as of parenting is not static but is subject to the sociohistorical context in which it is embedded.

ORGANIZATION AND FOCUS OF THIS BOOK

We will present a model to study child effect on parents. Throughout the years, many such ecological as well as some reciprocity of effect models have been presented, and there is unavoidable overlap among them and with ours (Belsky et al., 1984; Bronfenbrenner, 1979; Garbarino, 1982; Kahn and Antonucci, 1980; Lerner, 1986, 1991; Roskies, 1972; Tinsley and Parke, 1984; Whalen and Henker, 1980, to name only a few). The double advantage of the model herein presented, however, resides in its simplicity and in that it is *specifically geared toward child effect*, rather than child development, for instance. It can be used as a guide for future research, and is conducive to the development of precise research hypotheses. It suggests more areas of research than have been hitherto entertained in the literature and consequently opens up new avenues for future studies. In a nutshell, the focus of this book is strictly on child effect rather than on child development or parenting ability, as a large literature already exists in these areas.

Second, when we talk in terms of child effect, *we include both negative and positive effects*. That is, the pleasures as well as the burdens of parenting, or put otherwise, the happiness and the misery visited upon adults as a direct consequence of having children. A third difference with this book compared to previous works is that we will explore some of the specific *areas* in which children can affect their parents. In order to achieve this, we present a typology which is not meant to be exhaustive but which is nevertheless wider in scope than models focusing on broad familial subsystems (parental, marital, sibling subsystems [Minuchin, 1974]). Thus, the areas of parental lives will constitute the focus of the next chapter. Then, we will examine how children affect their parents depending on three sets of conditions: the characteristics of the children, of the parents, and of the societal response to parents and children.

In other words, it is posited that child effect on parents will depend on the types of parents and children involved, as well as the quality of the social environment within which parents and child interact (Bronfenbrenner, 1987; Bronfenbrenner and Weiss, 1983). It is interesting to note that Belsky (1985) has presented a related model to explain child abuse and the determinants of *parenting*. He focused on parents' personal background and resources, the child's individuality, and the "contextual sources of stress and support." His model clearly recognizes the feedback effect existing between child characteristics and parenting, as well as between the two and the quality of the societal response. The fact that his model and the one herein described were developed independently, each with a different focus, indicates the timeliness of such an approach.

The term "children" refers to nonadult offspring still living at home and dependent upon their parents for most of their subsistence. Adult children, and even grandchildren, constitute another promising topic of research that has yet to be well-studied from the point of view of child effect. Such topics have been omitted from this book because of space considerations.

The analysis of this book is informed by a multilevel ecological model (Bronfenbrenner, 1977, 1979; Garbarino, 1982). I have, however, placed all the ecological contexts within one caption, that of the societal response. In addition, this book is informed by a focus on *interactions* rather than unidirectional causality. One problem, as indicated above, is that circular or reciprocal interactions are difficult to investigate empirically (Lerner and Spanier, 1978; Lewis and Lee-Painter, 1974). Overall, however, no other theoretical viewpoint dominates this book. Such considerations are superseded by the model herein presented and the fact that child effect is viewed as a worthwhile research goal in itself in order to complement previous parental causality models. Thus, it is certainly not the goal of this book to invert conventional views of socialization and of parent-child causality or to replace them by simply presenting another unidirectional model. Rather, our approach rests on the complementarity and the interaction of these models.

The first set of chapters will delineate the mechanisms whereby children affect their parents. To begin with, Chapter 2 will outline the areas of parents' life which can be affected. The third chapter is devoted to child characteristics, parental characteristics, and the quality of the societal response as determinants of child effect. Chapter 4 presents a synthesis of this tridimensional model and elaborates on the new dimension of avoidable and unavoidable child effect. Two subsequent chapters, 5 and 6, will focus on certain very specific types of children. Thus, one chapter will discuss the effect that juvenile delinquency has on parents, a topic that is not studied *directly* at all in the fields of criminology and juvenile delinquency. We will then turn to emotionally disturbed children as well as difficult children and inquire into their effect on parents' lives.

These chapters will be followed by five chapters, each presenting the results of recent studies. In Chapter 7, we will look at students' perceptions and recollections of how they had affected their parents as they were growing up. Chapter 8 will present some data on the effect on adults of divorcing when they have children. In Chapter 9, we will look at the effect on parents (in mothers, in this case) of caring at home for chronically ill children who would not survive without the help of technology and advanced medicine. Chapter 10 examines the reciprocal child/parent effects in the definition and the direction of mothers' premenstrual syndrome (PMS). In Chapter 11, we will look at two case studies of mothers whose children are of a different race: what is the effect on mothers and children of "rainbow family" situations?

The book concludes with the content analysis of a literary biography in which mother-blaming is one of the key explanatory points (Chapter 12). The critique of this Hemingway biography not only fits the interdisciplinary tone of this book but provides an intriguing example of the perceived all-powerful parental causality. This is followed by the final, concluding chapter which wraps up the theoretical perspective of child effect on parents and, above all, offers additional research suggestions by focusing on topics not discussed within the framework of this book. Thus, this last chapter introduces, by way of conclusion, topics not generally presented anywhere else in the literature: we inquire about child effect on immigrant parents of Americanized children and the effect on parents of being adoptive. We also analyze child effect from a cross-cultural perspective. Finally, we conclude with a look at our ideology pertaining to "parental gratification."

Chapter 2

Areas of Parents' Lives

Our first object will be to delineate the domains of parents' lives which can be affected, whether by the mere presence of children or by specific children's behaviors, characteristics, and attitudes. Although there is an unavoidable overlap between some of these areas, I have divided parental lives into eleven major domains from which vantage point child effect can be studied with greater specificity. Another researcher who has attempted to outline areas of parental lives which can be affected by their children is Harper (1975).

As we delineate each area, we will present some examples of results from existing studies. Above all, as the chief task of this book is to generate ideas, research questions which could be studied at each level will be offered. The areas presented are those of parental health, place/space/activities, employment, economic, marital and familial, human interaction, parental relations with their community, parental personality, attitudes/values/beliefs, life plans, and feelings of control over one's life. To this list could be added the effect that the child has on parental behavior toward the child (see Harper, 1975): it is discussed under the rubric of child and parental characteristics in the following chapter.

PARENTAL HEALTH

Chronologically, the first child effect occurs in pregnancy and childbirth. The pregnant woman experiences many bodily changes and may even suffer from morning sickness, fluid retention, and, in some cases, diabetes. Her diet is likely to be changed, and if she is a smoker and drinker, she should abstain from both to protect the health of her future baby. Currently, because of sociomedical trends, often to ease the physician's schedule and insurance risk-taking, up to one-fifth of births are by caesarian section, in itself major surgery. In Quebec in 1983-84, 68.9 percent of all births were accompanied by episiotomies (Edginton, 1989:48). This procedure frequently causes subsequent sexual complications for women. Moreover, women hospitalized for childbirth are also subject to hospital-acquired infections (which afflict around 10 percent of any hospitalized population) and illnesses caused by medical treatment (iatrogenic problems, such as medication wrongly prescribed). Thus, the birth of a child becomes as much a medical event as a familial one for the parents.

Women who nurse both benefit from an enjoyable experience and have to adjust to certain hygienic conditions. It is also interesting to note another very direct child effect on the nursing mother: babies who nurse more stimulate milk production in their mother's breasts. Parents, especially mothers, report fatigue during infancy because of night duty and infant illness. Many mothers suffer from post-partum depression (Ballinger et al., 1979; Davidson, 1972). Estimates range from 20 to 80 percent depending on the definition of what constitutes post-partum emotional problems (O'Hara et al., 1990). In addition, small children are more susceptible to colds, for instance, than adults. They may have, on the average, five to nine episodes of flus and colds yearly, and even more than that in their first years in day-care centers. Parents of young children, especially mothers, who have to take care of the contagious little ones, often become ill themselves.

Research on impoverished families has found that mothers often skip meals so as to provide the basic necessities to their children. Mothers who have large families are less healthy than those who have smaller families. Not only is this difference caused by repeated child bearing and birthing, but it is so because of a heavy workload, sleep deprivation, lack of leisure, and concerns over children's health and behavior. For instance, Land (1977:175) has found that, in large families, "the mother . . . puts the needs of her husband and her children before her own." Single mothers who shoulder most childrearing responsibilities alone are especially vulnerable and are consequently a main consumer of medical resources (Belle, 1980).

Mothering disabled children has been shown to affect mothers' mental health (McAndrew, 1976; McMichael, 1971; see Chapter 9). Unfortunately, few studies have used control groups of mothers who do not have a disabled child, so that one has to be cautious in the conclusions that can be drawn (Gath, 1977; Rutter et al., 1970). In this vein, research has also been carried out to establish which maternal characteristics make mothers of handicapped children particularly vulnerable to negative child effect (Bradshaw and Lawton, 1978).

As this chapter was being written, a mother had just donated part of her liver to her ailing twenty-one-month-old daughter, a first in medical history. Physicians were very enthusiastic about this step because it opens the door to a larger supply of organs than is available when we have to wait for a person to be deceased for his or her liver to be transplanted. And, even here, it is often difficult to find as good a match as that provided when a parent-child dyad is involved, with a related genetic makeup.

The point here is that this type of organ donor program will have serious consequences for parental health, at least in the short term. Both the mother and the child will have to recover simultaneously. Who will care for them? Above all, this situation will put pressure upon parents to offer part of their liver to their children. In cases where parents already feel burdened physically or have a history of not recovering rapidly from surgery, this medical progress will represent a moral burden, and will add to their guilt load.

Cook (1988) has described well the stress suffered by mothers of mentally ill adults; added stressors consisted of physical violence from these same children. In my own research on divorce, I came across two mothers who were regularly assaulted by their teenage sons. It is obvious from the research on violent delinquents that violence against parents is not an isolated phenomenon. Unfortunately, I have not been able to locate a single study focusing specifically on the effect of such violence on various areas of the parents' lives. This is in part due to the fact that such parents go to great lengths to hide the abuse (Charles, 1986; Gelles and Cornell, 1985). Moreover, Straus et al. (1980) point out a researcher's bias in our failure to address the issue: even researchers need to preserve the myth that "all children love and respect their parents" (Agnew and Huguley, 1989:699). These few studies suggest that the mental and physical health of parents should be carefully mapped depending on the characteristics of their children. This issue will be further pursued in Chapters 9 and 10.

PLACE/SPACE/ACTIVITIES

"This area focuses on the *place* and *space* parents occupy in society as well as the *structure* of their *daily* lives. Generally, this area is considered 'natural,' and is therefore taken for granted and not studied" (Ambert, 1990:153). To begin with, parents may have to move after a child is born or may have to do so when the child begins school, whether for space considerations or to live in a neighborhood which is more appropriate to child rearing. For instance, in a Northern California study, 22 percent of the respondents who were parents replied that they had moved to the area specifically because it was "good for children" (Fischer, 1982). Moving carries economic consequences for the family in the form of a mortgage or the need to acquire furniture. In addition, this move may restrain or increase parents' community and leisure activities depending on the type of neighborhood they resettle in.

For instance, parents who move to a distant suburb may miss out on the social and recreational activities provided by the strictly urban environment. On the other side, certain parents may decide to move toward the urban core so that their child can be near a school with an advantageous curriculum. Such parents may also have to worry about the safety of their children in an area that, while educationally advantageous, may be more dangerous because of a higher rate of crime. Thus, basically, children influence where their parents will live, the space they will require and how the space will be organized (for instance, the necessity to "child-proof" a house), as well as the feelings the parents will develop concerning their space. For example, parents who cannot afford to move to a "better" neighborhood, either because of financial or racial restrictions, may find that the arrival and the growth of the child is particularly stressful. They may not have enough space and the lack of neighborhood safety will have long-term effects both on them and on their children.

Parents' *schedules* change. In order to meet their children's survival needs, especially when the children are very small, parents often have little control as to when they sleep, eat, or visit with friends and relatives. As the child ages, additional changes enter into play in the parental schedule in order to facilitate a variety of requirements from the school system as well as extra-curricular activities. One research question which immediately comes to mind in this respect is whether middle-class parents' schedules are more (or less) altered by their children's requisites than are the schedules of working-class parents. Indeed, middle-class children are frequently involved in a vast array of extra-curricular activities such as ballet lessons, competitions, and parties. It would seem that these middle-class requirements would have a particularly strong effect on the schedule of those parents who are responsible for the "chauffeuring" of the children. On the other side of the coin, in some inner-city neighborhoods parents are so afraid for their children's safety that they accompany them to school and return to pick them up — walking all the way.

Parents' *activities* are also altered (LaRossa and LaRossa, 1981). For instance, lovemaking may become less frequent and more inhibited. In addition, parents' freedom of movement becomes more restricted after the arrival of a first child: they can no longer simply leave the house whenever they so desire (Hoffman and Manis, 1979; Vinokur-Kaplan, 1977). Loss of freedom is indeed the disadvantage that both parents and adults in general mention the most frequently in this respect. Moreover, after the birth of a first or a second child, the mother may have to abandon her job (Burton, 1975; Baldwin, 1977; Moss and Silver, 1972), or find one that is less demanding, or is closer to home. Thus it can be said that *mothers'* activities will be even more affected than fathers'.

Parents experience varied degrees of restrictiveness in terms of activities they might have previously engaged in. But, at the same time, other activities related to their role broaden their horizon. For instance, parents have to meet with teachers, consult with pediatricians, play children's games, read children's books, and engage in a wide range of extra-curricular tasks at schools. In contrast, nonparents do not benefit from these contacts. When children suffer from behavioral, emotional or even academic problems, parents have to consult with a variety of professionals, not all of whom are competent. Thus, adults' activities as they become parents can be both a source of limitations and frustrations, and a source of personal growth.

Because so much time has to be devoted to child care, especially at the infancy stage, parents' *work loads* consequently grow. All the research evidence points to a more substantial work load increase for mothers than for fathers. Even studies of families with a disabled child show that only 25 percent of the fathers contribute sufficiently at home (Baldwin, 1976; McAndrew, 1976). One of the most basic domestic chores, cooking, can be greatly affected in frequency and complexity by a child's medical problems, weight, or even fussiness (Luiselli et al., 1985; Palmer and Horn, 1978; Traughber et al., 1983). Consequently, as the work load increases, additional effects are added to the list of changes in adults' lives, whether in terms of quality of the marital relationship, general well-being, time to socialize, or, as we have seen earlier, health. In our society, parents' time has to be managed more carefully (LaRossa and LaRossa, 1981) if they are to avoid stress and role overload.

But, as the child matures and acquires new skills, he or she may in turn contribute to reduced parental work load by sharing in the family's responsibilities. There is evidence, however, that parents are reluctant to resort to using their child's help for the sake of reducing their own work load. In a study by White and Brinkerhoff (1981), only 22 parents out of 790 who were given the question, "Why do you ask your children to work?" replied that it was because they needed help. Parents prefer to view child work at home as a means for the child to develop a sense of responsibility or to earn an allowance. Again, one sees here a well-ingrained reluctance to see children as social actors vis-à-vis oneself as a parent. Thus ideology has even biased sociological research, so that studies on the household division of labor have often neglected to include children. Nevertheless, there are studies indicating that older children, especially girls, help their mothers as caretakers of younger siblings or as helpers for such siblings (Cicirelli, 1976; Weisner et al., 1982; see, also, Benin and Edwards, 1990).

PARENTAL EMPLOYMENT

We have already mentioned that, upon the arrival of a baby, if a woman is employed, she is likely to take a maternal leave. She may also abandon paid employment altogether, at least until the children are older. Women physicians with children have been found, for example, to practice fewer hours than men or childless women physicians (Grant et al., 1990). Although there is a great deal of media attention on paternal leave and on fathers who become their children's primary caretakers because of maternal employment, these cases are still too few to alter significantly the general rule that maternal employment is more likely than paternal employment to be curtailed or restructured by the arrival of a child. Similarly, maternal employment can be stressful for certain women who have to juggle two roles (Cleary and Mechanic, 1983; Kessler and McRae, 1982; McLanahan and Davis, 1989; Ross et al., 1983). This may explain why mothers prefer to take some time off for the care of young children (Moen and Dempster-McClain, 1987).

It is generally mothers who are responsible for children when they are ill. Thus, the health characteristics of a child will be of great impact on a woman's occupational development during the child's infancy. A study by Galambos and Lerner (1987) has shown that certain child characteristics, such as "difficult," are important factors in determining whether a mother will return to work (also, Lerner and Galambos, 1986). (See also Chapter 6.) Carr (1988) has shown that mothers of Down's syndrome children are less likely to be employed, at all age levels of the children, than a control group of mothers. Furthermore, the characteristics of the societal response, such as the availability of quality day care, are more likely to affect maternal than paternal employment directly and to buttress negative child effect on maternal employment.

It has been suggested that the sex of the employed woman's child may have some effect on the extent of the role strain she experiences, with mothers of sons experiencing the most stress (Hoffman, 1984). For instance, Bronfenbrenner and Crouter (1982) found that employed mothers were more positive about their three-year-old daughters than their sons, while the opposite was found for nonemployed mothers. It is possible that boys' higher level of activity and lower compliance than girls' place more strain on employed women who are basically holding two jobs, one at home and one outside.

It would be interesting to compare the trajectory of the career development of married *men* who have children with that of married men who are childless. Countless studies have already indicated that career women are less likely to have children than noncareer women, and that career women with children may not advance as far as the childless ones. Now that the two-paycheck family is the norm, it is possible that children may come to affect *men's* careers more than they did in the past when mothers stayed home and could mediate between children and fathers, as well as serve as a backup in their husbands' careers. Is a man affected in his employment career differentially depending on the age at which he becomes a father?

Lein (1979) found that men were less likely to switch jobs after the birth of a first child. In other words, the new fathers felt a need for greater employment stability because of the added financial responsibility presented by the baby. When the addition of a child requires a move to a more expensive (larger) dwelling, both parents may feel obligated to seek a higher paying occupation.

FINANCIAL/ECONOMIC ASPECTS

I will be very brief in this section because this is an area of parental lives that has been much researched and discussed in the media. Moreover, the area of the economic and financial is very closely interrelated to other areas such as employment, life plans, activities, and even the health of parents.

Current estimates are that it will cost $180,000 to raise a middle-class child to age eighteen. Granted that this estimate varies slightly by region, having a child obviously represents a substantial investment for adults. At the same time, having a child may force one of the two parents to stay home, thus doubly reducing the family's financial resources. Moreover, in part because of inflation, but also because of the increasing consumerism around children, this cost has been steadily increasing. It had been estimated at only $85,000 in 1980 (Epenshade, 1980).

The period of adolescence can be a very expensive one for parents because of consumerist demands. Indeed, studies show that parents subsidize their children well into their university education and for a wide range of needs/possessions (Peters, 1988). The economic effect of children is especially acute in situations of unplanned single parenthood among teenagers and, as will be discussed in Chapter 8, in situations of separation and divorce. Divorced women with child custody are heavily penalized in this respect, and often have no other alternative than to go on welfare.

We have also summarized, in Chapter 1, the historical development of the financially expensive child phenomenon. Suffice it to say that this situation stems from the necessity to keep children dependent for educational purposes and thus to delay their economic contribution. Moreover, as we have seen, children in other types of societies are still seen as an economic asset to their parents (Miller, 1987).

MARITAL AND FAMILIAL RELATIONS

The husband and wife constitute a couple with its own dynamics. When the first baby arrives, this diminutive human addition means that the couple is transformed into a family. Or, alternatively, when a woman has a child on her own, she and her baby form a small family system. The first segment of this section focuses on marriage and, as such, does not apply to single parents who live alone with their children.

The arrival of the baby impacts on the parents as spouses according to the sex of the parents. Miller and Sollie (1980) carried out a longitudinal study of couples in the course of which the spouses were interviewed during the pregnancy, when the infant was one month old, and, finally, eight months old. One of their results showed that, while mothers became more stressed maritally, the fathers were not similarly affected (also Belsky et al., 1983).

We have, in an earlier section, mentioned the fact that the presence of children contributes to restricted spontaneity (timing, place) of sexuality between spouses. In fact, sexual spontaneity is often altered in some couples during the pregnancy itself, at times as a concern for the mother's health, but often as a result of cultural proscriptions or tastes. In addition, because of the restructuring of activities and the added work load, the spouses have less time to devote to the *marital* relationship, as its contents are often substituted for a coparental and instrumental relationship (Belsky et al., 1985; MacDermid et al., 1990). Consequently, it is not uncommon to meet middle-aged couples who have nothing to share after so many years of marriage except for their co-parental role. Such couples interact mainly within contexts created for or by their children and these interactions form the contents of their marital relationship. There is, in addition, some literature indicating that childless couples are happier maritally than those who have children (Callan, 1987; Campbell et al., 1976; Glenn and McLanahan, 1982; Glenn and Weaver, 1979).

In 1976, Thurnher found that adolescent children were the most frequent source of marital disagreement. Later on, in Chapter 7, we will see how children can affect their parents' marital life as perceived by students' recollecting on their own effect. The following is merely one quote from a student's autobiography. In this instance, child effect was negative.

> For my parents, the years fourteen through sixteen [of her life] were certainly the worse ones. I was difficult to be with to say the least. I was very sneaky and manipulative and I would play one parent against the other in order to achieve my goals which were boys, boys, boys. My parents were upset at me most of the time and used to take it out on each other because I think they were basically afraid that I would run away which I used to threaten to do all the time. They were also afraid I'd get pregnant although they never said as much. Looking back, I am surprised that my parents didn't divorce because of me. I am even ashamed as I write this.
> (*Twenty-year-old woman student*)

The literature on remarriage and stepparenting has recently focused on the effect of stepchildren in terms of marital stability and happiness (Ambert, 1986; Hobart, 1988; White and Booth, 1985). In Chapter 8, we will study the effect on adults of divorcing when they have children.

If we pass from the marital to the broader area of kin relations, we can hypothesize that the mere presence of children may contribute to better integration of a couple within the web of family relations. When the adult or the adolescent becomes a single parent, the effect may be quite different, depending on the age, class, and ethnic status of the families involved (Hogan et al., 1990). Single parenthood may place a great deal of strain on parents if they are morally opposed to such a state of affairs. They may not benefit as much from their status as grandparents, and may in fact merely inherit another child in the person of their grandchild.

While many children probably glue their parents more closely to their kin, certain children may actually act as a divisive force. For example, if grandparents meddle or disagree with the parents' childrearing practices, the adult children may resent them. Or, the grandparents could indulge the children so much that the parents may find themselves in a difficult position. These intergenerational conflicts and bonds beg to be researched, not only in themselves (as they have to some extent in the gerontology literature), but also from the point of view of child effect.

It would be interesting to learn more about what happens to siblings when one or more of them become parents. On the one hand, we already know that they interact less with the arrival of children (Leigh, 1982; Ross and Milgram, 1982). Still, do brothers and sisters see more of each other or less? If they have children of the same age, does this contribute to cement their relationship or do the children, with their varying aptitudes, become sources of jealousy and of friction? How do brothers fare in this respect compared to sisters? How do the relationships which their own children form with each other (cousins) affect, if at all, the siblings' own relationship?

HUMAN INTERACTION

Children contribute to expand adults' interactional repertoire because the parent-child relation, especially when children are very small, is a unique one. Thus, adults who are nonparents do not generally benefit from this educational experience. Indeed, as parents and children interact, they do so on a wide range of levels, whether in terms of body language, facial expressions, behaviorally, or verbally. In a unique study, parents reported that children widened parents' emotional repertoire, from intense rage to joy (Purrington, 1980). In another study by Patterson (1976), where normal preschoolers were observed with their mothers, there was a "rapid escalation in sheer decibels of noise when the mothers' attention was not rapidly forthcoming." For the better or the worse, parents have an advantage over nonparents in that they partake of a very special mode of human interaction.

Children directly affect their parents' speech pattern when the parents are in their company. Several studies have illustrated how parents use a simpler vocabulary and more repetitions when explaining something to children who are younger. As children age, parents' verbalizations to them become more complex because the parents know that the children can understand better. Thus, parents alter their speech pattern as a direct result of changes in the child (e.g., Snow, 1972).

Children may also be excellent companions to their parents. This might be especially so for younger parents, and more particularly for parents who are relatively isolated socially, or are physically disabled. Bolton (1983) reported that working-class mothers in England derived more companionable benefits by being with their children than was the case for women who were more educated. The latter found their children's conversations more boring.

At the affective level, children present additional sources of gratification or of frustration. We have already mentioned the companionable aspect to which we can add the close emotional and physical bond which generally exists between parents and child, especially between mother and child. Many mothers spontaneously comment on how surprised they were to find breast feeding their infant such a source of emotional gratification. Others mention the pleasurable physiological aspect.

In addition, children may contribute to socializing their parents to adopt new patterns of interacting. This phenomenon maybe more evident among immigrant families where the parents do not know English. In contrast, their children who are fluent in the language can explain North American attitudes, habits, as well as patterns of interaction to their parents.

Moreover, as we will see in the chapter on students' perceptions, children often nurture their parents (Boulding, 1980; deMause,

1974; see also Chapter 10). They may help their parents through bad times, may encourage them, may simply comfort them by offering to share a toy with them. They may give parents physical affection. For instance, in a study meant to test for something else (Cummings et al., 1989), children between the ages of two and five were found to offer verbal comfort to their mother who, in the course of an experiment, was being angrily confronted by a researcher. Even the proximity of a small child may have a soothing effect on parents. It would be interesting to learn more about the effect on parents of receiving physical affection from their children. Physical affection on the part of parents promotes well-being in children. We can only assume that the reverse may be equally important.

COMMUNITY

In order to meet their children's needs and to function as a family unit, parents have to reach out to the community more so than childless adults. For instance, they have to have recourse to physicians, schools, special classes, such as ballet or karate, to teams, such as hockey, to sitters, to name only a few. These social interactions can be positive or negative depending on the various contexts. For instance, parents of "gifted" children often have to organize themselves in order to procure a more enriched educational environment for their children. Had these persons not been the parents of such children, they may never have had the opportunity to form a community with other parents. Parents who have special-needs children who deviate negatively from the average may have to consult with a vast array of professionals (Kazak, 1987) and may even become advocates or activists dedicated to protecting the rights of the disabled. But, generally, it is women who serve "as mediators of outside services" in matters of health (Graham, 1985). As such, their community life is expanded with the arrival of children.

Mothers are more likely to be on welfare than childless women. Mothers, as a result, have to conform to the demands of welfare agencies and personnel who basically control their lives. Social workers and clerks scrutinize the mothers' personal lives who, in turn, have to accept the fact that "their family's boundaries will need to become highly permeable'' (Rubin and Quinn-Curran, 1983:89). In other words, as the double result of being poor and having children, these women's family life has to suffer the intrusion of nonrelated persons.

Although O'Donnell (1982) has found that parents are more active in community affairs, we would like to learn if parents' social networks are more or less *extensive* than those of childless persons. To begin with, children act as a resource in terms of augmenting the number of friends the family, as a sum of persons, has. Children have friends and the two sets of parents may become acquainted. As adults, children cohabit or marry: thus, two families become indirectly related to each other. It would also be important to know whether parents' social networks are more or less *positive* than those of childless persons. For instance, do the requisites of parenting lead adults to find their social interaction less fulfilling? Or more so? For example, Ishii-Kuntz and Seccombe (1989) have found that childless adults, especially the older ones, express a lower level of support from confidents than those who have children. But, in another study, Fischer (1982) found that women with children at home had less support and a smaller social network.

"Children may act as social facilitators (for instance, as mentioned earlier, in the case of immigrants who do not know the language of the host country) and matchmakers'' (Ambert, 1990:158). On the other hand, the requisites of child rearing may hamper adults' social relations. Children who are handicapped or difficult may also interfere with their parents' ability to form and maintain social patterns (Butler et al., 1976; Kew, 1975). We have also mentioned earlier the fact that parents have to reach out to teachers and other school personnel. Such official interactions have the potential of being either rewarding or detrimental. The latter outcome may be more likely when the child is deviant. Unfortunately, we possess relatively little information on these research questions.

PARENTAL PERSONALITY

What effect do children have on their parents' adult development? Certainly, how children impact on their parents' personalities will depend, in great part, not only on the child's age and sex, but on parents' stage of the life cycle (Elder et al., 1984). Young parents whose personalities may not be as stabilized as would be the case were they much older might be significantly more changed by having children and might be particularly responsive to certain types of children. The entire field of adult development (Clausen, 1986) would be a particularly rich laboratory for the joint study of child effect. Even family support programs are designed to some extent around the reality of parental development (Weissbourd and Kagan, 1989).

For instance, Cummings (1976) and Cummings et al. (1966) found that having a child with an abnormal development was a psychologically stressful situation that resulted in somewhat different personality profiles for the parents involved. Mothers and fathers seemed to be affected differently. Thus, the question of the effect that different types of children exert on their parents' own psychological life is a valid one and certainly needs further exploration. For instance, worry and anxiety over their children is, after financial matters, the cost that people mention most often about having children (Barnett and MacDonald, 1976; Miller and Myers-Walls, 1983). This being the case, one can only ask what the consequences are in terms of personality development at the adult level among parents.

The responsibilities of parenting frequently exert a tremendous "pull" toward maturation among young people. Having to take care of a helpless child and being faced with added financial constraints, parents may mature earlier in *some* aspects of their personalities than nonparents. At the same time, especially for women, parents may have a more restricted adult development than nonparents, perhaps especially if they became parents at a very young age and were cut-off from educational avenues.

In certain groups, a girl who has a child and a boy who fathers a child may experience, at least temporarily, a rise in their self-esteem and even in the male's sense of his own virility. Thus, in certain groups, it is possible that the failure to *produce* (as opposed to rearing) a child may be stigmatizing and may hamper adult development.

Child effect on parental personality is a theme which recurs, directly or indirectly, in subsequent chapters. Indeed, having children whose behavior deviates from the expected average is presumed to exert a strong impact on parents' adult development. Belsky et al. (1984:257) summarize the situation by suggesting that "the competence that one's offspring evince, as both children and adults (and perhaps even as parents), is likely to figure prominently in many persons' final appraisals of their own lives." At the very least, one study has shown that mothers who had difficult toddlers perceived themselves to be less effective parents (Meyer, 1988).

ATTITUDES, VALUES, AND BELIEFS

There is a great deal of literature on parental transmission of values to their children. Parents may pass on their attitudes and beliefs to their children by the example of their own behavior (as a reflection of their values), by direct teaching, and by acceptance or rejection of their children's behavior. But, while parents thusly fulfill their child*rearing* role, their children will have, at the very least, an indirect influence on their parents' own values.

New parents frequently point out that the arrival of their first child gave them an entirely new perspective on life: "I became more responsible. I now have a family to support and it is no longer me on my own." "Before, I used to not mind what went on the television set but now I do mind. I have become much more conservative because I know that these programs can affect my children." "I have always been in favor of free sex but now that my daughters are growing up it's a different matter. I simply don't see it the same way." "When I was younger I never cared much for money or material possessions but now that I have children I need these for them. I have become much more materialistic." "As a student, I did drugs but as a parent I am strictly against them. I no longer see anything positive in them."

These few comments made by parents during casual conversations point to an evolution in their value system as a result of their parental role, as a result of the age or even the sex of their children. The simple fact of having become a parent has an impact as a new perspective often opens up for the individuals. Some of these changes might have occurred because of age rather than being a parent. But it is reasonable to assume that being a parent is responsible at least in part for these changes. Although there is some literature comparing childless couples with parent couples, the issue of value change/stability as related to parental role (and child characteristics) has not been addressed.

Longitudinal studies of a group of new parents with a group of nonparents of the same age would be a first step in order to see which values change over time for both groups and which values change only for one of the two types of couples. It is also quite possible that single parents as opposed to single adults of the same age hold different values. We need to control for the possibility that people who choose to become parents have at the outset different values than people who prefer to remain childless or even people who become childless involuntarily. It might even be hypothesized that the values of the latter will be closer to those of prospective or new parents than those of nonparents by choice. Our question here is: what impact do children and the parental role have on men and women?

The presence of maturing adolescents and young adults who hold different values may be a catalytic factor in influencing parents' values. As a result, parents may become more conservative (or liberal). Or, yet, they may be presented with the more environmentally-conscious stands of their youngsters and their values may evolve in this direction. During adolescence and adulthood years, there is certainly a great deal of give-and-take which occurs between parents and children. And, of course, the children's influence may be even greater if they become highly educated, successful, or integrated into the new society in the case of immigrant parents.

One important area is parental sex-role orientation. Here as well, the entire literature has focused on the development of children's sex-typing and sex role orientation via the process of socialization, especially within the context of the family. It is possible that simply becoming a parent affects one's sex role ideology. For instance, Abraham et al. (1978) found that couples who were parents were more sex-typed than couples who were not. While the cause and effect is not clear, in the sense that it is possible that people who decide not to have children are less sex-typed, there is still the possibility that becoming a parent renders one more sex-role traditional.

Ganong and Coleman (1987a) compared parents with sons only, daughters only, and families with an equal number of both sons and daughters. They found that parents of sons were more sex-typed than parents of daughters. Specifically, fathers with sons were significantly less feminine than those who had only daughters, while mothers with sons were more feminine than those with daughters only. The authors propose that, since sons are more highly valued than daughters in our society, "then it is logical that parents would invest more in socializing them into" appropriate sex roles. "Sons have more to lose than daughters if sex role socialization is incomplete or inadequate, and parents, similarly, have more at stake" (p. 280). Consequently, parents of sons may try harder at providing an appropriate example in their own behavior and may, as a result, become more sex-typed themselves.

LIFE PLANS

Another aspect of parents' lives which we can logically expect to be affected by the presence of a child or of children is their plans for the future. These plans may refer to material resources, such as the desire of young couples who start a family to own a house. They can refer to their own career development as when a woman decides against pursuing a doctorate upon learning that she is pregnant. Or when a parent consciously decides to build his or her career in a certain geographic area so as to provide children with location stability.

It would be interesting to know whether childless persons, especially couples, plan their future more carefully and further ahead of time than do parents, or less so. It is possible, for instance, that childless persons are better able to predict their future and to plan for the outcome accordingly. They have fewer "hazards" to encounter in the form of illness in children, handicaps, expenses in the educational realm. Children, in the long term, represent more unpredictable factors. For instance, they do not always leave home when predicted (or even desired — some leave too soon, others too late), do not complete their education "on time," do not get employment as expected, or fail to marry and even to produce grandchildren! Thus, children can delay adults' plans and even wipe them out completely.

Childless persons can perhaps better afford not to plan ahead too carefully as they have more discretionary income and opportunities. Their time is more free and so are their movements. They may wish to leave certain things to chance and be more receptive to mere opportunities. Yet, one can also assume that they can plan ahead, say for an early retirement, more precisely than couples with children. Yet, in the short run, they may be more able to grasp opportunities as they materialize — be it in the form of geographic mobility, travel, or discretionary expenses.

Although the possibilities raised in the three paragraphs above seem logical, it is surprising that they have never been tested empirically. What expectations for the future do childless adults as compared to parents have? Are their plans different? Moreover, if there are differences, how do important sociological variables such as social class intervene to create additional differences or to simply attenuate potential differences? What about cultural differences?

FEELINGS OF CONTROL OVER ONE'S LIFE

The involuntarily childless, it has been found, feel less in control of their lives than those who have children by choice. One can also ask whether the voluntarily childless feel more or less in control of their lives than parents.

It could be argued that, in the old days, when children were an important resource and fecundity a source of pride, children added to adults' sense of control over their lives — and perhaps of control over life and others in general. The same argument could apply in societies that are not yet industrialized and do not have a large market economy.

Consequently, it might be argued that parents today are less in control over their own lives than the voluntarily childless. Not only do children represent many question marks in terms of the future, but the unpredictability of the life of a modern child may represent an element of instability and of insecurity in parents. As we have seen in several of the previous sections, parents are at the mercy of an array of professionals — from pediatricians, pedodentists, orthodontists, day-care workers, teachers — not to omit the demands made on them not only by their children, but also by their children's friends.

Thus, parents have to structure their schedule and have to restructure their own needs (or become burdened by guilt feelings if they do not do so) for the very survival of their infants and, later on, to meet the requisites of the development of the modern child. What effect do these requirements have in terms of feelings of control over one's life? Do parents feel as if they are controlled by an army of experts and professionals, each vying for the parents' time and imposing a variety of requirements on them?

Studies of chronically ill children, for instance, such as Chapter 9, have well illustrated how such requisites can place parents in a straightjacket. Yet, in our society, one does not need to have a chronically ill child to feel squeezed by the demands of the experts and semi-experts who care and "service" our children. A few examples will illustrate the point.

The mother of a ten-year-old girl takes the child for weekly piano lessons. The piano teacher suggests that the child is ready to become more involved, has the talent, and since there are no economic constraints on the parents, she sees no reason why the child does not come twice a week. But the mother is employed and has to chauffeur a son to *his* weekly lessons and feels that she cannot afford the *time*. She suggests that her daughter will be able to take more frequent lessons in two years when she is old enough to take the street car. The teacher shows her disappointment and replies that it is regrettable that the child "will be delayed." The mother feels guilty and annoyed. She feels that the teacher is too demanding.

In another case, a dentist requests that his young patients be checked and receive a fluoride treatment four times a year. The mother has two sons, one of whom already has to see the orthodontist several times yearly; both sons are driven to hockey or football practices weekly. In addition, the mother herself has serious dental problems and visits an assortment of dentists and doctors for a grand total of at least one visit every other week, when all her sons' dental and medical appointments are met. She feels harassed by all these health requirements. She explains to the children's dentist that her sons do not have cavities, have good oral hygiene, and two visits a year would suffice. The dentist becomes agitated and points out to her that "you are jeopardizing your sons' dental care." The mother leaves

> not knowing whether I should laugh or cry. If I listened to all of my sons' dentists and physicians and then mine, I would be in the taxi driving industry. On top of it all, I am supposed to feel guilty. They *all* seem to think that *their* own little narrow specialty deserves my unswerving priority. They're so myopic. What if I have a nervous breakdown because of their stupid demands? At least, if I were neglecting my children, they might have a right to complain!

At that point, her voice has reached a very high pitch: she definitely feels externally controlled.

A third mother (always a mother) recalls her latest "flap" with a child professional. Her eight-year-old daughter is taking gymnastic lessons: the mother drives her, half an hour from home, in the heavy traffic, three times a week. Because of the distance, the mother stays at the club where she knits, reads, and writes letters, as well as plans her meals while waiting for her daughter for three hours. But the little girl is so good that she has been promoted to the pre-competitive level which will require Saturday afternoons in addition. The mother explains to the head coach that the family goes to their cottage each weekend. "I told her that we are a busy family and we need this time to unwind. My daughter needs it as well." — "Well, you know that your daughter has all the markings of a future champion." — "I know, but she *enjoys* gymnastics and I find her too young to be at such an advanced level." — "But you may be depriving her of an exciting future." The mother does not know what to say and blurts out that she will discuss the matter with her husband.

They both decide to keep their weekends free. After a few weeks, the little girl is complaining that the coaches yell at her for nothing — and, in fact, the mother can hear it. One coach then complains that "she is falling behind." The mother is exasperated and feels sorry for her child. The child is simply "falling behind" the coaches' new expectations that have not been met by the parents. After two months, the little girl begs her mother to stop taking her to gymnastics as the coaches are always criticizing her. The mother is frustrated, feels that her child's enjoyment of life has been taken away and that the past four years have been wasted, both for the child and the mother who, at any rate, had made so many personal sacrifices for these lessons.

CONCLUSIONS

Children can affect their parents in a wide spectrum of situations. We have always taken for granted that children, by their very nature of helplessness as infants, do bring necessary changes in their parents' lives. Yet, because of the "naturalness" of this situation, we have failed to study it adequately. In the case of older children, we have failed to study it at all. When something is taken for granted, or is considered normal, it is often obliterated from our consciousness. What is taken for granted rarely becomes a topic for research as we fail to "see" the obvious and as we fail to transform the obvious into a problematic for research.

Moreover, the above sections clearly illustrate that parents can be affected by their children in many more areas or ways than has hitherto been presented in the scientific literature and in the mass media. Again, this oversight may stem from the apparent naturalness of the situation. In addition, I am certain that the entire realm of possibilities in these respects has not been fully exhausted, and that more could be added to this chapter by other researchers.

Because it is taken for granted that *parents* affect their children rather than vice versa, and because it is taken for granted that children have to be taken care of, we have also failed in our past research and discussions to distinguish between these effects which are positive and negative for parents and in which areas of their lives. In fact, it is not generally considered socially proper for parents to admit that they have problems with their children or that their children are affecting them negatively. Many parents, because of this ideology, do not even dare to admit it to themselves when the effect is negative. Hoffman (1975) and Hoffman and Manis (1979) have found that parents in the United States value having children for such reasons as kin extension, affectivity, fun and purpose in life. Other reasons mentioned were obtaining an adult status and teaching someone something. It should be noted that these valuations of children differ somewhat by sex with women placing more importance on affectivity and men more on identity and the fulfillment of their masculinity (Hoffman and Manis, 1979; Humphrey, 1977).

This chapter, however, has not offered a life span and life cycle approach. Because there is an absence of empirical literature in this field, we have not been able to look at all areas of parental lives to see how child effect can vary within the span of the parents' lives. The *development* or evolution of child effect as parents age, children age, as both age together could not be presented. Not only do we not have cross-sectional studies but longitudinal studies do not exist at all in this field. Thus, future researchers might want to inquire into the effect of children on parental health as children age and compare a group of initially very young parents with a group of late-timing parents. This technique would allow us to control for the respective aging processes of parents and children. Similarly, one might be interested in finding out how children affect their parents' self-esteem and feelings of control over their lives as both children and parents age. One could hypothesize that parents of adolescents will see a decrease, or an increase, in their feelings of control over their lives. These are only two examples of questions which could be studied from a life-span perspective.

Moreover, I have chosen to write a book on children who are below eighteen years of age. The effect of adult children, and even of grandchildren, therefore had to be left aside. Again, this should not be taken to mean that once children leave home they no longer affect their parents (and mutually, for that matter). As one parent recently put it to me, "Oh, no, the problems don't go away when the children go away, they just become different." And, as a greater proportion of our population reaches advanced ages than before, and as many of these elders may become dependent upon others for their well-being, child effect and parental effect come again to the forefront as if life had come full circle.

It is important to specify the areas of parental lives which can be subject to child effect (positive or negative) because it is logical to assume that the "goodness of fit" (Lerner and Busch-Rossnagel, 1981:26) between having children and being an adult in this society differs from area to area of life. For instance, there may be a better contextual fit between parents' life-style and children's needs than between parents' employment, sexual life, health and children's needs. Or, to be even more specific, the goodness of fit may be more deficient for some of the areas of parental lives depending on the type of child involved, the type of parents, and the adequacy of the societal response. These determinants of child effect are the focus of the following chapter.

Chapter 3

Determinants of Child Effect

In the previous two chapters, we have investigated domains in which children may affect their parents. We have alluded to some specific effects which can occur in these areas. We now take one additional step. That is, we turn to the factors which will determine whether and how child effect will take place, both in general and in any of the areas discussed in the previous chapter.

Because we are discussing *child* effect, we must now ask: what types of children affect their parents (negatively or positively)? Since the child effect studied is on parents, rather than on teachers, for instance, we also need to ask what types of parents are most susceptible to being affected by their children. Finally, since our model is ecologically oriented, and since parents-child interactions do not take place in a vacuum, we need to explore the social situations which allow for child effect, contribute to it, alleviate it, exacerbate it, or even cause it. Consequently, there are three sets of characteristics which will determine or influence child effect: the characteristics of the child, of the parents, and of the societal support for the parents and their children.

These three sets of characteristics are the focus of this chapter. Hypotheses covering the direction and the intensity of child effect are presented based on these characteristics and their combinations. Thus, when parents' and children's characteristics are considered, they are often examined jointly in light of the reciprocity of effect perspective. Throughout this chapter, we highlight topics that could be studied, and suggest research questions that have, to this day, been unexplored.

CHILD CHARACTERISTICS

The underlying assumption of this section is that not only do children enter the world "with a behavioral repertoire that actively" shapes their reactions to the environment, but also that this repertoire acts as a stimulus to influence their caretakers' responses as well as the caretakers' lives (Thomas and Chess, 1981:234). Children and parents influence each other so that the characteristics of each set of actors become a very important element in this circularity of effect.

Child characteristics are divided into demographic and personal ones.

Demographic child characteristics[1]

1. age
2. sex
3. birth order
4. singleton or twin
5. from a first marriage or a remarriage

Personal child characteristics:

6. IQ and other abilities
7. personality traits, attitudes, mental health, affectivity level, including attachment to parents
8. physical health, including birth weight
9. physical appearance/disabilities
10. school performance and achievement
11. performance and achievement in other activities (sports)
12. behavior (at home, school, with peers and in neighborhood)
13. relationship with other significant persons (peers, teachers, siblings)
14. quality and composition of sib group
15. quality and composition of peer group

---

1. The child characteristics included herein pertain to children who are eighteen and younger. Thus, the characteristics are less numerous than they would be were we to study adult children. In addition, some of the child's characteristics are assumed to be the same as those of parents (e.g., SES).

It is suggested that child effect will be greater on parents or on certain areas of parental lives depending on the above child characteristics. More specifically, I hypothesize that the more a child deviates from the socially accepted average in child traits 6 through 15, the greater the child effect on parents. This hypothesis is furthermore refined by recognizing a negative (A) and a positive (B) deviation from the average — although, in reality, we are dealing with a continuum.

(A) The more a child deviates *negatively* from the socially accepted average in traits 6 through 15, the more negative the child effect on parents.

The negative effect may be temporary, sporadic, or lifelong. It would be interesting to pursue hypotheses on the basis of temporality, but our knowledge of this topic is yet too fragmented to allow us to do so in a constructive way. To complicate matters further, many parents will also experience positive effects, in spite of the negative deviation, as they will draw on their own personal strengths to cope with the situation (Hardman et al., 1987). Above all, as will be discussed in the next chapter, I would hypothesize that the negative child effect could be largely mitigated by a favorable social response. It is also hypothesized that a child's negative deviation from the norm will impact more negatively on parents when the deviation is *perceived* to be avoidable. In this category, we would place juvenile delinquency and difficult child behaviors as opposed to, for example, a child who has cerebral palsy, a deviation which may be unavoidable at this point in time.

Each society has explicit and implicit expectations concerning what a normal child should look like, should be, and how he or she should behave. Thus, parents have expectations concerning their children even before they have one (Roskies, 1972). When the child arrives, their initial visual encounter with the infant will present the first test of how their expectations have been met (Klaus and Kennell, 1976). As the child ages, maturational expectations enter into play (Glascoe and MacLean, 1990). The child who deviates from the norm, including the normative parental expectations, will affect the parents differently compared to the child who meets or even exceeds these expectations. Varying child effect on parents ensues (as well as feedback parental effect on the child) depending on the nature of the discrepancy between norms and child.

In a research on "slow-learning" adolescents, Mink and Nihira (1986) found that "the social maladaptation of the child had a negative effect on parental community involvement; that is, the higher the social maladaptation was, the lower was the community involvement" (p. 12). But they also found that this child effect did not exist in some types of families, or was even reversed in that the parents' social involvement influenced the child's adjustment. Thus, the necessity to control for both child and parental characteristics in the study of child effect is obvious.

Researchers also have to be careful that the child characteristics we study are independent of the parental characteristics they are assumed to affect, otherwise it becomes impossible to disentangle the direction of effect (Crockenberg, 1986). For instance, one has to be very cautious when interpreting the results of studies which are based on parental reports of a child trait and of the parental response, as the parental response could have actually "caused" the trait which they perceive (but may not exist), or both could be caused by an unidentified variable external to the child-parent dyad. The same note of caution is to be given later on in the chapter on juvenile delinquency; in this instance, we urge caution when delinquents complain of parental traits which they themselves may have "caused" because of their own behaviors.

Research has shown that "difficult" children, at times called coercive children (a negative deviation), may be so uncontrollable that parenting skills break down as a result. The child in effect "replaces the parents as the dominant force in the household" (Loeber and Stouthamer-Loeber, 1986:39). The mother of a teenage runaway put it this way: "It's the most frightening thing in the world for parents to feel if they say or do the wrong thing the child will run away. Beth held running away over us like a weapon" (Chapman, 1976). In a study of chronically ill and impaired children, Tavormina et al. (1981) found that these parents often had doubts about their parenting abilities as a result of the difficulties encountered in their daily lives.

As discussed earlier, parents of children who deviate negatively from the socially accepted average have to readjust their conception of what is normal and reeducate themselves as to what to expect. A great deal of adaptation on the part of the parents is necessary (Wikler, 1981) and the discrepancy between expectations and reality may produce stress (Deiner, 1987). Two studies (Buckhault et al., 1978; Buium et al., 1974) comparing the maternal language of normal and Down's syndrome one- and two-year olds will illustrate parental adaptation. It was found that maternal language became more complex with normal children but remained constant with Down's syndrome children. These studies suggest that mothers adapt their expectations and their behavior to the characteristics of their children. Indeed, the normal children's own speech became more complex while that of the disabled children failed to improve. Similarly in a study of hyperactive children, it was found that mothers lowered their level of control after the child had been put on an activity-reducing drug (Barkley and Cunningham, 1979). These studies show that mothers *respond* to their children's idiosyncrasies, and do not necessarily "cause" them.

(B) The more a child deviates *positively* from the socially accepted average in traits six through fifteen, the greater the positive child effect on parents. For example, parents who have a musically gifted child (a positive deviation from the average) may reap praise from their relatives and friends.

This last hypothesis can be refined as follows: the effect on parents will be positive in *some domains* and perhaps even negative in others. The direction of the effect will depend on parental characteristics and the quality of the societal response. For example, an insecure parent may feel threatened psychologically by a high-IQ child while at the same time benefiting from social praise (Speed and Appleyard, 1985). If the child comes from a less-educated, lower-class background, his or her parents may feel inferior because the child overtakes them intellectually and role reversal takes place at some levels of functioning. These parents may feel helpless, especially so when the child performs well in school and they are useless to him or to her.

In contrast, more educated parents may not be negatively vulnerable to this child characteristic—quite the contrary: the "fit" between parents and child will be greater. In a majority of the cases, parents may, in addition to feeling proud, feel particularly close to the gifted child (Cornell, 1984). Educated parents may identify more with these children. On the negative side, they may also feel overwhelmed by the attention and the special lessons that these children require. Thus, the child's needs may compete for the parent's time for him or herself. The child may, in turn, make direct demands on parents for special attention and favors.

In terms of the demographic characteristics of children, there is a vast literature illustrating how a child's sex affects, first of all, the expectations that parents will have, their plans, their dreams for the child's future, the way in which they handle the child, even the color scheme of the child's room. This is where gender roles come into play. Moreover, some parents who have a daughter when they expected a son may be temporarily disappointed. Studies have documented that parents are more favorably disposed when their firstborn is a son (Pedersen, 1982; Teyber, 1983). Other studies have shown that couples with daughters or one daughter are more likely to have another child in the hope of having a son than are couples with sons. Thus, even the sex of the child affects parents' family planning.

The sex of a child combined with one parental characteristic — that of the quality of their marital relationship — has also been documented to impact on parent-child interaction. For instance, studies have found that parents of girls, especially mothers, will be more positive toward them (warmer, for instance) when the quality of their marriage is high. Less difference by parents' marital relationship, however, existed for boys (Cowan and Cowan, 1985, reported in Cox et al., 1989). Thus, when we combine the sex of the child, that is, boy or girl, with certain parental characteristics, differential parental as well as child effects are likely to be observed.

Throughout the chapters, the age of the child will come into focus as a potent determinant of child effect. For instance, there are many studies which point to the period of adolescence as one that is particularly stressful for parents because of the emergence of a variety of parent-child conflicts, especially in terms of daily life activities (Hill et al., 1985; Montemayor, 1983, 1986; Montemayor and Hanson, 1985; Smetana, 1989; Steinberg, 1981, 1988; Youniss and Smollar, 1985). We will present additional corroboration of this adolescent factor in a later chapter on students' own perceptions of their effect on their parents.

Another demographic variable which has been studied extensively in the literature on child development and mother-child interaction is the child's birth order. Studies have shown that not only later born children receive less attention than first born, but also that their arrival signals a decrease in maternal attentiveness to the older sibling (Feiring and Lewis, 1982; Kendrick and Dunn, 1980; for a review, see Peterson and Rollins, 1987:484). In turn, we should be interested in studying how later-born children affect their parents in comparison to first-born children. (The chapter on students' perceptions once again provides a glimpse into these possibilities.) The least that can be said is that the first born presents the framework within which most adults will learn firsthand their parental roles. Thus, the first born child unwittingly occupies the role of a socialization agent for his/her parents.

Twinship is a child trait which can also affect parents greatly. As Glaser (1987) points out, there are additional stresses to having twins over and above having a single child. Twins tend to be born smaller, have more medical complications, and their arrival brings in added emotional and financial strains on the parents (Ainslie, 1985). Mothers of twins spend much more time in infant-caretaking than other mothers (Gosher-Gottstein, 1979). Fathers of twins are also more likely to contribute to their care than other fathers (Glaser, 1987), although parents interact with twins individually less than parents of singletons. Twins often have a different parent as their main object of attachment.

Lytton (1977, 1980) calls twinship an ecological factor that has great impact, not only on their development, but on parental conditions as well. Parents often receive a great deal of positive social attention and may have feelings of pride that other parents do not experience. Unfortunately, the effect on parents of having twins has not been adequately studied after the early childhood period. It would be especially important to learn how teenage twins affect their parents in comparison with the average teenager. This question is particularly relevant in view of peer group effect. Are such children less or more likely to be peer-oriented, school-oriented, parent-oriented? Are they less or more likely to be cooperative with their parents? Are they less or more likely to be "rewarding" adolescents for their parents?

There is also very little empirical literature on parental adaptation to their growing (especially adolescent) children (Greif and Ulman, 1982). I am referring here to the *biological* growth and not to the psychological development of the child. What kinds of adjustments do parents of menarcheal girls have to make, for instance? And what about parents of pubertal sons? For example, early menarche is often related to poor adjustment, probably because of a lack of preparation (Brooks-Gunn and Ruble, 1983). If this is the case, then what effect does it have on parents when their young daughter suffers from anxieties and even social ostracism because of her early physical maturation? Research by Hill et al. (1985) has implied at least a temporary disturbance in parent-child relations if menarche occurs at a modal age, while the effect may persist for a longer period of time when the menarche is premature.

Similarly, there has been very little research on children's friendship networks (Rubin and Sloman, 1984) or peer groups, in terms of how these affect parents. Not only do parents often move to provide their children with a better social environment, but they choose schools and camps for their children so as to maximize their chances of forming friendships with other "good" children. How are parents affected, perhaps especially immigrant parents, by their children's peers? How does the necessity to accommodate and facilitate their children's relationships with peers change the structure and the quality of the parents' daily lives? What do parents learn through their children's friends? It is reasonable to expect that children's peers (or lack of) will have an effect on at least certain aspects of parents' lives.

As illustrated in the above selected examples, child characteristics are a key determinant of child effect on parents. We will return to this topic at greater length, as in subsequent chapters we will study the effect on parents of child characteristics which deviate negatively from the average. Juvenile delinquency, children with emotional problems, children who exhibit difficult episodes, and chronically ill children will be discussed in this respect.

PARENTAL CHARACTERISTICS

Child characteristics alone are not usually sufficient to cause *directly* an effect on the parent (Sameroff, 1975), although there are probably many exceptions to this rule, particularly as the child matures. Parental characteristics will in great part magnify, mitigate or prevent child effect. Another way of putting this is that certain parents are more vulnerable to child effect than others because of their own characteristics. The term "vulnerable" is not used with a necessarily negative connotation. It means that certain parents are more open to receiving enjoyment from their children, while other parents are more likely to be casualties. It also means that, given certain child characteristics, some parents are more likely to suffer from a negative effect than other parents with similar children.

Unavoidably, a few of the following parental characteristics overlap with areas of parental lives which can be affected. This is particularly evident for health. Moreover, several parental characteristics can themselves be the direct result of child effect. I have in mind as an example here variable 17: commitment to parenting. One could easily see how parents of difficult or rejecting children could *become* less committed to parenting as a direct result of the type of children they have. Thus, it is important to keep in mind, when studying such parental characteristics, the child and societal characteristics which could affect them.

Demographic parental characteristics:

1. parent's age (at birth of child and currently)
2. sex
3. socioeconomic status (SES): education, income, occupation
4. adoptive vs. biological
5. ethnicity and minority group status
6. immigration status
7. marital status
8. religion and religiosity

Personal parental characteristics:

9. quality of parenting they themselves had received as children
10. IQ and other abilities
11. personality, affectivity, responsiveness
12. gender role ideology and implementation (including division of labor)
13. coping patterns
14. parenting skills
15. parenting expectations
16. perception of child
17. commitment to parenting
18. health (mental and physical)
19. physical appearance/disabilities
20. material resources
21. social resources (such as friends, often referred to in the literature as "social support")
22. quality of marital relationship and family system
23. parents' other children; these children's characteristics; their number and spacing

To begin with the demographic characteristics, children affect mothers more than fathers (parents' sex — Kazak and Marvin, 1984; Veroff et al., 1981), largely because mothers are the primary caretakers. In this role, they interact with their children more than fathers do and the interactions range over a wider variety of patterns (Umberson, 1989). When parental divorce occurs, children are again generally in the single care of their mothers, while the father role vanishes in 50 percent of the cases. Thus, much of what children *do* and of what children *are* (child characteristics) is likely to affect mothers much more than fathers. Children often consciously attempt to change or influence their parents, and these attempts are directed more at mothers than fathers (Baranowski, 1978). Moreover, as Arlie Hochschild (1983) has so well illustrated, people expect more of women than of men in terms of nurture, support, and feelings. Children certainly do not escape this rule of expectations, and, as a consequence, may place more demands of this kind on their mothers than on their fathers.

To move on to other parental characteristics, a child with a low IQ (child characteristic), for instance, may have a differential effect on parents depending on their social class (parents' characteristic). Single parents may be more affected by their children's behavior than married parents, even if only because there is no other parent present to mediate (or aggravate) the relationship or to support the parent; studies have indeed found that children more often comply more to a parent's request when the other parent backs up that request (Lytton, 1979). In our society, single parents are often poorer than other parents, and this situation may exacerbate the parent-child relationship and contribute to negative effect from and for both parties. Studies also indicate that children may have a positive effect on the well-being of widowed parents (Umberson and Gove, 1989) and that divorced fathers who remain in touch with their children or have custody may also be positively affected (Ambert, 1982, 1984; Umberson, 1989).

Another example of the role of parental characteristics in child effect can be illustrated as follows: immigrant parents may be more affected, both negatively and positively, by their Americanized children than nonimmigrant parents or immigrant parents who know English and are more educated. The former have less power and are less in control of their own situation. To pursue still other examples, parents who have an autistic child may be less stressed if they have the material resources that will allow them to hire a caretaker and go on a vacation alone. Parents of a delinquent child who have just resettled to a new neighborhood where they have no acquaintances (social resources) may be more stressed than other parents who also have a delinquent child but benefit from a *supportive* group of friends.

The parents' age is another important characteristic which will impact both on parental effect and on child effect. There is evidence that very young parents, specifically adolescent mothers (as similar studies on adolescent fathers are lacking), are less responsive to their children's needs than are older mothers and provide children with less intellectual and verbal stimulation, even though they are affectionate mothers. (For a review, see Parke and Tinsley, 1987b:616-617.) But, as Crockenberg points out, "displays of affection may be an expression of the mother's emotional needs rather than evidence of her responsiveness to the baby" (1987:7).

In turn, the baby, and later the child, will influence its young mother's life differently than if the mother had been older at the time of the child's birth. Such children may present the mothers with more problems and will be a proportionally greater financial burden, as a young mother is less likely to have a high income. On the other hand, as they grow older, children who have a smaller age difference from their mother may be more rewarding companions to her as young adults than are children of older (and more educated) mothers. Because of the economic disadvantages early in their lives, these children may not reach a higher educational level than their own mother's, so that the cultural gap between mother and child may not be wide and may be advantageous to the mother as she ages.

Father's age has not been given much attention in the literature (exc. Daniels and Weingarten, 1982); nor, for that matter, has child effect on fathers. There are a few studies, however, which indicate that an older father is more likely to become more involved in the care of his first child than a young father. From this perspective, it could be suggested that the first child will have a greater impact, at least on the father's structural situation, than a subsequent child. As reviewed by Parke and Tinsley (1987a), father-infant attachment may not be affected by the age of the father, but the older father may participate less than the younger father in children's physical activities. It would also be interesting to know if the older father is more or less at risk of being negatively affected by a variety of adverse child characteristics.

Parents' employment may be an important variable. For instance, mothers of handicapped children find relief in their work. It provides a "break" in their demanding routine and, as such, may contribute to lower the potential of negative child effect.

> It's marvelous because when I get to work I forget all about, you know . . . you're with women who haven't got mentally handicapped children . . . You're in a more normal environment.
> (*Mother of a four-year-old girl with epilepsy and cerebral palsy, quoted in Baldwin and Glendinning, 1983:66*).

On the other hand, parents whose employment situation is stressful may be particularly vulnerable to child effect — both positively (the children may act as a compensation) or negatively (the children may be an *added* stress). Feldman et al. (1983) have found that fathers with a low-salience job were more involved in child care than fathers whose jobs had high salience. In turn, we could ask how the type of job parents have will promote or lessen child effect.

The number and spacing of children belong to parental, rather than child, characteristics because the latter are related to individual children. Thus, parents who have several children may be affected differently than parents who have a small family. Large families in turn will produce a differential impact depending on how closely spaced the children are: research indicates that parents cope with a large family by adopting more managerial and less flexible childrearing techniques (Kidwell, 1981; Peterson and Kunz, 1975; Richardson et al., 1986; Scheck and Emerick, 1976). Moreover, such parents are less able to devote as much individual time to each child as is feasible in smaller families (Blake, 1989). This may be one of the reasons why, on the average, children from large families do less well in school than children from smaller families. We also have to document the consequences on the parents of having a large family, or two or three small families from different marriages. The socioeconomic conditions of the parents would be a very important intervening variable in this respect.

Large sib groups may be better able to form coalitions against parents who would then be less able to socialize their children as they see fit. It has indeed been found that children in closely spaced families are more influenced by their siblings and less by their parents than children from more widely spaced families (Koch, 1955; see also Powell and Steelman, 1990). The vast literature on juvenile delinquency, which we review in Chapter 5, points to higher rates of delinquency in large families. We can also hypothesize that parents who have several children may feel less in control of their family life, and may feel that they cannot contribute to their children's future as much as they would like to. This may result in lower self-esteem as well as health problems, especially for mothers.

In the previous chapter, parents' marital and familial lives were placed among those aspects which can be subject to child effect. Here we can also inquire as to how marital quality and familial quality can contribute to prevention or reinforcement of negative as well as positive child effect. We will see in the chapter on juvenile delinquency that parents' marital relationship is one of the many background characteristics that have been constantly used in the literature on child socialization and development. But here, we would like to know if and how a good marital relationship can contribute to increasing positive child effect and serve as a buffer against negative child effect.

To begin with, it seems logical to expect that a couple who is happy with each other and provides companionship and support to each other is more likely to be positive toward the children and be affected by them in a more rewarding manner (Cox et al., 1989; Howes and Markham, 1989; see also Deal et al., 1989; Owen et al., 1989). Similarly, if such a couple has a problematic child, as these spouses will support each other, they will find in each other a compensatory outlet; in contrast, an embattled couple will not benefit from this advantage. Thus, the former parents should be less likely than the latter to suffer from negative child effect.

Studies have also found that paternal involvement and successful paternal parenting are more affected by the quality of the marital relationship than is maternal involvement (Dickie and Carnahan Gerber 1980; Belsky et al., 1984; Lamb and Elster, 1985). Such results add further proof to the theory that children affect mothers and fathers differently. In this case, additional parental characteristics, besides sex, act as mediating variables (see also Simons et al., 1990).

In the realm of the extended family system, if parents have maintained a warm relationship with their own parents, they are all more likely to share in the joys of parenting and grandparenting than in situations where parents and grandparents do not get along, where grandparents meddle or disagree with their own children's child-rearing practices, or where grandparents do not help out when they actually could. However, we have no literature on the family as a system in terms of *child effect* and, especially, on the *processes* involved. There is certainly a vast literature on the family as a system (e.g., Feiring and Lewis, 1984), but this literature fails to address the questions raised in this book.

We have, in this section, proposed research topics and hypotheses stemming from parental characteristics. One of the goals is to identify parents, as has been done for children (Felner et al., 1985), who might be more vulnerable to negative child effect. Another goal is to identify parents who are the most likely to reap positive child effect. Parental characteristics and child characteristics interact with each other to produce child (and parent) effect in a feedback model. Certain parental (and child) characteristics may be active only at given stages in the family life cycle — whether to promote negative or positive child effect. For instance, it is possible that parental commitment to their role may fluctuate over time, so that a parent may be very committed while the children are small and may become much less so during adolescence. Such fluctuations in commitment might make parents more or less vulnerable to child effect over time. Thus, the characteristics discussed herein are meant to be looked at within a dynamic perspective. We now turn to society's characteristics, which will act as a catalyst to or a buffer for child effect on parents.

CHARACTERISTICS OF SOCIETAL RESPONSE

Parents' and children's interactions do not take place without external influence but within a social context. Each society offers a set of structural constraints and opportunities as well as a cultural content that guides behavior. "How society supports or fails to support both parents and children will in great part determine parents' reaction as well as the direction of child effect on parents" (Ambert, 1990:162; see also Bronfenbrenner, 1979; Zigler and Black, 1989). In addition, subcultural and class requisites within various social groups also contribute to determine which child characteristics will affect parents (Super and Harkness, 1981; Thomas and Chess, 1977). What is important to parents is the help and moral support they receive from society at large (Belsky et al., 1984), as well as the resources that society offers their children to maximize their development and enhance positive parent/child interaction (see Kazak, 1987; Weiss, 1989). Bronfenbrenner (1979) points out that the opportunities a child has in terms of development are in great part related to the extent to which the parents' social situation helps or hinders them (also, Osofsky, 1986; Zigler and Weiss, 1985).

Societal support refers to the resources that a society places at the disposal of parents in order to facilitate the fulfillment of their role (Ambert, 1990:162). When a society has few resources available or chooses, out of socioeconomic and political considerations, not to invest in these resources, parents are effectively deprived of societal support (Kagan and Shelley, 1987). The use of the word "societal" instead of the more commonly utilized term of "social" support is intentional. Indeed, social support has generally been defined in research as the support one receives from *individuals,* and more specifically, from individuals that one should be close to such as family and friends. While our family and friends may indeed be sources of support, they represent only a minute portion of what we call here "societal" support or response. In this chapter, we refer to aspects of the *society* rather than of individuals; *we refer to the way the society is organized to meet parental needs and children's needs.*

The term "social support" has been over-utilized in the literature on health and on stress, for instance, and has been measured to include support that could be at the same time negative as well as positive. It is not necessary to digress into a lengthy discussion of this factor here. Suffice it to say that individuals who are viewed as supportive may also be a source of stress in other aspects, so that one can question which way the support goes. For example, a husband who is supportive of his wife's employment may also be highly critical of her performance as a homemaker. Therefore, that mother may be caught in a cross-fire and, as a consequence, may be more vulnerable to negative child effect — even though she receives support from her husband in one area of her life.

Characteristics of the societal response:

1. adequate housing
2. quality and existence of early day care systems
3. quality of schools
4. quality and existence of after-school programs
5. income supplements for impoverished families

6. adequate dental, medical, and psychiatric resources
7. availability of parenting-skills education programs
8. quality of the contents of mass media (two adverse qualities are media violence and sex role stereotyping)
9. safety of neighborhoods
10. appropriate recreational facilities for youngsters and families
11. home and community support for parents who have special-needs children and for special-needs parents
12. society's open acknowledgement of parental contribution (labor reproduction)
13. fostering of a positive peer group culture among children and adolescents
14. society's acceptance of minority-status parents and children (as opposed to discrimination)
15. society's acceptance and fostering of gender equalitarian ideology

Any one of these characteristics can lessen or even prevent the potentially detrimental impact that children with certain negative characteristics could have on their parents, who in turn have their own set of characteristics. Moreover, these societal characteristics can also increase the potential for positive child effect in general. Obviously, a combination of effective societal characteristics will have even greater positive potential than just one or two considered in isolation. In contrast, absence of societal support can increase the negative effect of children on parents as well as the reverse: parents living in situations of low societal support can have a negative impact on their children (Parke and Tinsley, 1987b). An example is child abuse, which is more likely to occur when parents are stressed or isolated and, as a result, may respond to a negative child behavior (such as constant crying) in an abusive manner (Fried and Holt, 1980). It is obvious that the adequacy of the societal response *helps* parents cope and helps them, in turn, respond more appropriately to their children's needs (Telleen et al., 1989). A study by Lempers et al. (1989) showed that economic hardship impacted negatively on marital harmony as well as parental nurturance and discipline with attendant negative consequence in adolescents' levels of distress.

Crnic et al. (1983) found that high-stress mothers who received adequate support were better equipped to foster a healthy emotional growth in their babies than similar mothers with low levels of support. Parents who benefit from organized forms of societal support may at the same time receive information on child rearing and on problems which may afflict children (Affleck et al., 1989). Such information has a positive effect on parents as it allows them to understand their child better and, consequently, be less negatively affected or less threatened when inappropriate child behaviors occur. Seitz et al. (1985) found that societal support extended to impoverished mothers had a long-term positive impact when these mothers were compared to a control group who had not received the same support. In this case, mothers had been provided with medical as well as social services, including day care.

A study by Crockenberg (1981) showed that mothers and irritable babies who had received societal support were more securely attached than mothers and babies who had received inadequate support. Societal support did not, however, have much of an impact when mothers had nonirritable babies. These results could be interpreted to mean that *social response adequacy is of greater consequence to parents of children with problems*. Thus, parents who have impaired, difficult, or disturbed children should receive more societal support than parents of average children (Koeske and Koeske, 1990).

Particularly important for these parents are special classes and after-school programs, which could give them a respite from their parenting responsibilities. Such services reduce the negative impact that these children potentially can have on their parents and increase parental enjoyment. This should be especially evident for parents who themselves are poor, isolated, in ill health, or are going through difficult times, such as separation, death in the family, or unemployment. Strober and Dornbusch (1988) present a comprehensive review of public policy alternatives that would go a long way to offer support to parents and their children and, consequently, alleviate mutually negative effect.

For instance, there are several studies indicating that single parents do not have as many contacts (such as Parent-Teachers Night or Open School Night) with schools as other parents and that, at the same time, there is a correlation between parental attendance at such functions and children's grades (Dornbusch et al., 1987). Single parents may be unable to attend such functions because the schools fail to provide day care during these hours (Dornbusch and Gray, 1988) or because teachers are prejudiced and do not treat such parents with dignity (see Chapter 11). The societal response (of the schools, in this case) does not meet the needs of single parents and their children.

It is consequently obvious that the societal response has the potential to compensate for negative child characteristics as well as negative parental characteristics which would make parents particularly vulnerable to child effect. Such a statement has widespread application because there are very few parents who do not have at least one or two negative characteristics that place them at risk for child effect. Neither should we assume that negative child characteristics cannot affect "perfect" parents. Thus, appropriate societal response and societal resources are key determinants in parents', as well as children's, welfare (Eichler, 1988).

Twenty years ago, Rodman and Graves (1967) called for "parent-education television" which would place that medium at the disposal of parents. The goal was to teach them effective parenting skills and educate them about various child problems. Television is a societal resource in potential in that it has yet to respond to parental needs. Indeed, instead of helping parents, television, with the exception of certain educational and family-oriented programs, submits their children to a barrage of fabricated and artificial "needs" via advertisements, and exposes children to violence, racism and sexism, as well as values and life-styles that are antithetical to most parents' own values in terms of what they want for their children.

If we take quality of mass media, one of the societal characteristics listed above, we can advance the notion that violence as portrayed on television, movies and videos is problematic. It is so not only for the healthy human development of children, but also for parents' well-being. Most parents do not consciously encourage their children to be antisocial or violent. Consequently, the least that can be said is that most parents may be uncomfortable with the idea of their children being exposed to so much violent material. Moreover, many parents are very upset when their own children become victims of their peers' violence. And finally, parents with violent children, as we will see in a next chapter, are negatively affected. In sum, from many parents' point of view, the media expose their children to values which they oppose or to situations which are detrimental, whether it is because the parents belong to a minority which is irresponsibly portrayed, because of parents' sex role ideology, or their opposition to violence and the degradation of women.

How society conceives of the roles that men and women play will have a great impact on parents (Cohen and Katzenstein, 1988), especially on mothers, in terms of child effect. As our society continues to place child rearing squarely on women's shoulders at a time when individualism and financial pressures for outside employment operate, women with children are bound to suffer from work overload and role conflict. Thus, currently, the societal response in terms of gender roles is detrimental to mothers in terms of negative child effect and may cheat fathers in terms of the positive child effect they miss out on because of their remote role in child care.

Another important societal characteristic that contributes heavily to either negative or positive child effect is neighborhood safety. While, on the one hand, studies abound concerning the negative influence which impoverished and crime-ridden ghettos have on children, little is said about the heavy cost that these children's parents pay. Parents may not be able to allow their children out to play, not only because they may fear the criminal influence but because they may be afraid that the child will be attacked, robbed, raped, or caught in the cross-fire of gang warfare. Such parents will suffer doubly because their small apartment may already be overcrowded and the cooped-up children may become noisy and aggressive.

In many neighborhoods parents have to walk their children to school, again because of the above-mentioned fears. These parents become captive, due to their neighborhood's dangers, and as their children's constant keepers. We can surmise that such parents might suffer from premature burnout, high levels of stress, and a cornucopia of physical and psychosomatic ailments as a consequence. Thus, lack of societal resources to offer safe neighborhoods to the poor, to educate the poor, and to offer police protection exacerbates child effect to highly undesirable negative levels.

Finally, one aspect of the societal response which has to be taken into consideration is its timing. Crnic and Greenberg (1987) suggest that there may be periods in the parents' and children's lives when social support is more necessary and more influential. Their study on the first year in a child's life leads them to conclude that parents benefit more from individual social support during the immediate transition to parenthood than later on in that first year. I will suggest that, for certain types of parents (very young or ill) and/or certain types of children (special needs), the societal response will be needed even more as the child ages.

PRELIMINARY CONCLUSIONS

The *results* of child effect may be positive or negative, and this can be so in any of the areas of the parents' lives outlined in the previous chapter. For instance, a researcher interested in adult development could use this tripartite model to study child effect on parental personality over the life cycle of parents and of children. And, more specifically, such a researcher would be interested in studying how certain types of children affect parents under given societal circumstances.

Another researcher whose expertise resides in career and job development could study the impact of children on adults' work performance, work satisfaction, and employment trajectory. Again, the matter of the children's characteristics would loom large in such studies. Another person might be interested in the area of leisure, and might want to compare the leisure activities of adults of various ages who have children with certain characteristics with adults who have different types of children and childless adults. Finally, a scholar in the area of adult health could well utilize the same model to study the effect of children on adults' health.

A multitude of additional conclusions are necessary to do justice to the contents of this chapter. Moreover, a synthesis is needed that combines all three determinants into a more sophisticated model. The following chapter is designed to complement and synthesize the material we have just presented.

Chapter 4

Theoretical Synthesis

We will now offer a synthesis and a conclusion to the preceding chapter. As well, the concepts of avoidable and unavoidable child effects will be introduced to further our understanding of child effect in general. The model proposed is multidimensional and dynamic. It consists of the interplay between child characteristics, parental characteristics and societal response to produce or not produce an effect in parents, to produce a negative or a positive effect, and a strong or a mild effect. Moreover, certain child characteristics are more likely to produce an effect than others, and this effect will be positive or negative depending on the direction of the deviation from the socially accepted average in a given society or subcultural group. In addition, certain parental characteristics produce greater vulnerability to child effect and, ultimately, the appropriateness of the societal resources or response is a key variable in the final equation.

INTERACTION BETWEEN CHARACTERISTICS

I have summarized the interaction of the various sets of characteristics on child effect in Diagram 1. In the upper part of the diagram, the quality of child effect is placed on a continuum. To the left, parents experience mainly positive effects; at the very least, the positive predominates over the negative. At the opposite extreme of the line, negative effect is hypothesized.

In turn, each one of the three sets of characteristics which will determine the quality of child effect has been placed on the continuum. We have ranged child characteristics from, on the left, very positive, all the way to very or totally negative at the extreme right.

DIAGRAM 1

Presence and quality of child effect on any

given area of parental life

Quality of effect on parents

positive
effect
predominates
∧
|——

negative
effect
predominates
∧
——|

Mixture of
positive/negative
∧
|——

positive <—— child characteristics ————> negative

compatible <—— parental characteristics ————> incompatible
(congruent)   (non-congruent)

appropriate <—— quality of societal response ————> deficient

No effect on parents will take place when:

. children or child characteristics are not salient to area or to
  parents;

. parental characteristics preclude child effect;

. societal response is compatible with no effect.

According to the hypotheses presented in the previous chapter, positive child characteristics are more likely to affect parents positively, as indicated by the direction of the arrow.

Parental characteristics are presented on a continuum of compatible-congruent. It should be noted here that we could also range parental characteristics from very positive (which would mean here compatible-congruent) to very negative or incompatible-noncongruent. But the adjectives "compatible-congruent" are preferred, although another researcher might wish to use different labels with similar results.

Parents' characteristics are seen in terms of how compatible they are with the child's own characteristics. For instance, a normally physically active child (who would fall in the middle of the continuum of child characteristics) whose parents are fifty years old and relatively sedentary may have parents who are less suitable to this physical demand than a same child with twenty-five-year-old parents who themselves like physical exertion. It can be predicted that the latter set of parents will be more positively affected by that particular child trait than the older, more sedentary set of parents. In other words, the "goodness of fit" between parents and child will determine in great part how each will react toward the other (Lamb and Gilbride, 1985; Lerner, 1985; Thomas and Chess, 1977; Windle and Lerner, 1986).

If we pursue the continuum, most negative parental characteristics would fall at the incompatible extreme to the right: parents who are alcoholic, addicted, disturbed, criminal, violent, or have poor parenting skills, to name only a few. Such characteristics are basically incompatible with the requisites of good parenting. These extremely negative parental characteristics are, in fact, more likely to impact on the children. The children of such parents will, in turn, have a negative effect on them *indirectly* as a consequence of their distressed reactions to having abnormal parents. Moreover, these parents, having fewer personal resources and being less able to utilize societal resources placed at their disposal, will be more at risk of being further burdened mentally, financially, and socially. But it is also possible that many such parents will be immune to child effect, as is often observed currently among crack-addicted parents who reach the point where they forget about their children who are, in effect, neglected. Such parents are more likely to impact on children than vice versa (and would fall in the lower part of the diagram).

Children who maintain positive characteristics in the face of adversity with such parents, what one could call "survivors," could even affect these parents *positively* by showing them affection (nurture), helping them, standing by them, giving them a goal in life, and perhaps, providing them with good role modelling, and an emotional anchor. It would be very important to have studies on families where parents exhibit serious dysfunctional characteristics but have children who function well—what Werner calls "resilience in the face of life's adversity" (1989:72).

The knowledge I have acquired throughout the years via my students' autobiographies indicates that such children generally pay a heavy personal price during their youth, but that many do "recover" sufficiently to lead a happy adult life. There are many indications that such students are providing a great deal of support to at least one of their two parents. But, it should be noted, the writers of these autobiographies are fortunately few and constitute a self-selected group: they are all students. One can therefore only wonder about those who never reach this educational level. For them, the parental effect, combined with a detrimental social situation, may have been overwhelming.

We can also analyze parents' *normal* characteristics, such as being immigrant and non-English speaking, within the framework of being incompatible to a child who is brought up "American." There is nothing wrong or abnormal in being an immigrant per se. But, from the point of view of *child effect*, such a set of characteristics may be negative as they may open the door to a great deal of child effect, much of which *can* be negative as such parents are particularly vulnerable. This would especially be so once the children reach school when parents may be frustrated because they cannot help them with their schoolwork and may not understand the demands of American school systems.

If we return to the diagram, we see that the quality of the societal response to the particular parent-child configuration is presented on a continuum of appropriate to deficient. Again, it is expected that the more appropriate the societal response is, the less likely it is that child effect will be negative. Or, put otherwise, an adequate societal response can prevent a poor parent-child configuration or fit from affecting both parents and children as negatively as will be the case when the societal response is deficient or inappropriate.

Actually, I propose that negative child characteristics could affect parents much less than is currently the case were parents/children provided with more social services (including education) to help them. Similarly, many inappropriate parental characteristics could be greatly reduced in their impact both on parents and children if, for instance, poverty and social isolation were relieved. This, of course, can happen only when we place loneliness and isolation within a social framework rather than continuing to see it as a personal problem or attribute. Basically, in a society such as ours, where men and women go into space and even walk on the moon, much more energy could be harnessed to alleviate *human* problems. Because of its *potential*, the societal response holds the balance of power, so to speak, in terms of child effect, as well as in terms of parental effect. The strength and the direction of both effects become matters of the inadequacy or adequacy of the social structure.

I have proposed, in Chapter 3, that the vast literature on parental causality in the field of child development represents a bias in yet another direction: it has prevented us from studying the preventive and buffering effects of the societal response, and perhaps even, its main or direct effect in some circumstances. Above all, the literature has placed the blame on parents rather than on the social situation in which parents are embedded. This is well illustrated in the case of juvenile delinquency in the next chapter. Extreme examples of the results of this position are currently being implemented in certain states. For instance, parents of teenagers who skip school too frequently receive reduced welfare checks. In other areas, parents have to pay for their teenagers' vandalism. A priori, these policies appear to make sense. But when one realizes that such parents are generally helpless in curbing their teenagers because of the external social situation (neighborhoods, schools, peers), it is evident that parents become the victims both of society and of their children.

These policies return us to a discussion initiated in an earlier chapter concerning the greater facility that social agencies have in controlling, policing and "treating" families as opposed to attacking the real social problems which are at the root cause of "familial" problems. (See also Sigel, 1983.) In times of budgetary cuts at the national and regional levels, welfare and policing agencies fall back on their old scapegoat, the family, more specifically the parents, in a last-ditch attempt at solving their problems. This action also has the added advantage that they do not have to question the global social situation — nor do they have to redress it.

One could legitimately ask which of the three sets of characteristics is the most important in determining child effect. Belsky (1985) has concluded that negative child characteristics "are relatively easy to overcome" (p. 91), and that psychologically sound parents are the primordial buffer. It should be noted, however, that his discussion pertains mainly to infants who are at risk. Even here, I would propose that psychologically mature parents with a disabled child, for instance, may easily become unravelled if the societal response to their plight is adverse or simply insufficient. On the other side of the coin, multiple-problem parents may be less negatively affected by their children (and affect their children less negatively) when an adequate support system exists. Earlier I offered the possibility that, in our type of society, it is the societal response which may well be the key set of characteristics in child effect. This point of view is directly and indirectly shared by researchers who advocate and evaluate family support programs (e.g., Bronfenbrenner, 1987; Bronfenbrenner and Weiss, 1983; Zigler and Berman, 1983; Zigler and Black, 1989).

As the child becomes an adolescent, the societal response, *as defined in this book*, may be the ultimate buffer and even main effect (Rutter, 1988). Emotionally and socially stable parents can be wrecked by abusive and delinquent teenagers who are ruled by a disruptive peer group. At that level, the child characteristics are of such magnitude that only a forceful societal intervention will help parents (the buffering function). However, many are the children who *become* delinquent and abusive as a direct consequence of peer group association (a main effect in this case).

Thus, *which set of characteristics has primacy will depend on where there is imbalance, the degree of the imbalance, as well as the stage in the child's and the parents' lives that is reached.* Although I hypothesize a primacy of the societal response in fostering/preventing child effect (both negative and positive), one also has to consider that certain parental or even child characteristics may be so extreme that no amount of societal support could prevent them or compensate for them. As well, there are certain characteristics (serious mental illness, hard-core criminality) which prevent parents from utilizing the societal resources which exist. Parents and even older children may actually resist societal efforts at reaching them.

Because most of the available literature which has addressed child effect has focused on early childhood rather than later years, it is possible that far too much strength and influence have been attributed to parental characteristics (as will be illustrated in the following chapter). The active social role of the child is minimized once again in this context, as is the role of the societal response. In fact, *we could hypothesize that parental characteristics become less important than child characteristics as the child ages and passes into adolescence. At that point, both child and societal response characteristics may supersede parental characteristics in child effect.*

The importance of the societal response, and of its effectiveness, is made more salient because parents and children together probably face more difficulties and external threats than in the past. Social forces such as urbanization, technology, economic difficulties, and media influence, to name only a few of the sources of obstacles families face, place additional barriers and stressors on parents and children (Zigler and Black, 1989), and on adults in their parenting role. Poverty is one of the most salient social characteristics influencing both parental and child effect. It lowers parental effectiveness (Gelles, 1989), raises children's risks (Comer, 1989; Rutter 1987b), exacerbates negative child effect and may hamper positive child effect. Poverty highlights individuals' vulnerabilities and creates additional ones (Halpern, 1990; Schorr, 1988; Solnit, 1983).

As parents and children age, different characteristics from each, as well as from society, will assume a greater or lesser importance in this equation of child effect. Similarly, areas of parental lives which can be affected will change over time. The literature reviewed in the previous and the following chapters illustrates quite well the dynamic as opposed to static state of parents' and children's lives, as well as the impact they have on each other throughout their own life cycles. Child effect should be studied developmentally as opposed to the "snapshot" approach.

It is important to mention in this chapter that concepts such as reciprocal effect or bidirectionality of effect could be misleading if they are construed to mean that parents' and children's effects are equivalent or equal in strength at all times. Here again, the respective characteristics of the actors, including age, will determine the source of the stronger effect. Most human interactions are not equal at all times: parent/child interactions do not escape this rule.

Bidirectionality simply means that two actors affect each other, even though one may predominate. Reciprocal effect between parent and child should be interpreted similarly and should not be taken to mean that the effect emanating from one of the actors is as strong as that from the other. Moreover, one actor's effect can predominate in certain circumstances (during an illness, for instance) while the other's can predominate at other moments.

Finally, the diagram takes into consideration the fact that not all parents are affected by their children and that not all areas of parental lives are equally affected by their children (lower section of the diagram). Again, for such a case to occur, the three sets of characteristics have to offer a very specific configuration. When are children totally or nearly totally devoid of any effect on their parents? First, when the child characteristics are irrelevant to the parents or to the parents' area of life under study. For instance, an average child or even a very gifted child may have no impact on a parent's employment, social, community, or health areas of life. At the same time, from the vantage point of parental characteristics, for a child to produce no effect, the parents would have to place no importance on children in certain areas of their lives or in their entire lives. In the latter case, such parents would have to be either very deviant and/or can afford to have their children raised entirely by others.

A parent who deserts his family (studies show that fathers are more likely to do this than mothers) and starts life somewhere else, never contacts his children again, nor cares about their existence, may be one example of such a parent. Another could be a parent who becomes so mentally incompetent that he or she has to be institutionalized, no longer recognizes who anyone is, and thus is no longer aware of his or her children. This parent will no longer be affected by the children as they have no relevance to his or her life. I have mentioned crack-addicted parents as another possibility which could fall in this section of the diagram. Very well-to-do parents who have never cared much about having children, or never cared much for children, may abandon them to the responsibility of a staff of nannies, governesses, boarding schools and summer camps so that the children's presence rarely intrudes in their lives. The children will not affect them.

Finally, the societal response will have to be compatible. For instance, if a father deserts in this society, not much is done to help children and mother. The social response *allows* the father to go unfettered, unencumbered, and start his life all over as if his children did not exist. When the law regarding support of these children will be *effectively* put in practice, such fathers may find that they are still affected by their children — at least in their pocketbook. In the case of the hypothetical well-to-do parents, or even parents who *have* to institutionalize a severely disabled child, such parents can remain unaffected by their children only if society allows them to or provides them with the means to do so. The parents in such a case, if presented with no feasible alternative, may be encouraged to have another child and start their lives over again. In the case of the well-to-do parents, they can "buy" the appropriate social response in the guise of retainers and boarding schools. They may also care very little about people's reaction to their life-style as their financial status allows them this luxury.

UNAVOIDABLE AND AVOIDABLE CHILD EFFECT

In order to complete this synthesis, I would like here to bring a distinction between two types of child effect: unavoidable and avoidable child effect, for want of a better terminology. Child effect that is *unavoidable* results because infants and young children are helpless in terms of the fulfillment of their immediate needs and have to be protected from dangers. *Someone* has to take care of them if the species is to survive. This rule applies to most of the nonaquatic animal world. Young ones have to be fed, sheltered, and need help in bowel and bladder elimination. Generally, they have to be protected from predators or dangers (such as falling off a crib for a human or off a tree branch for an ape) and, in many instances, need emotional stimulation, including bodily contact with a parent (for example, with the mother in the context of nursing).

Moreover, because human infants and young children are less knowledgeable than their parents about the dangers and rewards of their environment, and are less knowledgeable about future outcomes, it is unavoidable that parents have to teach, or socialize, young children purposively (Baumrind, 1980). Because infants are helpless, their caretakers have to adjust to the infants' characteristics (Sroufe, 1985), if the infants are to survive. Only a minimal infant adjustment to caregiver needs and characteristics can be expected at that age. "Reciprocal" effects exist but are not equal nor equally purposive.

So long as parents are the primary caretakers in a society, then it becomes unavoidable that parents will be affected, both directly and indirectly, as a result of their parenting roles at that stage. This child effect, because it is so unavoidable, is natural. It is also universal and is not species-specific. Only the contents are species-specific as each type of animal lives in a specific environmental niche and has a distinctive biological constitution, thus different needs and capacities.

As the child ages, learns skills in self-help, becomes more alert to dangers, and generally becomes more self-sufficient and aware, the level of necessary and unavoidable care should be expected to diminish. Consequently, unavoidable child effect should also diminish as the child matures. At some point (and this point in time differs from child to child and from society to society) much of child effect on parents could be termed *avoidable*. That is, in theory at least, it should no longer be necessary for parents constantly to alter their lives to minister to every need of a growing child. The child, by then possibly an adolescent, should be able to take over the responsibility for his or her immediate needs with the help of appropriate societal support. This ability to become more reliable and self-reliant in itself impacts positively on parents as it allows them more freedom, more time, and fewer worries, more energy to spend on activities other than parenting. Some parents, however, may react negatively to the loss of the (unavoidable) part of their parenting role as they may have enjoyed having a totally dependent child. Many individuals enjoy giving this type of unavoidable and unconditional nurturance.

At a certain point in time, or at a certain age, a maturing child should exert fewer demands on parents, thus lowering the potential for effect, especially negative. It is at this juncture that societal norms concerning children's rights and parental obligations as well as society's support will determine in great part whether child effect will diminish. In much of North America, for instance, adolescents, their peers, teachers, and a variety of professionals expect parental obligations to continue at a very high level. Educational expectations are heightened, extra-curricular activities for middle-class adolescents and pre-adolescents increase rather than decrease, often requiring parental involvement. At the same time, parents are informed that children have to become independent and go through the process of "individuation." Consequently, parents often have to prolong their socialization role within the stressful context of what has been called intergenerational conflict.

These child effects can be called avoidable. *They do not arise from the intrinsic nature of children or of adolescents but from the demands of a particular cultural setting.* They arise from definitions we construct about children and adolescents. Often, these definitions merely serve capitalist, materialistic interests and ensure them a market. We can hypothesize that the adequacy of societal response will have a direct bearing on the quantity and quality of avoidable child effect on parents when children reach a certain age. As well, child and parent characteristics will contribute to the prolongation of avoidable child effect. Both parents and children can create, however unwittingly so, avoidable child effect. For instance, a domineering parent who does not allow any freedom may prevent an adolescent from reaching a normal level of self-sufficiency in this society. In turn, that adolescent may place demands on the parent. The circularity is totally avoidable.

While unavoidable child effect is a universal phenomenon, albeit responded to differently depending on the cultural context, and even applies to most other animal species, avoidable child effect largely is a cultural phenomenon. Avoidable child effect arose as a direct result of the prolongation of the socialization period required to produce an adult person in industrialized societies. It is a direct result of longer educational demands, of the increased economic dependence of adolescents and young adults on parents, of the formation of peer group subcultures, of the requisites of the capitalist system, and of the compartmentalization of the nuclear family as compared to the familism of agrarian as well as tribal societies. Avoidable child effect is a sociohistorically specific, not species-specific, phenomenon. It is not found in nonhuman species. By its very definition, it can be avoided.

In societies which cannot afford avoidable child effect, adolescents become an integral part of the familial and village life. They become contributing members, unless of course, they are disabled or emotionally disturbed. Such societies have fewer *material* resources than our own and a less technologized labor force. Parents cannot afford older, dependent children. Rather, parents and adolescents become interdependent and contribute to one another's well-being, with the parents' contribution diminishing substantially with age. At that stage, parents begin to harvest the rewards of having children.

In animal species, a parallel situation takes place. The natural offspring disappears to join another group or stays in the maternal group, but the animal mother is by then entirely relieved of any responsibility for her child. It could be said that she also harvests, unconsciously, the rewards of having had children: she recaptures her freedom to mate and to reproduce again. Negative avoidable child effects do not exist in other animal species.

Thus, basically, when we talk of avoidable child effect for human beings, we refer to *negative* child effect which, if society was structured differently and held different values, would not necessarily occur. Ideally, as a child ages, negative avoidable child effect should be replaced by positive child effect. While unavoidable child effect can be both positive (the joy of taking care of a baby) and negative (worries over a sick child), avoidable child effect is largely negative.

In turn, if we refer to negative child effect and its impact on parents, we can hypothesize that the more avoidable negative child effect is, the more negatively affected parents will be. In other words, when parents perceive (rightly or wrongly) that certain problems created by the child or society are avoidable, they may be more upset. An example would be parents of chronically ill children who contract an acute (temporary) illness while in hospital as a direct result of misguided or careless treatment. Such parents (and children) will become doubly burdened. Another example is parents who perceive that their children's peers are delinquent and relate the difficulties they themselves are experiencing to their children's peers. Such parents may feel particularly helpless and frustrated. Dangerous neighborhoods, demands arising from advertising seen on television, and poor-quality schools are all additional examples of avoidable situations leading to avoidable child effects.

CONCLUSIONS

The analytical model described herein is of universal application in terms of its broad lines. Societal characacteristics, however, will differ somewhat for each society. Thus, a hunting-gathering society's supportive characteristic for parents will bear few similarities to the ones described earlier. It is extremely important to keep in mind the *cultural* context of child effect. In the United States and Canada, this cultural caveat would be particularly relevant to Native and Inuit societies, Mexican-Americans, as well as, for instance, Amish and Mennonite communities, to mention only a few.

Moreover, our analytical model applies to all types of children and parents in that it allows for the fact that certain parents will be more "vulnerable" to child effect than others due to their own characteristics or even situations, and that certain types of children will be more likely to affect their parents. Here as well, however, the cultural context has to be kept in mind when we do cross-cultural research. Thus, a given type of American, middle-class parent may not be as vulnerable to child effect as the same type of parent in Ethiopia, for instance.

Within a North American context, the model proposed in this book is suited to all types of parents and children. Special-needs children, average children, delinquent children, and gifted children can all be studied within this model in terms of their parental impact. Then, poor or rich, young or old, mentally unstable or healthy parents can be studied in terms of their vulnerability to child effect. As well, all types of children and parents are subject to different societal responses and resources. These can be studied to see how they facilitate positive child effect or foster negative child effect.

It is interesting that Roskies long ago recognized the importance of this triumvirate of conditions (which we call here characteristics). She used this model, consisting for her of child/mother/society, to discuss the impact of the birth of a thalidomide child. She pointed out, in 1972, that this birth upset "the delicate network of interlocking needs and obligations — child's, mother's, and society's — on which the successful rearing of a child depends" and, within our own analytical model, from which child effect on parents will flow. She further explained that "what makes this event so disruptive . . . is that the failure does not occur on one level, or in one partner. Instead, there is a chain reaction in which the needs of mother, child, and society, rather than working in harmony, become embroiled in a complex conflict of interests" (1972:289). Unfortunately, Roskies' words have too frequently been ignored in the literature.

In summary, the model proposed herein can also be utilized from a psychosociological perspective as well as from a larger macrosociological framework. It is basically interdisciplinary, as will become obvious in subsequent chapters. It is relevant not only to researchers, whether psychological, sociological, or even anthropological, but can also be used by clinicians, social workers, and experts in the various domains of special education. Moreover, because of its flexibility, this model is especially appropriate cross-culturally and in multicultural societies. In North America, child effect will differ depending on the ethnic background of the parents and the societal support offered to or withheld from various ethnic groups (see Chapter 11). We could point here to the lack of societal support that immigrant and refugee parents receive, not only as a collectivity and as individuals, but as parents. The same remark would apply to Native Americans. These topics in themselves would deserve entire chapters. We will conclude by saying that the model would be particularly helpful in formulating social policies in the domain of family life in general. It would be most beneficial for families with special-needs children or for families in which the parents are socially disadvantaged whether financially, educationally, and/or as a result of discrimination.

Finally, let me add that the theoretical synthesis herein advanced is informed by a sociohistorical perspective of family life. Each society constructs its definitions, not only of childhood, adolescence, and what a family is, but also of what good parenting is. These constructs are buttressed by the ideologies and institutions prevailing at any given point in the history of a society. Thus, one of the tenets of the theory herein proposed is that the contents of the three sets of characteristics discussed at great length in the previous chapter will evolve over time. And so will their interaction. The relationship between parents and children is largely a cultural construct. I suggest that this construct should perhaps be added to the list of societal characteristics for this construct is an ideology — and ideologies do contribute to increasing negative child effect as well as enhancing positive child effect. As we have seen, ideologies and social institutions determine in great part avoidable child effect as well as the contents of unavoidable effect. This is particularly relevant to the following chapter.

Chapter 5

The Effect of Juvenile Delinquency

As we have seen in the previous chapters, the vast literature on the sociology of the family and child psychology has generally focused on the effect that parents have on their children. Conversely, child effect on parents has been largely neglected, as has been circularity of effect between parent and child. This neglect is particularly striking in the field of juvenile delinquency where child effect, as a topic of study, is practically nonexistent. Research on juvenile delinquency has yet to benefit from the more recent advance in psychology and sociology concerning the redirection of the parent-child-parent effect patterns (but see Rutter, 1985:353).[1]

The literature on juvenile delinquency itself is particularly extensive. Not only are there scores of textbooks and monographs, but the topic is covered in a wide variety of journals in the fields of sociology, psychology, social work, psychiatry, penology, and criminology. A thorough search of this vast literature has failed to uncover any significant work *focusing directly* on the impact of juvenile delinquency on the delinquent's *parents* or even on the delinquent's family. Yet, every *textbook* on juvenile delinquency devotes a chapter to "the family and delinquency." These chapters typically focus on the familial causes of, antecedents to, or correlates of juvenile delinquency. The causality model depicted is generally unidirectional. The question asked is: What kinds of parents do juvenile delinquents have? And, directly or indirectly, an inference is made between type of parents and delinquency.

To illustrate the flavor of such texts, we read in Trojanowicz and

---

1. Additional references applicable to the contents of this chapter can be found in the next chapter.

Morash (1987:94): "Aichhorn [1969] states that so strong is the influence of the family in shaping behavior that pathology undoubtedly exists in all families where there is a delinquent youngster." No rectifying commentary follows in the text—an otherwise excellent book. Additionally, textbooks on adolescence in general usually include a chapter on delinquency and a section on its familial antecedents. For instance, in Jensen's commendable text (1985: 421), one reads in bold captions: "What kind of family is likely to produce delinquents?" There is no equivalent section asking "What kind of familial environment do *delinquents produce?*" This book also contains a section on the effect of parental types on adolescents but no section on the effect of adolescent types on parents.

Until recently many of the family variables considered as sources of delinquency have been structural (for a review, see Geisman and Wood, 1986), such as family size, birth order, broken homes, or even indirect (Haskell and Yablonsky, 1982), such as the quality of the neighborhood. First, it is important to point out that, taken together, the results and conclusions of these studies express a great deal of disagreement (Rankin, 1983; McCord, 1982), especially concerning broken homes and maternal employment. Moreover, the conclusions drawn from many of the studies repeatedly quoted in college texts may be outdated. One may question the relevance in the early 1990s, where divorce is more socially acceptable and maternal employment the rule rather than the aberration, of studies on these topics done in the 1930s, 1940s and even 1950s. But it is interesting that, *even then*, studies on the effect of broken homes were far from unanimous in their conclusions, even in past decades. Nevertheless, since college texts are often the only source of information that students and even practitioners utilize, one can immediately see the problem which these texts perpetuate. Indeed, if they keep referring to outdated studies and fail to take stock of the new trends in the field of juvenile delinquency and child development, we will keep turning out generations of students who are exposed to a very one-sided, and perhaps even biased, perspective.

In one study, Johnson (1985) found no relationship between family structure and self-reported delinquency, except for boys in mother/stepfather families. But he found that children, especially girls, from mother-only families were more likely to be *apprehended*. He concluded that school and justice officials may discriminate on the basis of family structure. Rosen and Neilson (1982) have also concluded that there is no important relationship between broken homes and actual delinquency. Whatever relationship exists is probably the result of functional variables, such as inadequate parental supervision (Elliott et al., 1985; Stouthamer-Loeber et al., 1984).

The functional family variables recently studied are parental involvement (neglect), discipline, supervision, rejection and parental deviance (Rankin and Wells, 1990). Reviewed well by Loeber and Stouthamer-Loeber (1986), these variables are credibly correlated with juvenile delinquency. But, as indicated by Agnew (1985), Elliott et al. (1985), and Feldman et al. (1983), such parental influences can be greatly overshadowed by peer group effects at certain ages, and by the sib structure and gender composition (Dishion et al., 1991; Loeber and Stouthamer-Loeber, 1986; Offord, 1982: 146). More to the point here, a great deal of interaction between parental influence and child influence surfaces upon critical examination of the studies. Several researchers themselves are pointing out that many of the observed correlations may stem from parental reaction to coercive child behavior (Loeber, 1982; Patterson, 1982). Rutter, for one, asks (1985:354): "Did harsh and inconsistent punishment cause the boy to be aggressive or was it that the parents were led to take extreme measures just because the boy's disruptive behavior failed to respond to more ordinary methods of discipline? Again, there are reasons for supposing that both may occur." In spite of warnings from such authors, the bulk of the research on functional family variables is still largely unidirectional.

In the next section of this chapter, we will situate the inquiry within the framework of more recent perspectives. In the following section, we will identify biases present in the research on juvenile delinquency which have contributed to inflate parental causality. In the third section, we discuss parents as a ready-made explanation. In the last section, we present suggestions for future research which could begin to redress the unidirectionality of the existing literature.

THE OVERALL PERSPECTIVE

One general result of the emphasis on parental variables in the causation of delinquency is that it has deflected energy from studying more global causative agents such as community resources (Rosen, 1985; Weis and Sederstrom, 1981). The family has been studied, not only *because of the influence of clinical theories and ideologies*, but also because *it is more easily accessible* than schools, mass media, neighborhoods, and other community variables. It is even more accessible than the frequently studied peer groups (Giordano et al., 1985). The delinquent's family is a "captive" population, easily accessed *and more easily policed* or controlled (Donzelot, 1979; Meyer, 1977) than other social units. Moreover, it is deceptively easy to study through the delinquents' own perceptions.

Not only have delinquent children been related to problematic parents or problematic childrearing practices, but the *context* of parenting itself in our type of society has rarely been scrutinized as a possible cause or even an intermediate cause of delinquency (Bronfenbrenner, 1979). In other words, while parenting difficulties may themselves be caused by juvenile delinquency, the other aspect is that detrimental parenting difficulties and incompetencies may be in great part caused by an inadequate societal response or by a lack of fit between society and the needs of the modern family. Society is not providing families with sufficient support in their various roles. Familial roles are not buttressed by society. But theoretical and empirical analyses of the family structure rarely examine this lack of fit.

The effect of parents on their children's delinquency is certainly not disputed (Cernkovich and Giordano, 1987; Gove and Crutchfield, 1982; Loeber and Stouthamer-Loeber, 1986), and *is not even the topic of this chapter*. A unidirectional focus on parents, however, is dangerously misleading. Indeed, we can infer from a critical reading of the literature that delinquency may be unrelated to familial background in at least a small percentage of *very young* offenders and possibly in a *large* percentage of *teenage* delinquents for whom peer associations may be more important (Elliott et al., 1985; West, 1982). It is not unreasonable to assume that, in cases where children become delinquent despite parental efforts, the emotional and social costs to the parents must be very high. Parents who have difficult children in spite of their best efforts to the contrary must suffer from a great deal of stress and a diminished sense of self-esteem and control over their lives. They must feel stigmatized socially; moreover, the critical tone of the literature and of the experts must exacerbate their feelings of guilt, isolation, and failure.

Second, even in the majority of the cases where parental/familial characteristics (whether lax supervision, lack of attachment, alcoholism, violence, marital conflicts, mental instability [McCord, 1990]) may be at least in part responsible for the development of delinquent behavior, it is valid to assume that the children's delinquency is not usually a result sought by these parents (Elliott et al., 1985). Consequently, even in these families, which too often are already malfunctioning, delinquency will be an added stressor which may further imbalance parents socially and emotionally, and feedback negatively on the already delinquent children.

None of the above assumptions are disproved by the available research—they are simply ignored or are granted a sentence or a paragraph in an entire article, chapter and even book (for exceptions, see Elliott et al., 1985; Gove and Crutchfield, 1982; Loeber and Stouthamer-Loeber, 1986; West and Farrington, 1977). A relatively early exception to this unidirectionality can be found in Nye's book on Family Relationships and Delinquent Behavior (1958). Nye even used statistical manipulations to try to highlight the impact that juveniles had. Unfortunately, his example was not immediately followed. But he certainly proved that it is as valid scientifically to explore the effect of juvenile delinquency on parents as to explore the effect of parents on juvenile delinquency; it is startling that only the latter has been studied.

RESEARCH BIASES AND THEIR IMPLICATIONS

In the data gathering methods of many studies on juvenile delinquency, there are biases which contribute to inflating parental causality. The first, which is well-recognized by experts in the field, arises from the fact that a majority of studies on juvenile delinquents have used *official statistics*. Consequently, juvenile delinquents and their families are studied *after* they have been apprehended and labelled. Studies on self-reported delinquency generally indicate that a much higher percentage of teenagers are *de facto* delinquent but never come to the attention of the authorities, and are never labelled (Johnson, 1985). Among others, Johnson (1985) and West and Farrington (1977) have indeed shown that adolescents admit to many more offences but proportionally far fewer contacts with officials.

In other words, adolescents "get away" with a majority of their offences: the official delinquent may not represent the average delinquent. Thus, obviously, many more parents have delinquent children who are never caught by officials than there are parents whose children are caught. This means that many parents have to cope with delinquent children on their own. It would be important to know of their coping mechanisms; as well, it would be important to know whether this situation is less or more detrimental to parents than the situation in which their children are apprehended, labelled, and officially punished.

It is also known that a great proportion of legal juvenile delinquents, especially the repeat offenders, were delinquent or exhibited problematic behavior long before they were caught and labelled (Loeber, 1982). Some may have been charitably remanded to their parents' custody many times before being arrested. Months or years of delinquent behavior may pass (Farrington, 1986), even after the legal labelling, before parents of delinquents are studied. During this time, these parents' self-esteem may plummet. They may become disturbed, stressed, stigmatized, alcoholic, hardened, and even rejected by their own families as a result of the delinquency episodes and labelling processes.

Parents of delinquents may also suffer from parental "burnout" (Rubin and Quinn-Curan, 1983:84). Unfortunately, burnout is a phenomenon which tends to be studied as an affliction of professionals, whether in nursing or teaching, rather than of parents. However, the concept and the reality it represents apply equally well to parents, especially to parents of difficult children (Procaccini and Kiefaber, 1983). Yet, this reality is only beginning to emerge in studies. In summary, as indicated by a few of the researchers mentioned earlier, in many cases, parental malfunctioning and instability may be the result of delinquency or may have been exacerbated by it. The causality pattern may actually be a reverse one in many cases and, in others, an interactive or circular one (Gard and Berry, 1986; Patterson, 1980; Wahler, 1975).

A second bias is found in those studies whereby *researchers interview the delinquents only*. While delinquents' perceptions of their parents is a legitimate research topic, it ought to be taken for what it is: *perceptions*. The reality may be entirely different. (It is interesting that when researchers interview both parents and adolescents, they often obtain divergent results [Rittenhaus and Miller, 1984; Tims and Masland, 1985].) It is possible that delinquents' perceptions are part of a distorted thinking system as their behavior often is. In other words, if the thinking system of many adolescents is out of step, is it not possible that they may not be very good judges of their own parents? It is also possible that the social distance which exists between delinquents and their parents prevents them from knowing their parents well.

I further propose that children who are delinquent may need to explain away or rationalize their acts to others. They need to look good, a need they share with everyone else. They may seek scapegoats on which to blame their problems, and parents are vulnerable targets because of societal ideologies. Researchers who report that delinquents are more likely to have negative perceptions of their parents than nondelinquents have an interesting research result to publish. The error resides in that another conclusion is often drawn from these results: that the parents always are the way they are described by their delinquent children. And even if they were as described by their delinquent children, another error is then committed: the direction of the causality. Indeed, the parents may be as described by their children because of the children's behavior.

In this vein, many researchers report that delinquents often complain of low family cohesiveness and not getting along with their parents (Brennan et al., 1975; Canter, 1982). It is reasonable to conclude from these studies where a control group of nondelinquents is utilized that there are more problems of communication, of hostility, and of lack of affection between delinquent children and their parents than between nondelinquent children and their parents. It is premature, however, to place such results in the middle of a discussion or of a chapter which focuses on parental causality or antecedents. Indeed, it could as well be concluded that the children's difficult behavior has pushed their parents away, that after having failed to reach their children for years, many parents with-draw; that after years of hostility from their children, parents may become hostile.

In a comparison of delinquents and nondelinquents, Andry (1971) found that delinquents perceived their parents, especially their fathers, to be embarrassed at openly showing affection for them. These adolescents, however, also felt more embarrassed at showing their feelings for their parents than did nondelinquents. This, he concludes, implies a causal link from the parents to the adolescents. Instead, we propose that there may be an interaction between parents' and adolescents' inhibitions rather than a unidirec-tional causality. Moreover, the adolescents may actually be project-ing onto their parents their own affective problems. (See also Lin-den and Hackler, 1973.)

Similarly, Alexander (1973) videorecorded discussion sessions involving families with a delinquent child and families with no de-linquent children. He found that the former were less supportive of each other and less integrated than the latter. Again, the inferred direction of causality is from the family to the delinquent. This is certainly not an unreasonable conclusion. But the alternative might be equally worth exploring: families with a delinquent child may not be able to communicate as smoothly when the child is there because the child is the focus of a great deal of stress, friction, and threats. The act of being a delinquent is not a supportive act in itself. Therefore, it is possible that (a) these families have become less communicative because of the problems caused by the child and/or (b) had these families been tested in the absence of the prob-lematic child, they might have scored much higher on integration. Indeed, in Chapter 7, some students describe how the moment they entered their house, the family situation became explosive because they were so difficult to be with. Moreover, researchers have found, in studies of schizophrenia, that the presence of a schizo-phrenic child in an experimental situation hindered parents' ability to perform cognitive tasks; moreover, parents of nonschizophrenic children did not differ from parents of schizophrenic children when experimentally paired with a normal and then a schizophrenic child (Liem, 1974; Mishler and Waxler, 1966; Waxler, 1974).

From the point of view of the delinquent, Tolan (1988:328) has intimated a similar explanation for the often-reported finding of a lower sense of cohesion in families of delinquents. "It could be that delinquent adolescents desire less involvement with the family because that is the site of conflict and turmoil. Their delinquent and antisocial behavior may have made family contact painful for everyone, lessening its attraction." This perspective certainly allows for the analysis of delinquents as social actors who may have a negative effect on their families and produce their own negative familial environment.

Other intriguing studies presented within the same unidirectional vein show that delinquent males are less likely than nondelinquent males to identify with their fathers' characteristics (Andry, 1971, 1950). This is at times interpreted to mean that the *parents* are faulty role models. But it could also be interpreted to mean that the delinquents have rejected the parents as worthwhile models. The adolescents' peer culture may be the culprit; or the adolescents' own personality characteristics may have prevented appropriate identification and role learning.

A third bias arises when researchers, especially social workers and probation officers, *inadvertently reward* delinquents who verbalize negative perceptions of their parents. It is significant that this phenomenon has not been studied. But this lacuna is hardly surprising in view of the fact that our ideology is slanted in the direction of parental fault. Rather, it would be worthwhile to consider that delinquents may have some ready-made or subcultural theories to proffer for their behavior. Even among nondelinquent adolescents, it is part of the peer group culture at many schools to be "against" one's parents. Richards (1979) has found that 25 percent of her middle-class high school respondents were angry at their parents most of the time. Brennan et al. (1978) have found that, as they age, adolescents evaluate their parents more negatively. Nye (1980) discusses parents in terms of the costs and rewards adolescents incur from them.

PARENTS AS A READY-MADE EXPLANATION

Researchers and authorities may unwittingly reinforce these adolescent "theories," either by their line of questioning, the interest they show suddenly when the delinquent broaches a topic, or the sympathy they give the delinquent when he/she expounds on familial misery and parental abuse/neglect/malfunction. It may not be coincidental that this "cause" of their delinquency may be the source of the only sympathy they will receive in their careers as delinquents. These adolescents proffer explanations which meet the expectations of the child-saving agencies. These perceptions of parents are then *shared* by delinquents and agencies: the *parents* can then be targeted for blame and "treatment." This ideological perspective then justifies an entire array of interventions with the families (e.g., Leyton, 1979), for which perhaps the peer group or the school system should be targeted (Elliott et al., 1985; West and Farrington, 1977).

We have seen in previous chapters that research and conclusions derived from studies have been heavily influenced by clinical ideologies and theories that see parents as the main agents responsible for their children's personalities and maintain that personalities are irrevocably formed during the first years of life. Moreover, we have seen, in a previous section, that students learn about the causes of juvenile delinquency from textbooks which are still largely under the influence of old theories and which have yet to be exposed to new psychological and sociological orientations. Some of these students become probation officers or social workers who deal with delinquents. The vicious circle of parental causality is therefore perpetuated and passed on to the clients and their unfortunate parents.

Sixteen years ago, I initiated a study of various types of sexual abuse. But, as other research commitments entered into competition, the project had to be abandoned. Nevertheless, by that time ten teenage "hookers" had already been interviewed—all runaways, it turned out—aged thirteen to sixteen. I was intrigued by the widely accepted clinical opinion to the effect that young prostitutes inevitably have been the victims of abuse, especially sexual, within their families. I did not broach this topic, however, until the end of each interview. By that time, only four girls had volunteered such information without being queried. (In two other cases, the girls had been active sexually with peers, but not within their families.) Noticing my sudden interest at their volunteered information, the four girls went on at great length on this topic, details and all. But, in two cases, there were many obvious contradictions.

Towards the end of these interviews, I questioned parts of their stories. One girl laughed and said: "I nearly got you, didn't I?"

Both girls explained, each in their own words, that familial sexual abuse is a "good line" to tell at the police station and to case workers. They get a sympathetic ear when they come up with such a tale. They explained that, after a few months on the street, "most girls" use a similar story. The only thread common to these ten girls was that their familial background was generally economically deprived and that they didn't get along well with their parents. Some seemed to be coming from disturbed families while others seemed to have had good families—that is, when one could read between the lines of their stories.

Therefore, of the ten teenage prostitutes, only two (20 percent) probably had a true background of abuse at home. This 20 percent hardly matches journalistic and clinical claims that "nearly all" these girls have such a background. An alternate explanation which deserves exploration is that it is the young prostitutes' subculture which encourages this "parental causality." Parental mistreatment becomes one of the "badges" worn by these youths in their yearning for belonging with street peers. As well, *it may be the encouragement they receive from police, media, and case workers which reinforces this explanatory behavior*.

These facts came to haunt me through the years: students write a structured autobiography, *anonymously*, in nearly all my classes. Throughout the years, approximately 20 to 25 percent of all female students have recounted sexual abuse from family members or persons they knew well. This statistic is remarkable considering that these students *are not asked any question about sex*: they simply bring in the sexual abuse under the rubric of "things that have been painful to you" at given ages. What is more remarkable is that the percentage of sexual abuse is the same for both groups of girls: the ten teenage prostitutes and the hundreds of women students who have written their autobiographies (see also Government of Canada, 1984). Yet, none of the women students had a history of running away or becoming prostitutes. Moreover, none used the sexual abuse as an excuse for subsequent failures.

We may be in the presence of a circularity of explanation among "street kids," welfare personnel, police, and clinicians. On the one hand, as discussed in earlier chapters, we are loathe to attribute agency to children, even to adolescents. And we are perhaps still living the dream of the "natural innocence" of children, even though these children are practically adults. From such a double ideology, it is only a small step to believe (and to find out — one often finds what one is looking for) that delinquents are not responsible for their acts. Then, who is? Since societal causes are too "difficult" (costly) to tackle, it is easy to blame the nearest, most "obvious" and most vulnerable cause — parents. Parental causality is discussed in the media, among adolescents themselves, and by the child saving industry. All these sources of information feed on each other — circularity of explanation.

Although I have analyzed only a tiny fraction of the wealth of information contained in the students' autobiographies (see Chapter 7), one overwhelming impression garnered from the entirety of the material is that there are two main groups of persons who are at the source of a majority of children's and adolescents' miseries in our society: their peers and some of their teachers. (Peers are both described as the main source of problems and the main source of joy, by many.) Siblings come next followed in the distance by parents. When students describe their most painful experiences as they were growing, peer cruelty and influence loom above all else. This is followed by teachers' insensitivity, and even mental abuse. Although they exist, parents who have been cruel, abusive, and insensitive to their children's needs are by comparison far fewer. In fact, students — even those who went through a period of delinquency — generally attribute the onset of psychological, academic, and behavioral problems primarily to their peer associations.

THE MISSING LINKS: SPECIFIC RESEARCH SUGGESTIONS

The literature surveyed in the previous sections was condensed for space considerations. Similarly, the following section is not exhaustive. It is meant to present a sample of research suggestions which could begin redressing the unidirectionality of the research on delinquents' parents. Moreover, many of these suggestions could be applied to the study of reciprocal parent effect/child effect in general, and, might thus offer additional perspectives to those presented in the first chapters of this book.

Longitudinal Research

Thomas and Chess (1977) propose that children's temperament can contribute to negative interactions with their parents (see also Webster-Stratton and Eyberg, 1982). In this respect, there are indications that traits which are highly correlated with certain types of criminal acts persist over time. Such is the case with aggressiveness which has proven to be highly consistent from early childhood onward (Farrington, 1978, 1982; Huesmann et al., 1984; Lefkowitz et al., 1977; Lerner et al., 1988; Loeber, 1982; Nylander, 1979; Robins and Ratcliffe, 1979). Consequently, many delinquents have, from infancy, exhibited personality traits that created tension, stress, and a variety of failed attempts at controlling the child on the part of the parents (Loeber, 1982).

So far, society has not taken these problems seriously as they have evolved mainly within the mother/child dyad, that is, at a psychological level with low social visibility and between individuals with low social value (mothers and children [Sidel, 1986]). By the time the problematic child is ten years old, the parents may be more stressed, less functional, and more hostile and rejecting than parents who have children without dysfunctional personality traits. At that point, researchers observe "maladjusted" parents correlating with delinquent children and conclude that such a familial background has contributed to the delinquency.

Therefore, it is suggested that causality would be more effectively studied within the context of a longitudinal study beginning either during *pregnancy* or at the *birth* of the targeted child (so as to know how parents were before the arrival of the child), progressing through the child's infancy and adolescence (to learn the child's characteristics and the development of the parents' behavior and attitudes). At any point in time, parents whose children are to become delinquent and/or particularly difficult could then be compared to parents whose children will not become delinquent or difficult. Most importantly, as difficult child behavior is detected, parental antecedents could be separated from parental reactions (or child effect). While it is obvious that the timing of these happenings could not always be disentangled (because of the rapidity with which circularity of effect can set in), less biased results would be achieved *if child effect is built in the original design* than when it is ignored at the outset of the research project and merely thrown in ex post facto.

Although a few extensive longitudinal studies exist, none has been specifically designed *from the outset to include child effect* (Rutter et al., 1983). In the studies herein suggested, it would be important to include official delinquents as well as self-reported delinquents who have not come to the attention of the law. Certain types of self-reported delinquent behavior may indeed be more problematic to parents than official delinquency. For instance, children who are violent toward their parents or steal from them may affect them more than children who are caught shoplifting.

Sibling Research

Siblings have been studied in the context of families containing multiple delinquents (Farrington et al., 1975), sibling conflict and aggressiveness (Loeber et al., 1983; Steinmetz, 1981), and the negative influence older children can have on their younger siblings (Stott, 1966; Rittenhaus and Miller, 1984). In keeping with the premises of our earlier sections, it would be worthwhile to compare nondelinquent siblings' perceptions of their parents to delinquents' perceptions of the same parents. Similarly, these nondelinquent siblings' interaction with the parents could be observed in the absence and then in the presence of the delinquent child.

I have hypothesized earlier that many ''delinquent'' families function at a normal level when the delinquent child is absent or removed from the situation. Second, I hypothesized that certain delinquents' perceptions of their parents may be faulty or deficient. We would further hypothesize that parents' interactions with their nondelinquent children *are* different from their interactions with their delinquent child. Or, conversely, it could be that parents react to nondelinquent siblings just as negatively because their entire parental experience has become clouded by the delinquency (halo effect). It is relevant that studies in the area of disabled and chronically ill children have found difficulty in family functioning because of the requisites of the handicap (McKeever, 1981), as well as problems of adjustment among siblings (Falkman, 1977; Klein,

1976; Spinetta and Deasy-Spinetta, 1981). It is only logical to suggest that similar familial deficits are created by delinquents at the expense of their siblings (Spurgen, 1984; Wilkinson et al., 1982).

Family Reconstruction Research

Family reconstruction after a delinquent child has been removed or has left home is a topic which has not been adequately researched. In a longitudinal study on divorce, there were families who had extremely difficult teenagers at the time of the first interview (Ambert, 1984). By the second interview (two years later), the most difficult (hostile, aggressive, acting out) children had been removed from these families. *All* the single-parent mothers were happier, healthier, had better control over their remaining children, and were more satisfied with their children than they had been at Time 1. (See Chapter 8.) All were *relieved* that the problematic child was gone. Rutter and Giller (1983) have gone so far as to recommend that problem children whose parents have difficulty accepting the problems be adopted at an early age. (See also Hawkins and Meadowcroft, 1984, regarding trained foster parents.)

Researchers might want to explore what changes occur in a family, especially in parents, after a delinquent is removed from the family. What are the processes involved? Admittedly, the stigma remains and damage-control can therefore be only partial. Parents may still worry about the future of the child and of this child's future children. If parents are viewed as *victims* of delinquency, it then follows that they should be offered the moral support that is belatedly being offered to victims of rape and of crimes in general. But, in order to offer the help needed, one has first to learn about the damage done and what the needs are.

So far, when evaluation or outcome research is carried out with a view to preventing the recurrence of delinquency, the positive outcome is measured mainly in terms of a reduced delinquency, of the delinquent's adoption of functional attitudes and behavior, and of the familial reintegration of the delinquent. Such studies are necessary but the other question is: at what cost, if any, to the parents? At what cost emotionally, physically, and socially?

Research on Parents' Adult Development

How does the marital relationship of delinquents' parents change through various phases of delinquency, arrest, treatment or incarceration? What are parental patterns of alcoholism, drug use and abuse, psychiatric treatment, and physical health through the same phases? If longitudinal studies cannot be carried out step by step, retrospective accounts from *both* parents *separately* should be correlated with the stages on the delinquent's official record and recollection of the timing of first nonrecorded offences. The underlining assumption to be investigated here is that delinquent behavior (a stressor) will negatively impact on parents' happiness, marriage, health, and overall functioning (with the exception of parents who are themselves so deviant that they are immune to child effect). This could be so even in those cases where familial disorganization was a cause of delinquency.

We should also study the effect of juvenile delinquency on parents' adult development. There is a burgeoning literature illustrating how adults go through stages of development (e.g., Anderson et al., 1983; Clausen, 1986 for review). Teenagers and middle-aged parents both face problems of identity (Hill, 1980). Steinberg (1985) and Silverberg and Steinberg (1987) suggest that the phase of the parents' life cycle is an important consideration in the study of adolescents; as well, they propose that understanding parent-adolescent relationship may be helpful in studying the parents' adult development.

In fact, Baruch et al. (1983) have even suggested that it is because of the presence of adolescents that parents reevaluate their own lives, and experience psychological strain. Moreover, Hoffman and Manis (1979) have found that parenting adolescents is more likely to provoke anxiety in parents than parenting children of other ages. Montemayor (1983, 1986) has also shown that 20 percent of parents experience difficulties with their adolescents while another 20 percent experience "intermittent relational problems." Yet these adolescents are not even delinquent.

It could then be inferred that middle-age development for parents of delinquent children could be significantly disturbed by the consequences of having a delinquent child. If, as Silverberg and Steinberg (1987) point out, there is no research studying the effect on parents of their adolescents' individuation processes, we are all the more in need of studies on the impact of adolescent delinquency. Not only are we interested in short-term effects, but we also want to know: What are the long-term implications for these parents in later life? In old age?

For instance, Silverberg and Steinberg (1987) found that mothers, but not fathers, reported a much lower level of general life satisfaction when they experienced conflict with their sons and tended to show more psychological symptoms when they had intense conflict with their daughters. Thus, not only does the sex of the child impact but so does the sex of the parent. It would be highly important to have longitudinal studies of parents who experience severe conflict, including delinquency, with their adolescents to see how such parents recover or fail to recover in the long run. Would such parents continue to experience lower self-esteem as they did when their children were delinquent? Would their marriages be more likely to be disrupted at a later age?

At a more advanced developmental level, we would want to know how middle-aged and senior persons who have had delinquent adolescents might differ as *grandparents* compared to those who did not go through such problems earlier. Do these grandparents perceive their roles differently? Do they have additional responsibilities for their grandchildren? Do they distance themselves from their grandchildren? We have yet to read one single study addressing these issues.

Research on the Impact of Agencies of Social Control

In view of the fact that the clinical and much of the empirical literature is slanted toward parental causality in delinquency, it is certainly reasonable to assume that such parents may be viewed very negatively by agencies responsible for the apprehension, treatment, rehabilitation, and incarceration of delinquents. Even the literature on disabled children emphasizes guilt-based theories of parental behavior (Darling, 1983). As Darling (1987:54) points out, "When parents seek help for their children's problems, they are often treated as though they, and not their children, were the patients or the clients." Anderson and Spanier (1980) have found that the ideology held by probation officers affects their perception of their work and their labelling process. Surely, a similar process can be at work vis-à-vis delinquents' parents. Consequently, what is the quality of the parents' interaction with these agencies? What feelings do these agencies arouse in parents? What control do these agencies exert on parents? What demands do they make of parents? Do these agencies help parents or do they burden them (with guilt, blame, unnecessary advice and requests)?

The literature on disabled children documents well that parents are often made to feel helpless as well as incompetent in dealing with their own and their children's lives by various service delivery personnel (Budoff, 1975; Strickland, 1982; Yoshida et al., 1978). It is not difficult to see how this could even be more so in the case of delinquent children's parents because the official ideology generally holds them responsible. As Rubin and Quinn-Curan (1983:73) point out, "Seeing the parents as 'the problem' assumes that the parents are emotionally disturbed. Professionals under siege sometimes begin to fall back on their perception of parents to justify their desire to excuse themselves from their responsibility for responding to parents' concerns." Later on, they point out that, when society cannot meet a request for services, the assumption is that there is something wrong with the parents (p. 74). This preempts the need for an examination of systemic failures. "Too often in American life, problems that are institutional in nature are treated as problems of the individual" (Dornbusch and Strober, 1988:4). Zigler and Black (1989:10) advance a similar criticism when they point out that past social service programs were based on a "deficit model" and on "curing deficiencies." (We should add here that these models are still practiced as a regular matter of course.)

Moreover, professional and agency intrusion means that parents' personal and family lives will be scrutinized and "their family's boundaries will need to become highly permeable" (Rubin and Quinn-Curan, 1983:89). For instance, Spillane-Grieco (1984:165), in a study of parents of runaways, quoted parents as "reporting some reservations about seeking help because they felt that they would be blamed." At a different level, a study on the relative merits of "intensive supervision programs" for delinquents at home concluded that such programs were viable without a single word as to the costs or the benefits to the juveniles' *parents* (Barton and Butts, 1990).

We have already alluded to the role which agents of social control (clinicians, social workers, and police) may play in the explanations offered by some categories of delinquents concerning specific aspects of their familial background. Space considerations preclude an in-depth presentation of research strategies on these formal reactors to delinquency, who are both products and reproducers of a wider societal ideology. What effect do these agencies have on delinquents' subcultures and/or explanations? And, in turn, what effect do these explanations (such as parent blaming) have on family relations, parental well-being, and rehabilitation prognosis? To what extent is parental blaming in delinquency a social construct which is perpetuated to serve the interest of at least a segment of the child-saving industry? To what extent is parental blaming used to hide the failure and the inadequacy of the societal response to parents/children and, especially, to delinquency and to the families of delinquents?

CONCLUSIONS

As the focus of a unidirectional ideology of causality, and as targets for various child-saving industries, parents bear a double burden of vulnerability. Parental vulnerability is not only a valid scientific topic of research but it is also a topic which begs to be addressed in a socially responsible manner.

In sociology, child socialization has been emphasized and has been accompanied by the failure to consider how children socialize their parents. Similarly, we have generally failed to inquire into the effect of children on parents. This gap in the general literature is reflected in the field of delinquency, and is also magnified therein because the societal costs of delinquency are calculated from the costs that the delinquent incurs to the social system but only rarely to the familial system, and even more rarely, if at all, to parents. Delinquency is generally analyzed as a social problem; we have yet to address the question of how it affects parents directly and indirectly.

The study of the effect of juvenile delinquency on parents is multifaceted. On the one hand, various areas of parental life can be touched, including self-concept, health, and marital and familial relations, to name only a few. As well, the effect may vary in strength and in the areas affected depending on the stage of the delinquent trajectory which is targeted for research. For instance, oppositional child behavior preceding the official episode and labelling may not affect parents in the same manner as might officially labelled delinquency and, later on, recidivism or a return to adolescent conformity. Furthermore, the effect on parents will be mediated by parental characteristics, as explained in previous chapters. Thus, parents' material, personal and social resources — including their marital, class and ethnic status — will act as buffers or as facilitators of adolescent effect. In turn, the adequacy of the societal response will also act as an exacerbating or mitigating agent on the effect on parents.

The study of the effect of juvenile delinquency on parents not only constitutes a "new" field of inquiry (in the sense that it has not been researched previously), but it is also a field which is at the intersection of many theoretical and substantive traditions. Research in this field should take place in the sociology of the family, psychology, and juvenile delinquency.

Chapter 6

Children's Emotional Problems and Difficult Child Episodes

We will now turn to the impact on parents of two types of children. First, children who have emotional problems, whether diagnosed (such as schizophrenia) or undiagnosed and, second, "difficult" children — that is, children whose behavior is problematic for parents, teachers, and even peers. There is certainly a great deal of overlap between the two categories of children, as a good proportion of the children who exhibit difficult episodes over a long period suffer from emotional problems. But not all do. Similarly, not all emotionally disturbed children are difficult children. Many are actually very compliant and withdrawn children who cause no difficulties whatever to others. It should finally be added that there is also overlap between delinquency and emotional problems and, especially, delinquency and difficult child episodes. Thus, Chapters 5 and 6 are to a great extent complementary.

As was the case for juvenile delinquency, a survey of *textbooks* on the sociology of health and medicine, as well as of mental illness, produces only a few paragraphs acknowledging the impact of a person's emotional problems on his/her family. Even less is written on the effect of *children's* emotional problems on their parents. Authors who do discuss the topic (e.g., Litman, 1974) admit that there is very little to go on. Consequently, their presentation of the subject has to be very sketchy, and this further compounds the general difficulty of addressing this question and of educating students and practitioners on the matter.

THE FAMILY IN PERSPECTIVE

This lack of material on the effect on parents of their children's emotional problems is related to the fact that, as pointed out by Spiegel (1982), etiological explanations of emotional problems have, over the centuries, moved closer to the home, namely to childhood experiences within the family circle. As already explained in Chapters 1 and 5, parents have been targeted as the major cause of their children's problems. There has thus been no ideological or theoretical incentive to focus on child effect or even on reciprocal effects between parents and children.

The lack of material on the topic herein discussed is especially vexing in view of the fact that the issue of the responsibility of families for the care of their sick members has been debated for well over two centuries (Moroney, 1981). One would expect that caring for the sick has consequences for the caregivers and that these consequences should at the very least be mentioned (see Chapter 9). Similarly, the treatment of the emotionally disturbed has also been moved closer to home: deinstitutionalization has meant an increased responsibility for the family (Hatfield, 1978; Spaniol et al., 1984; Test and Stein, 1980), especially for mothers (Hatfield, 1978). The assumption has been that care in the community is better than institutional care. Not only has this latest ideological shift placed an enormous burden on families (and patients), but the assumption may be faulty. This may be so because familial care in the community has been judged superior to institutional care, which has a long history of providing poor and mismanaged care (Finch and Groves, 1983:10). However, *quality* institutional care may be just as good as familial care. In fact, it might also be so at a lower cost to parents, both emotionally, physically, and socially.

The family provides a service to the community by reproducing the labor force (and the future tax base). This service becomes magnified when the family has to shoulder the added cost of caring for citizens who are disabled or emotionally impaired. As Mumford (1983:199) points out, "the stresses and strains imposed by the rather isolated small family, the confined living space in cities, and the great expectations we now have for how much parents should do for children all can impose tremendous strain on parents of young children." Again, it is only logical to assume that this is the more so when the children have emotional problems. In the case of adult children who are chronically ill, their parents often become responsible for the search for services as the patients exhaust various avenues that have successively failed (Eckholm, 1986).

In the previous chapter, I reported having found no direct research on the effect of juvenile delinquency on parents; however, there is a sizeable literature on the effect of having a mentally delayed, an autistic, and a physically disabled child. I wonder whether the total absence of research in terms of delinquency may not stem from the more masculine character of the researchers in the field. In contrast, mental retardation is generally studied by educational psychologists who are often women. It is possible that, as a field of expertise becomes more feminized, the focus is less likely to be so unidirectional. *Women* researchers may be more likely to empathize with these children's parents. Since *they* raise their own children, they may be better able to perceive the effect the children have on them than men, who are generally less involved and less affected as fathers.

LITERATURE ON CHILD EFFECT

In spite of the fact that the literature is still slanted toward the traditional unidirectional causality path of parents as the independent variable in their children's illness, there is a sound, albeit small, body of literature describing the deleterious effects on parents of having psychiatrically ill children (Arey and Warheit, 1980; Cook, 1988; Holroyd, 1974, 1975, 1976, Ricci, 1970; Doll, 1975; Thompson and Doll, 1982) especially where the child, often an adult, resides at home with the parents (Arey and Warheit, 1980; Cook, 1988; Herz et al., 1979; Kreisman et al., 1979; Holroyd, 1975) and there is a great deal of contact (Anderson and Lynch, 1984).

There is also some literature which documents how demented seniors exert a considerable degree of stress on their adult children and spouses. Although the focus of this book is on children eighteen and under, it is relevant to take note of this literature (Eagles et al., 1987; Gilleard, 1984; Gilleard et al., 1984a, 1984b; Robins et al.,

1982), inasmuch as these seniors and mentally ill children both require high-density care and supervision. Recent research also indicates that abuse of the elderly is often associated with living with spouses or adult children who are themselves emotionally unstable or dependent financially on the elderly (Pillemer and Finkelhor, 1989). Thus, emotionally disturbed children can exert a negative influence on their parents through the parents' last years of life.

In 1972, Brown et al. found that relatives' low-quality level of expressed emotion toward schizophrenic family members was strongly related to relapse (see also Vaughn and Leff, 1976; Leff et al., 1982). But they also found that a decrease in the patients' symptoms led to a reduction of negativism in relatives. They added,

> We are unable to comment on claims that factors in the relative's personality and handling of the patient as a child cause the first onset of the illness, except to say that the fact that expressed emotion acts as strongly in marital partners as in parents argues for a reactive rather than a causal model. (p. 255)

When we assume that the parents' handling of the child caused schizophrenia, we may be wrong, "in which case harm may be done both to relative and patient" (p. 256). The relative may needlessly feel guilty or outraged, while the patients may turn away from a relative whom they erroneously believe to be at the source of their problems. This concept of reverse causality is also supported by Kanter et al. (1987), Cook and Cohler (1986), and Seywert (1984), who argue that relatives' "negativism" may be *caused by* rather than be a cause of the difficulties encountered because of the child's mental state and consequent aberrant behavior.

It is relevant here to note that mothers of hyperactive children whose symptoms diminished after taking medication showed corresponding behavioral changes (Barkley, 1981; Tarver-Behring and Barkley, 1985), and the same parental changes have occurred in children trained to behave differently (Brunk and Hengeler, 1984). For instance, in studies of schizophrenia, researchers have found that the presence of a schizophrenic child in an experimental situation hindered parents' ability to perform cognitive tasks; moreover, parents of nonschizophrenic children did not differ from parents of schizophrenic children when experimentally paired with a normal and then a schizophrenic child (Liem, 1974; Mishler and Waxler, 1966; Waxler, 1974). These studies taken together seem to indicate that the emotionally disturbed do influence others' responses to them, including behavioral responses. The emotionally disturbed are social actors with agency, even though they may not necessarily be responsible for their acts. Thus, they affect others, especially their parents.

Brown et al. (1988) have found that parents of children who suffer from ADD (attention deficit disorder) score significantly higher on depression scales than parents of nondisordered children. "ADD children often have a way of disrupting activities, wherever they may be." The authors add that, as a result, "these parents become discouraged, demoralized, and depressed." They also suggest the possibility that "parents who have emotional difficulties react less well to provocative child behavior, a reaction that may exacerbate the child's behavioral difficulties" (p. 126). Hence, circularity of effect between child and parental characteristics, as discussed in Chapters 3 and 4.

We know very little of the impact of emotional problems on parents at various stages of the development of the problem. Which stage is the hardest? The pre-diagnosis stage? Or is it more difficult once a diagnosis has been rendered, or treatment initiated? Raymond et al. (1975) detail the stages family members go through as the illness progresses, including guilt, anger, blame, shame, grief, confusion and acceptance of reality. There is a great deal of similarity here with the results of studies of bereavement and diagnostics of handicaps such as retardation. Often, the impact on the parents of mentally handicapped children begins occurring at the infancy stage (Gath, 1977, 1978).

The impact of emotional problems or illness on parents can be studied practically only where treatment is sought or given; otherwise, obtaining a sample of emotionally disturbed children to study is difficult and perhaps impossible. This leads to another research problem: parents probably seek treatment only after they have reached the limit of their understanding or of their patience. This may be especially so in lower-class families where the ratio of medically unattended symptoms to attended ones is very high (Alpert et al., 1967). Moreover, lower-class persons have also been found to understand emotional problems less well than their more educated contemporaries (Hollingshead and Redlich, 1958). Therefore, one could expect that the impact of children's emotional problems on parents may differ by class. It may carry a heavier objective burden (such as financial costs), but a lighter subjective burden in the lower-class, when subjective burden is defined as "the family's perception of duress and oppression caused by the patient's presence in the home" (Arey and Warheit, 1980:160; see also Gubman and Tessler, 1987).

Another effect of children's emotional problems on parents may be that, when difficulties persist and demands mount on parents, the latter may begin to resent their child. Parents may become less interested, less overtly affectionate, less communicative. It would be interesting to study which types of parents go through detachment. As Loeber and Stouthamer-Loeber (1986:54) point out, "it is also difficult to love children who make one's life miserable," although the ill children are not responsible for all their actions.

> . . . and I would sit and pray for seven o'clock to come . . . and I would say to myself, "Tomorrow is going to be like today, and the day after tomorrow is going to be like today as well, and how am I going to live this way because my life is just impossible. I just have no joy from this child." (Mother of an autistic boy [Mack and Webster, 1980:36])

What kinds of mechanisms do parents utilize to maintain a high level of commitment to their emotionally-disturbed children? As it is normal for parents to supervise their children less as they grow older (Goldstein, 1984; Patterson and Stouthamer-Loeber, 1984), what kinds of strains does continued supervision entail? Parental characteristics such as commitment and expectations will be important variables in this outcome.

IMPACT ON THE MOTHER

Health studies unanimously show that the mother is overwhelmingly responsible for the care of ill family members, including deciding when to seek medical assistance (Litman, 1974). An elaboration of these points can be found in Chapter 9. The few studies which have explored the topic have discovered the impact of a child's emotional problems to be higher on the mother than the father (Cook, 1988; Kazak and Marvin, 1984). Similarly, the effect of a mentally or physically handicapped child is greater on the mother (Gath and Gumley, 1986), especially in terms of work (Dupont, 1980; Pahl and Quine, 1984; Wilkin, 1981).

But now that well over 50 percent of mothers of small children are in the labor force, with even higher percentages among mothers whose children are in school, one can only wonder about the added impact on the working mother, or on the one who would want to be employed, of having an emotionally disturbed child. We have already reported in an earlier chapter that studies of employed mothers indicate that they are responsible for most of the housework and child care. In view of these facts, several research questions could be explored on the effect of children in the area of maternal employment:

1. Are mothers of emotionally disturbed youngsters less likely to be employed full-time or more likely to be employed part-time?

2. Are employed mothers less or more successful at work than mothers who have no emotionally disturbed children? On the one hand, it could be argued that the stress and requirements resulting from parenting an emotionally disturbed child would take a toll on a woman's work efficacy and on her career development. But it could also be argued that such a woman may seek a compensatory outlet in her work to make up for the problems at home and, therefore, would be a more dedicated worker (Lerner and Galambos, 1986a).

3. At what point in the development of the child's illness or disorder does the mother leave work, if she does?

4. When the child's symptoms become too disruptive, is there a greater maternal vulnerability depending on the mother's age as well as stage in her work career? In other words, are younger or older mothers more affected? Which are more likely to choose to stay home? Similarly, when a woman has already been employed for many years, how differently will she react compared to a mother who has only recently begun working?

Another series of effects on mothers which should be explored are related to the area of their health. It is reasonable to assume that parenting an emotionally disturbed child is a stressful situation. What kinds of physical and emotional symptomatology may the mothers themselves experience as a result? And how do these mothers treat their symptoms? Medical drugs would be a highly pertinent focus of inquiry in this respect. It could be hypothesized that mothers of emotionally disturbed children will use more medical drugs than other mothers. Psychotropic drugs in particular could be used as an escape outlet, as well as a stress-reducing outlet. Moreover, even the physical health of the mothers is likely to be affected, especially as a result of stress. In addition, a study of parents of adult children who were chronically mentally ill found a large amount of physical violence directed toward mothers (Cook, 1988). There are, consequently, many potentially valuable avenues of research concerning the health status and behavior of mothers of emotionally disturbed children.

RELATIONSHIP WITH PROFESSIONALS

An important aspect of the effect of children's emotional problems on their parents concerns the parents' relationship with professionals, especially psychiatrists, psychologists, and clinical case workers. We have already broached questions arising out of the professional ideology of parental blaming in the previous chapters. Additional material on professionals is presented in Chapter 9.

It is worthwhile here to reprint a paragraph from the chapter on juvenile delinquency as it is so well related to the topic at hand. The literature on handicapped children documents well how parents are often made to feel helpless, as well as incompetent, in dealing with theirs and their children's lives by various service delivery personnel (Budoff, 1975; Darling, 1988; Strickland, 1982; Yoshida et al., 1978). It is not difficult to see how this could be even more so in the case of parents of emotionally disturbed children, especially where the official ideology and the research literature generally hold them responsible. As Rubin and Quinn-Curan (1983:73) point out, "Seeing the parents as 'the problem' assumes that the parents are emotionally disturbed. Professionals under siege sometimes begin to fall back on their perception of parents to justify their desire to excuse themselves from their responsibility for responding to parents' concerns." Later on, the authors point out that, when society cannot meet a request for services, the assumption is that there is something wrong with the parents (p. 74). This preempts the need for an examination of systemic failures. Moreover, professional and agency intrusion means that parents' personal and family lives will be scrutinized and "their family's boundaries will need to become highly permeable" (p. 89).

Often, as the illness prolongs or recurs, family members come to believe that professionals view them as inferiors and even as intruders in their relatives' well-being. The psychiatrist Terkelsen emphasizes that, "When either therapist or family harbor the belief that schizophrenia is caused by personal experience with family members, therapeutic misalliance is bound to follow" (1983: 91). He came to this conclusion after having first misinterpreted the patients' parents' words. He describes how he "listened to the parents talk about life with the ill person, abstracting from their reports those interactional phenomena that I thought suggestive of parental pathology" (p. 192). He finally came to realize that abnormal patterns of family interaction were interpreted in terms of parental causality (also, Schopler and Loftin, 1969). Related to this, Beels (1974) noticed that family members' thinking was clearer when he met with them separately from their patients. Thus, how professionals perceive families may depend in large part on the circumstances under which they meet them. The presence itself of the patients seems to have a negative effect.

The concept of burden has been used in relation to emotional problems. It has been pointed out that one person's poor social performance is another person's burden, and, moreover, that it is important for clinicians to map out familial burdens (Gubman and Tessler, 1987). While the work force in mental hospitals, social agencies, and some professionals have *chosen* to care for the emotionally ill as their profession, the patients' families have made no such choice. They have no choice. Moreover, the family's potential in the treatment of the emotional problems of its mentally ill members is not actualized: the family is simply given a custodial role (Hatfield, 1979). As Falloon and Pederson point out, "In this capacity, they are often denied access to information concerning the nature of the patient's illness and guidelines on its management" (1985:156). However, an increased role for the family, especially the parents, may be at the expense of such parents. Falloon and Pederson (1985) have also shown that an effective family management program on the part of the therapeutic community substantially reduces parental stress and burden. In contrast, a program focusing intensively on the patients did not relieve family burden (Grad and Sainsbury, 1963).

Many parents feel that mental health professionals do not have a realistic view of the patient whom they often see socially under very limited conditions. The mother of a schizophrenic adolescent explained the matter thusly in an interview:

> The psychiatrist has not the slightest inkling as to how difficult it is for us to care for Jimmy. Right now he thinks that he is doing better. I mean, he says that because these days Jimmy communicates better and he was able to have a good conversation with him [his psychiatrist]. But his *behavior* isn't any different. He doesn't *see* it . . . At other times, we beg him to hospitalize him and he only tells us that we exaggerate. Strange thing is that when *we* think he's doing better he disagrees. That's when he starts digging up a few new symptoms. You know, it's enough to drive parents to become schizophrenic themselves.

THE CHILD'S APPEARANCE

A study of autistic children found that parents of normal *looking* and particularly attractive autistic children were more stressed than those parents whose autistic children did not look normal. In the latter case, the child's abnormal behavior was more socially acceptable because it was more easily explained. Its cause was visible. In the former case, relatives, friends, neighbors and observers expected the child to be normal and were less accepting of the disruptive and erratic behaviors which would occur. These parents felt that they were being blamed for not being able to control their child better.

> I was told off by a lady in the supermarket one day . . . he grabbed a tomato out of this lady's basket . . . She gave me the dirtiest look and looked at Jeremy and said, "A fellow your age should know better." And then looked at me as if I should be a parent who should teach him a few manners. (Mack and Webster, 1980:33)

> And she said, "Why don't you let your kid play out on the street?" She was quite serious! . . . And have him run over? If you did, he'd sit right down in the middle of road. (Mack and Webster, 1980:35)

In other words, where there is a lack of congruence between a child's appearance and behavior, parents may be more likely to blame themselves for the child's problems and be blamed by others. Moreover, if the child looks normal from birth and is reasonably well-adjusted in several spheres of behavior, and a delayed diagnosis is made, parents may be utterly confused by the discrepancies within the child. Thus, we can hypothesize that parents of children who look normal, who may even be gifted and socially pleasant with strangers or with relatives whom they occasionally see, are particularly vulnerable to stress, self-blame, loss of social support, and loss of physical and mental well-being.

It can be safely assumed that a large proportion of children and adolescents who suffer from emotional problems go undiagnosed and are never treated. Thus, they do not appear in clinical statistics and cannot be studied. Neither are their parents. Many children who are gifted in some areas and/or physically attractive are able to "pass" for normal. Others simply do not live in an environment which possesses the resources to diagnose and treat problematic children. Therefore, it would be very important to locate such a sample of children and compare their parents to the parents of children in treatment. While the parents of nondiagnosed children do not have to suffer the ignominies of public disclosure and contact with professionals who are at times unsympathetic, the parents of nondiagnosed children may suffer from confusion, lack of understanding, self-blaming, and lack of social support because their child's behavior is inappropriate in certain key contexts (whether with peers, at school, with them at home, or with them in public places). If such parents confide to their relatives about their problems, they may receive negative reactions as the relatives may see only the positive or pleasant aspects of the child. Jimmy's mother, whom we quoted earlier, had this to say on the topic:

> Jimmy is more than just a schizophrenic. He is it off and on. Naturally, when he's better, we take advantage of this to visit his grandparents on both sides, but that's difficult for us because they practically always see a normal Jimmy so to speak. And when he is normal, well he is charming. His grandparents *adore* him [he is the only male grandchild] and that's fine but the problem is that they don't want to hear us talk about him when he isn't OK. You should even see the incredulous looks they give us, or the long silences over the phone. They think *we*'re crazy. I'm sure they think we're bad parents and let me tell you that this creates a great deal of distance between us. We, my husband and I, are *their* children and they don't believe us. It's a big strain on us, as if we needed one more.

Moreover, such children may be particularly difficult to manage and can be very manipulative. Patterson (1976) has found that parents who try to suppress coercive behavior in a normal child generally succeed; but in a problem child, the disruptive behavior continues and is even accelerated (see also a replication by Snyder, 1977). Parents may become prisoners of the child who needs constant attention lest he/she disrupt the entire household, hurt himself, steal, run away, etc. These parents may even resort to bribing the child on a daily basis in order to obtain one hour of peace. One would expect a high rate of marital discord in such families as the two parents do not have the benefit of a label or a diagnostic around which they could unite and organize their family lives. Instead, they may blame each other and the child may pit each against the other.

DIFFICULT CHILD EPISODES

We have already focused on two types of children who are particularly "difficult" to cope with: the delinquent and the emotionally disturbed. Not only do these two types of children present particular difficulties to their parents, but the parents are faced with a public labelling of their children, or at the very least, a professional labelling. The emotionally disturbed child in treatment may actually not present many overt problems as far as the parents are concerned. For instance, one symptom of emotional problems is passivity and/or withdrawal. A child with such symptoms may be very easy to cope with from the parents' point of view.

But, as these children come to the attention of treating agencies, parents lose a certain degree of control over their own lives and even feel stigmatized. Thus, as we have seen, the effect that these children have on their parents may be exacerbated by social agencies. As we hypothesized earlier, the societal response will determine in large part how much and how positively/negatively parents will be affected by their children; and, as explained in Chapter 3, professionals are part of the societal response.

In contrast, the "difficult" child is much less likely to come to the attention of the social order, unless the behaviors spill into school dysfunction. All children are probably difficult during some stages of their young lifespan, that is, at certain age levels. This is well illustrated in Chapter 7, where students recall having had a more negative impact on their parents during their adolescence. Additionally, all children have their ups and downs as do adults. By the same token, difficult children have their moments of charm. Therefore, the problems created by the difficult child apply to a great extent to all children. There is a very thin line between the average child and the difficult child.

WHAT IS A DIFFICULT CHILD EPISODE?

We truly do not know how many difficult children there are. Galambos and Lerner (1987:899) and Lerner and Lerner (1983) talk of a difficult temperament existing when a child has a "low child-context goodness-of fit." Nevertheless, however interesting this definition is, it still refers us to contexts in the plural. Thus, it is fair to contend that researchers would probably have a hard time defining what constitutes a difficult child. Moreover, there may also be a great deal of disagreement among parents themselves. Indeed, because of their own needs and their own personalities, some parents may accept certain types of behavior more easily than others. For instance, hostile parents may not see anything unusual in a similarly hostile child, unless the child disrupts their lives. Quiet parents, on the other hand, may not tolerate so well an even lower degree of child aversion and may find their child's outbursts of hostility to be quite problematic.

It may actually be more practical to define difficult children in terms of *episodes* of problematic behavior rather than as a definite *type* of child. As pointed out earlier, even children who are considered difficult have their moments of charm and may make their parents quite happy. Naturally, the more frequently a child exhibits difficult episodes and the longer these episodes last, the more likely it is that this child will be perceived as difficult. The timing of the episodes may be another key variable: episodes which occur when parents are particularly tired, vulnerable, or busy may be more disruptive. Episodes which are displayed in public may also be more noticeable to parents — and more humiliating.

So far, we have been defining difficult behavior from the parental perspective, as if an independent observer could not spot such a child, or as if difficult behavior per se did not exist as a separate entity from parental reaction. Actually, most researchers agree on certain categories of behavior which can be labelled difficult. Examples are oppositional acts, especially when consistently displayed by the same child, who then becomes an oppositional child.

Whether this is a personality configuration or the child's reaction to a specific environment or even stimuli is irrelevant to the current presentation and will be left to specialists in the area to determine. Another set of examples are hostile acts: yelling, pushing, shoving, fighting, punching, hitting, name calling, banging objects, breaking objects. Another set are aversive acts which may include the previous category but to which can be added fussiness, whining, crying (not because of pain or hurt feelings), interruptions, sharp and immediate demands that are difficult to meet, disobedience, and refusal to comply. Another category would fall under dishonesty: lying, cheating, stealing. The hyperactive syndrome, although considered as a separate entity, can also be exhibited as episodes by children: moving about constantly, short attention span, shifting from one topic to another or one activity to another. Attention-seeking behaviors can fall in any one of the above categories but a child who is so inclined may exhibit a great many episodes of aversive activity.

In this section of the chapter, we are looking at the effect on parents of oppositional, hostile, aversive, dishonest, and hyperactive episodes exhibited by their children. Children with such profiles are often referred to as having conduct disorders (Herbert, 1987).

INCIDENCE OF DIFFICULT CHILD EPISODES

Patterson (1980) has found in one study that middle-class mothers of nonproblem children ("normal") experienced 3.4 disturbances per hour. Moreover, even normal children's sounds rose sharply when their mothers' attention was not immediately forthcoming. Minton et al. (1971) have found that mothers of two- to three-year olds issue a command or a disapproval every third minute. Patterson also found (1982) that problem boys engaged in aversive-coercive behaviors with their mothers at the rate of 0.75 per minute compared to 0.31 for nonproblem boys. The types of behaviors included under this rubric were crying, destructiveness, dependence, humiliation, ignoring, noncompliance, negativism, teasing, whining and yelling.

As children come to behave more and more in a way that could be labelled "difficult," not only does the rate of their aversive behavior go up, but so does the severity of the behaviors. Attempts to control such children often result in an escalation of parent-child adversity until the conflicts spill outside the home (Patterson, 1982). In extreme form of parenting breakdown, the children control the house (Loeber and Stouthamer-Loeber, 1986; Madden and Harbin, 1983).

Studies indicate that the younger a child is when behavior problems emerge, the more likely they are to persevere and to diversify, and the more serious the problems are likely to be (Loeber, 1982; Farrington, 1986). Research also indicates that mothers of difficult children become habituated to misbehavior and accept it as normal: such mothers have been found to be less able than mothers of non-problem children to distinguish misbehavior episodes from regular behavior. Loeber (1982) has also found that college students exposed to coercive child behavior were also less apt to notice coercive behavior in a laboratory setting.

Moreover, some children develop overt forms of difficult behavior (confrontational, aggressive) while others develop covert forms (stealing, vandalism, truancy, drug use). Loeber et al. (1983) point out that a third group of children develop both types of problem behavior. This group appears to be at higher risk of being eventually arrested for criminal acts.

Certain types of problematic behaviors appear quite stable over time, especially aggressiveness (Farrington, 1978, 1982; Fishbein, 1990; Huesmann et al., 1984; Lefkowitz et al., 1977; Loeber, 1982; Nylander, 1979; Robins and Ratcliffe, 1979). As children grow older and spend less time at home, problem behaviors may take place outside the home so that parents are not even aware of them. Teachers, peers, bystanders and even shopowners become the targets.

EFFECT OF BEHAVIOR

Mothers have been studied more extensively than fathers in their interactions with their children, in part because, until recently, mothers have been more available at home, but also because our ideologies have led us to believe that fathers are rather peripheral in parent-child interactions. But, as Patterson (1980) points out, "The role of mother is structured in such a manner as to almost guarantee higher rates of aversive events than does the role of the father" (p. 10). He adds that mothers "may be overselected as targets for responses such as dependency, destructive, noncomply, negativism, whine and yell" (p. 27).

Fathers, on the other side, have been found to engage more in play interactions with their children (Lamb, 1983). Fathers of difficult children show little difference from fathers of normal children in terms of stress reactions (Patterson, 1976). "This leads to the conclusion that the role label most appropriate for fathers might be that of 'guest!'" (Patterson, 1980:24). Studies of parents of handicapped children also describe fathers as less affected than mothers.

With regard to infants, several studies have shown that mothers who describe their infants as difficult at three months (Campbell, 1979) or at four months (Kelley, 1976) are less responsive to them, even later on, and more negative when the infants respond negatively. In other words, certain types of mothers may become affectively turned off when their infants are temperamentally fussy or nonresponsive. Stevenson-Hinde and Simpson (1982) have established that mothers of three-year olds who are rated as difficult correlate highly on anxiety and irritability. The authors tend toward an influence of child's temperament on mother's mood rather than the reverse. Related results for maternal depression were obtained by Wolking and De Salis (1982). In the same vein, a study by Kochanska et al. (1989) found that maternal satisfaction correlated with child compliance.

One effect of difficult child behavior, at least on the mother, is an increasing tendency on her part to issue directives, commands and threats so as to try to reduce the negative behavior (Patterson, 1980). Although parental reprimands do lower negative child behavior in normal children, it does not generally affect the behavior of problem children. The latter may simply increase the frequency and severity of their coercive and oppositional episodes.

One further effect, as pointed out earlier, is that parents, especially the mother, lose control over family life and over their children when the oppositional behavior becomes chronic (Patterson, 1982). "Some children ultimately 'win' when they perform in such a way as to stop virtually all parental behaviors aimed at changing the misbehavior" (Loeber and Stouthamer-Loeber, 1986: 110). As Loeber et al. (1983) and Madden and Harbin (1983) conclude, these children effectively become more powerful than their parents.

At some point in the escalation of parent-child conflict, the mother may become afraid of disciplining or even contradicting the child. Patterson (1980) also found that "mothers tend *not* to provide an aversive antecedent for these chains" of behaviors and desperately try "to avoid/escape from confrontations with a practiced aggressor" (pp. 32-33). Bates (1987:1132) has also hypothesized that infants and children who are difficult might learn less about their parents' attitudes and feelings than easier children. This inability to learn might, in turn, contribute to friction between the parents, as well as between child and parents.

Studies also show that mothers of aggressive boys have a negative self-concept (Patterson, 1980). It is possible that mothers with low self-concept, especially low self-esteem, are less skilled at parenting or do not have faith in their skills. This situation would lead them to undersocialize their children. Indeed, one very powerful predictor of difficult and even delinquent behavior in children is lack of parental supervision. For instance, Patterson and Stouthamer-Loeber (1984) found that 21 percent of the nondelinquents in their sample were poorly supervised by their parents, compared to 50 percent of the one- and two-time offenders and 73 percent of the repeat offenders. Farrington (1978) has found that aggressive children were also less supervised while McCord (1982) found the same for aggressive and antisocial children.

It should also be said that no study has ever investigated whether parents who offer poor supervision have a lower self-esteem than parents who monitor their children more closely. What we do know is that certain categories of parents are less able to monitor their children when their *own* life conditions are less than optimal. Such is the case of single mothers who have no child support, of unhappily married mothers (Stouthamer-Loeber et al., 1984), and of parents who have deviant tendencies themselves (Bandura and Walters, 1959, for aggression in children; Canter, 1982, for self-reported delinquency; Offord et al., 1978, for official delinquency). There are also currently upper-middle-class households, with two-career families, where both parents are too involved in their career and even in just climbing the social ladder to be involved at all in child supervision, especially at the teenage level. Unfortunately, we have no studies of such parents, nor on reciprocal parent-child effects, although an interesting case study appears in Chapter 8.

We can even hypothesize that, when children become too difficult, certain types of parents (more individualistic, perhaps) will choose to distance themselves and to ignore the situation. This behavior would serve as a protective mechanism on the part of parents who may have tried "everything," and for whose children nothing has worked. At some point, they may simply decide to "get on with our own lives," and let the youngster pick up the pieces.

ADDITIONAL RESEARCH QUESTIONS

We would want to know more about the effect on parents, in terms of self-esteem, marital happiness, and health, of having children who are so out of control that parenting becomes difficult. In terms of self-esteem, the negative children's reactions, the sense of having failed as a parent, and the disorganized household may be quite sufficient to lower a parent's self-esteem or to exacerbate an already low self-esteem.

Moreover, there are no studies which have focused on what happens to parents' relationship with their own kin, friends, and neighbors when they have behavior-problem children. One may hypothesize that it may be difficult for such parents to maintain an active social life as their children may be unpleasant, disruptive, and even aggressive. The children may in effect act in such a way as to isolate parents socially. Or parents may simply isolate themselves in anticipation of problems, because they are embarrassed, or because they fear being blamed.

There is also another group of parents who may be heavily penalized, but for another reason: their disruptive and oppositional children may be so only at home. Such children are often very charming and well-behaved outside the home, so much so that people may be drawn to them. The problem for the parents here, perhaps especially for the mothers, may rest with their own family. As women have been found to be more kin oriented than men and to have more confidantes than men, it is logical that women may seek moral support from their kin about their children's problems. Yet, the kin never *see* what the mother complains about: they actually see the opposite, as is well illustrated in Jimmy's case above. Thus, the kin are presented with a clear discrepancy between the observed and the reported. They may tend to believe what they can see and dismiss the mother's complaints or, yet, may feel sorry for such poor children who are not appreciated by their parents.

Several studies have shown that difficult children are more likely to grow into adult criminals (although by no means is this universally true), while the *absence* of difficult behavior in childhood virtually precludes its appearance in adulthood (Robins and Ratcliff, 1980; Elliott et al., 1985). Therefore, one long-term consequence of difficult child behavior is that parents may become saddled with a child who will perhaps become delinquent and may also exhibit adult behavior problems, including criminality. Indeed, little is known about the parents of criminals and of adults who are deviant, especially so in terms of the effect that these problems have on the ageing parents. For instance, these parents cannot boast of their children's achievements as any normal parent likes to do. They may have to lie to cover up for the adult child and to avoid embarrassment and personal stigmatization.

What additional social and psychological costs do the adult children place on the parents? As they age, do these parents continue to help their children or are contacts limited and even discontinued? Do the parents choose to sever contact or do the children choose to? Also, such parents may already have been problematic individuals themselves: how then do these ageing and problematic parents differ from similar problematic parents whose own children turned out "all right"?

CONCLUSIONS

In conclusion, as was the case for juvenile delinquency in the previous chapter, it is evident that much research needs to be carried out concerning the effect on parents of having emotionally disturbed and difficult children. I have presented above only a small sample of the questions which should be researched. Moreover, such questions should be addressed from a life-span perspective to see how the effect unfolds over the life of the parents.

But, contrary to the case of the juvenile delinquency literature, the psychological and psychiatric literature has at least initiated a discussion of child effect. In fact, recent trends in the psychology literature have allowed for the beginning of a reorientation of the unidirectional causality. In contrast, the literature on juvenile delinquency has apparently failed to take advantage of this new development and is still mired in ancient discussions, especially as far as textbooks are concerned.

There has not been a sufficient use of the concept of children as social actors in the literature on childhood disorders. The fact that some people, whether adults or children, are not responsible for every aspect of their behavior does not exclude them from the category of social actors. All human beings are social actors and, as such, have an impact on their immediate environment. Because disturbed and difficult children deviate negatively from the average, as explained in Chapter 3, their impact on their parents is likely to be quite substantial and generally negative. Yet, most analyses forget this possibility and choose to focus on the parents as causative agents.

Moreover, as suggested in at least a few studies (e.g., Brown et al., 1988), certain types of parents will be more vulnerable to the negative child impact. As emotional problems frequently run in families (probably as genetic chemical disorders), parents who are already disturbed themselves will inherit an added source of vulnerability in their own problematic children. Such families are doubly handicapped and a strong interaction or feedback effect undoubtedly takes place.

Similarly, studies on children's emotional problems have rarely offered a critical analysis of the lack of support offered by social institutions to parents and to such children. While it is true that often little can be done to cure the children, at the very least much could be done to alleviate parental burden.

Chapter 7

Students' Perceptions of the Effect
They Have Had on Their Parents

In the previous chapters, we have presented an analytical framework for the study of the effect of children on parents. While reviewing the existing literature, we have found that the research which already exists is not only very scarce but most of it focuses on infants and preschoolers (Bell, 1968, 1971, 1974; Lewis and Rosenblum, 1974). In contrast, the current chapter will focus on university students' recollections of the impact they have exerted on their parents throughout *all* stages of their own lives.

Not only was I interested in what students would have to say in general about child effect, but I wanted to know if they would apply to their own cases the influence of the three sets of characteristics described in Chapters 3 and 4. As well, would they recognize certain areas of their parents' lives on which they might have had a particularly strong effect?

OVERVIEW AND METHODS

My students have written structured autobiographies as one of their assignments in most of my classes for the past fourteen years. Although the autobiographical assignment is optional, in the sense that they are presented with the alternative of a more traditional research paper, 99 percent choose the autobiography. They do so both because they feel it will be easier than the research paper (only to find out that it is actually quite a difficult and time-consuming task) or because they like the novelty and the experience of writing about themselves.

The assignments are anonymous: students write their number on the cover sheet and, once I have read the autobiography and placed a mark on the cover sheet, it is torn off, and placed in a separate file; later, my assistant registers the marks. I retain the autobiographies for research purposes. Last year, I asked students to evaluate this assignment in terms of how confident they were that their anonymity was preserved and in terms of the type of experience the assignment had been for them.

Of the 105 students who completed the evaluation questionnaire, 40 percent and 39 percent respectively reported the experience as having been excellent and very good, for a total of 79 percent. Another 17 percent rated it as having been quite good, 9 percent as good and 4.5 percent as neutral. No student chose the option of "not much of an experience for me." In terms of confidence in the anonymity process, 82 percent answered, "yes, completely confident," 16 percent felt "yes, overall confident," and 2 percent were "more or less confident." No student ticked any of the two lower alternatives of confidence.

It is also important to point out that students are graded on the basis of the completeness of the autobiographical profile presented, rather than on the sheer number of pages or on any more subjective criteria. These precautions have been taken to prevent "made up" autobiographies. Moreover, a few questions have been introduced to insure that the data gathered through this method are reliable and valid. These are questions for which the answers are well known. The students' profile on these match that of other statistics. Answers to several questions placed at different intervals in the autobiographical questionnaire tend to produce a congruent entity rather than a contradictory profile with the same themes recurring. Thus, I am very confident that students are "truthful" in their responses. Of approximately 1,400 questionnaires collected over fourteen years, only five have been thrown out as "dubious."

RESULTS

A first set of questions focuses on what students recall as having made them happiest and then most unhappy at different stages in their life, beginning with early childhood. In these questions, when parents are mentioned, and they always are, students write about the happiness and the pain their parents inflicted upon *them*. But 20 percent mention pride parents felt for them as well as the pain *they* brought upon their parents. Thus, a proportion of young adults, when reconstructing their past, *spontaneously* and directly comment on the impact they have had on their parents. On the other hand, 30 percent of the students seem totally oblivious to any impact they might have had on their parents, directly or indirectly.

In order to focus more attention on this child effect dimension, a question is added toward the middle of the questionnaire focusing specifically on their perception of any effect they might have had on their parents.

Here, one finds that there are certain themes which run through the students' perceptions of the effect they have had on their parents up to age eighteen.

First, because they were asked to evaluate this effect at various age levels (0-5; 6-10; 11-14; 15-18), students generally differentiate between childhood and teen years. Most of those who describe a different effect depending on *their* age see their effect as *more negative when they were teenagers*, a result which is consistent with our discussion in the previous chapter. A second theme is the matter of pride. Many students describe how they made their parents proud. A third theme is the perception of having had a greater impact when their *parents'* life circumstances were unusual or out of the average. Fourthly, children from large families (four children or more) feel that each child has had a lesser *individual* impact on their parents than if they had belonged to a smaller family. A fifth theme revolved around being the first born or only child: a greater impact is attributed to this situation. A sixth theme emerged in that students whose parents were immigrants unavoidably had more to say than the other students about their impact on their parents. The last theme is that of an effect on their parents' marriage.

It is interesting to note that all but one of these themes represented "structural" situations or, if you wish, demographic child or parent characteristics, as presented in Chapter 3. Only the matter of pride departed from this. In terms of areas of parents' lives affected, only marital life, finances, and general happiness were recognized by students.

I will examine each theme separately and provide examples of how students expressed their effect in these domains. Before doing so, one salient result to be noted is that more *advanced* students (year four versus year three; year three versus year two) were much more specific in terms of the effect they had had on their parents. Not only did they write a far greater number of lines on the subject, but they were less vague, less moralizing about it (many younger students simply wrote "sermons" stating that "all children affect their parents," period), and provided more details. It is as if, having gained a certain perspective with age or education, they were in a better position to evaluate the situation. Or, perhaps, they felt more settled and secure in their relationship with their parents and were, consequently, less biased.

Adolescence

Eighty percent of the students differentiated the quality of their effect by age; all but seven of the 109 autobiographies analyzed for this chapter directly pointed to a negative impact on parents during adolescence or a *more* negative impact at that age level. For some of them, the negative peak was seen as occurring early in adolescence (eleven to fourteen) while for others it was later (fifteen to eighteen). In that sense, students' perceptions matched psychology and developmental textbooks which present adolescence as a time of conflict with parents, especially over issues of individuation and independence. A few students, on the other hand, indicated that they had had a more positive impact on their parents during adolescence, often under the rubric of the pride they had occasioned or of the help they had provided their parents who, for instance, were divorcing or needed special understanding.

The theme of adolescence was frequently tied to that of having immigrant parents with "Old World" values, and we will examine this aspect later. We will note, however, that these students generally come from Italian, Greek and Portuguese backgrounds. Students from the Caribbean countries or Great Britain and Israel did not, as a rule, link their adolescent impact to their parents' immigrant status.

Why did the students perceive having had a more negative effect during adolescence? Being "rebellious" and "challenging parenting styles" were frequently mentioned. "I was a frustrating teenager." "I was difficult to be with." "I always talked back."

> During the ages eleven to sixteen, I feel I had a negative effect on their lives for I began to challenge their style of parenting which frustrated them very much as their methods that were used from childhood years were not effective for me.

This student goes on to explain that, as her *parents* adjusted to her, and as their parenting style became more to *her* liking, her negative impact slowly wore off. In her very long discussion of the subject, it is obvious that this student was socializing her parents and teaching them their "proper" role as the parents of a young person her age. She then adds that the education she provided her parents "worked out for the benefit of my brother and sisters whose path I think was somewhat easier" (a theme linked to her role as first born).

Another female student places her negative impact after age eighteen because "my parents, mostly my mother, did not approve of my choice of boyfriends and this created a lot of tension and vocal dispute." Another one describes her behavior toward her parents between eleven and fourteen as one of "resentment." She blamed them for all that ailed her at the time: "I hated my new house. . . . I blamed my parents for making me ugly. . . . they had to deal with a child who was impossible." Between the ages of fifteen and eighteen, she resented the fact that they did not allow her to go out as much as she wanted to:

> They had to change their views about boys and me going out. It was a long and emotional battle. My father didn't sleep, he always yelled at my mother (because she was always on my side), and my mother was depressed a lot.

Again, the student was socializing her parents.

An observer from a different culture reading these autobiographies would notice that students who report these experiences definitely believed that, when they were adolescents, their *parents'* mentality had to be changed. Not a single student ever questioned their *own* mentality or the need to change it, with the exception of a rare few who had been truly delinquent. The adjustment was a parental one, they felt, and should not come from them. Their peer group subculture supported this mentality. Students perceived that they had changed their parents more or less forcibly, against the parents' will, while they themselves had simply changed as a normal consequence of normal growth.

Yet, to balance out this picture, in another question, students were asked who or what had most influenced them. Parents, or one parent in particular (the mother more often than not), were generally mentioned as having contributed the most to shaping their personalities and values. At the same time, students also perceived this parental influence as having been far greater *before* their adolescence.

On the one hand, the influence which students attributed to their parents was not surprising. The influence they attributed to themselves, however, was of a magnitude that was rather unexpected. The *tone* and the choice of *words* used to express this were quite definite and were so in a way that did not exist for mature students over thirty-five years of age. These older students rarely expressed such a clear cut impact on their parents during their adolescence — whether or not these same older students themselves had children. Therefore, it is not unwarranted to conclude that more recent generations of adolescents perceive themselves to have a greater and a more negative impact than previous generations. To use Thorne's terminology, they see themselves as having more "agency" than did previous generations. One has a very clear example of adolescents perceiving themselves as *teenagers*, a conceptual distinction I will discuss at greater length in the last chapter of this book.

It would be interesting to know whether adolescents who are employed as opposed to being in school would describe their adolescent impact similarly. It is possible that economic independence creates a lesser impact or even a more positive one as parents would consequently treat them as adults; or, it is possible that the economic independence creates a greater and more negative impact as parents try to restrain the independence thusly created. Unfortunately, all my respondents were students who had been in school during adolescence. Still, the matter of *part-time* employment and its effect on parents would be another interesting topic to explore, as there is a burgeoning body of research on the effect of part-time employment on high school students themselves.

Of the few students who perceived having had a more positive effect on their parents during adolescence compared to other stages in their own lives, some referred to the theme of pride. Others pointed out that their siblings were so difficult that they themselves presented a counterpart source of gratification for their parents. A student with a disability felt that her parents had grown "to be stronger" because of the coping required. Another mentioned that he "broadened" his parents' values: they were immigrants. Still another pointed out that he "would like to think I gave them hope. My father was from an exceedingly poor family. . . . My mother was from a very strange family. Somehow my making it gave them something."

A male student of yet another immigrant family felt that he had had a positive impact on his mother by helping her to become more independent, taking her to driving lessons. His impact on his father, however, had been negative because he questioned his father's patriarchal attitudes.

Pride

This theme was extended mainly to the students' late adolescence and young adulthood but appeared at other earlier stages. Twenty percent of students mentioned the fact that their parents were proud of them as an indicator of a positive effect. This may not be a large percentage but it is the only category mentioned with such a frequency and using the same terminology.

One of the contexts in which parents were reportedly proud of their children was when the students were the first in their family to go to college. Bar and Bat Mitzvahs were often mentioned by Jewish students as a source of parental pride. Scholastic and athletic achievements were also mentioned.

A student who discusses all the sacrifices her parents made to give their children a middle-class education puts the situation this way:

I really do not think that they regret the sacrifices they have made because they are very proud of my academic accomplishments as I am the first one of my entire family to have completed high school and am on my way to becoming a university graduate this year.

Another, after describing herself as a "terrible teen" who protested and "took everything the wrong way," concludes that her later teens had a redeeming value for her parents:

From fifteen until eighteen, I think I had again regained their positive feeling towards me as I was no longer rebellious and I matured. I entered university which made them proud as neither of them had been to post-secondary school. I was overall becoming successful.

In this category, a student points to her going to university as a mitigated plus for her parents:

However, I must say that they are not thrilled over the prospect that I am going to be a teacher. They are happy but not overwhelmed. They were hoping for something more prestigious such as a doctor, dentist or lawyer.

Parents' Life Circumstances

Many students pointed out that they had had a more negative or a more positive impact on their parents because their *parents'* life circumstances were unusual or difficult. Circumstances such as having had parents who were very young or very old at the time of the child's birth; parents who were unmarried; parents who divorced; who were struggling under the burden of poverty; who were in ill health; who had a problematic marital life.

Since my mother was divorced at the age of twenty-six, and left to raise three children on her own, I feel I have had a great impact on her life at all stages . . . I am sure that my mother's opportunity to remarry would have been far greater if she had

had no children. . . . between eleven and fourteen . . . she would often ask for my opinion concerning someone she was dating . . .

Being young themselves when they had me, they realized that they had to find means to support me . . . [gives other effects] . . . especially due to the fact that they were young and unmarried when I was born.

A student pointed out that she was the first child of her parents' *remarriages* and, as such, had a highly positive impact on them, a theme that will be mentioned again in the next chapter. We also recall the student who described his parents as having been unbearably poor and who represented hope to them. Another explained that she arrived late in her parents' life and they then had to "start a second family. From age eleven to fifteen, I can honestly say that I kept them young . . . in the sense of the word that they were always running around with me." Basically, these students were referring to parental characteristics, as described earlier on in Chapter 3. They were aware that their parents' young age, poverty, or divorce rendered them particularly vulnerable to child effect.

Immigrant Parents

The unusual circumstance in parents' lives which was most frequently discussed was that of immigration, generally from Italy, Greece or Portugal. Toronto has a large immigrant population and many of these new Canadian families are sending their children to college for the first time. But, above all, the most striking aspect is that students of immigrant parents were more expansive on the average than others on the topic of their parents and of their effect on their parents (as well as vice versa). These students were definitely very conscious of having had a great impact on their parents, both negative and positive.

The negative consisted in the fact that, as North Americanized children, they generally resented and questioned their parents' Old World ways. The friction reached an apex during adolescence and was especially acute for *girls* as Southern European parents tend to be more protective and prohibitive with their daughters than with their sons. Typically, these girls were raised quite differently from their peers. The need to conform to these peers' norms pushed the first-generation Canadians to rebel, withdraw, and have recourse to more drastic coping methods than many of their peers, or caused their parents to react to them in a more negative and stressful way. Parental impact, during the teen years and even into young adulthood, was often described by these young women as restrictive, even coercive and highly difficult to cope with emotionally. But the women could also perceive that *they* had impacted upon their parents.

One woman explains all the sacrifices her parents made (such as working shift jobs) in order to be able to buy a house in a middle-class neighborhood. This sudden upward mobility, as a front, created deprivation problems both for the teenager and her parents:

> I am certain that it must have been detrimental to my parents' self-esteem to have to come home from work all dirty in an old unattractive car while the neighbors were coming home in business suits and Porsches. While they mentioned their grievances at times, they really did not complain a lot because they were convinced that they were doing the best for the kids.

Another young woman presented the following profile:

> Everything they were brought up with I challenged and put little value to them. . . . I challenged all their Italian beliefs. I opened up so many questions to them that they found it mindboggling.

A female student elaborated further on the link between child effect and immigration:

> If my parents had been raised here things would have been easier for them. But my mother never learned much English and my father remained the typical chauvinistic Greek male . . . My mother was very frustrated because she could not understand what I was talking about over the phone all these long hours with my friends which means that she was deprived

of her opportunity to contribute to raising me when I was a teenager. Basically I lived as if she did not exist. I know that she was very depressed . . . My father was another story. He was overprotective of me and I was not allowed to go out til last year [she is now twenty-two] without my *younger* brother as a chaperon. I really resented this as you can imagine. I think that my father was so powerful at home that I didn't have much effect on him but he had an overbearing effect on me as a female. He had much less of an effect on my brothers though.

Another young woman, this time Italian, felt that she had had a profoundly negative impact on her father as he was very threatened by her development as an English-speaking female:

My father spends all his time with his Italian buddies and he does not bother much with English. At least my mother is trying because she has always tried to understand what we were doing in school, she even tried to help us. But my father couldn't control me forever because I always sneaked in his back and went out anyway. He did beat me up a few times when I was sixteen or seventeen but I threatened to leave and for him this would have dishonored him so he relented. He got so upset about my rebellious years that he stayed away from home more and more and drank up the money so that my mother had to take a job in a factory. I definitely think that I contributed to my parents' misery and that I created it during these years because they didn't know any better and were so afraid of my losing my Italian identity.

This and the previous quote illustrate so well the vulnerability of parents with certain characteristics of their own. In these examples, parents are vulnerable because they are immigrants, do not know their children's language, and are relatively uneducated. The children's characteristics of age (teenagers), English-speaking ability, and of rebellious mentality interact with the parental characteristics to increase vulnerability and create negative child effect.

First-Born Child

We already have had glimpses in the previous sections of the effect of one particular child characteristic, that of being a first born. A majority of the students who were first born emphasized that their birth order *had* to have resulted in a greater impact on their parents than would otherwise have been the case. Students explained that the first born is a "new experience" and that parents "learn how to be parents." Many mentioned that they had actually "raised" their own parents as parents and, as such, had "smoothed" the path for their younger siblings. A young man explains that his teen years had a negative impact on his parents:

> This was a period of experimentation for me, i.e., heavy metal music, different clothing, staying out late and drinking. Being that I was the first child, this must have been new and difficult for them. I was struggling against good behavior, and they would have to learn to handle it.

The theme of parental education is again well illustrated below:

> Because I was the first child going through the teen years, they weren't quite sure what to expect, but now that I have showed them the "ropes," as they say, they know what to expect when my various brothers and sisters enter into that very difficult time in their lives.

She is referring to her younger half-siblings from her parents' remarriages. Another explains the situation as follows: "Being the first and only born I changed their lives a great deal." Three additional examples follow:

> At the age of zero to five I feel that I had a great impact on my parents' lives in that I was their first born and they seemed to feel that they had so much to look forward to . . .

> I was the first child in the family and I can remember taking care of my sister quite a bit. I am sure that I influenced my parents positively . . .

I think that being the oldest in my family has always meant that I've had a big impact on my parents' lives at different stages.

Large Families

Students who had three or more siblings generally perceived that they did not have as much of an *individual* impact on their parents as would have been the case had they been part of a smaller family. Rather, they felt that the sheer *number* of children was the salient child effect in their parents' lives. Others emphasized that, in their families, only the oldest, or the youngest (especially when born much later than the other children), or a child with a particular gift or difficulties had had an individual effect on their parents.

It is interesting that these students' perceptions coincide with those of psychologists who have found children of large families to be at a disadvantage academically (and also in terms of the potential for delinquency [Loeber and Southamer-Loeber, 1986; Offord, 1982]), as parents do not have enough time to devote to each child. Consequently the children socialize each other and this same-age socialization is not as favorable to advanced language development and thinking. In smaller families, in contrast, children are in a position to receive more individual attention (as well as to produce an individual effect) and to be socialized by adults rather than by siblings of nearly the same age.

A student who, although not belonging to a large family, was the third and last child sees her influence, or lack of it, quite clearly:

> By the third child, they were used to the routines of having a child and what parenting was all about. They also had two other children who, although still young, were able to assist in my upbringing.

She goes on to explain, however, that she had a more positive impact on her parents as a teenager because her older siblings were troublesome children who created serious problems for themselves and for their parents.

The financial strain of having several children was mentioned by many students.

I sometimes feel that my parents had to do without luxuries because they had so many children. I often wonder if they regretted having so many children.

In all honesty I do not think I had much impact on my father's life other than the fact that I was another mouth to feed.

Others pointed out that the sheer number of children kept their parents "young" and, in some cases, kept the marriage together or kept the parents together longer before a separation finally followed.

Keeping Parents Together

Of the 109 autobiographies reported on in this chapter, six contained references to the fact that, either by their very presence or because of the problems (health or behavior) they had, the students had kept their parents together. They either mentioned that their parents stayed together longer than they would otherwise have done if they had not had young children, or that their presence kept their parents together and, for better or worse, these parents are still together. These students' perceptions relate to at least two studies which have found that the presence of young children acted as a strong deterrent against marital instability (Ferguson et al., 1990; White et al., 1986).

I also think that I had a positive impact on my parents' lives when I was six to ten years old. This is because I made them delay the idea of separation. My dad told me that he would have separated from my mother earlier had it not been for me and my youngest brother.

Another woman student puts the situation in these terms:

From eleven to fourteen [years of age]. . . my parents were suffering from a bad marriage and my mother sort of blamed the children for her staying in the marriage. She never said it directly but I know it is because of us that she is still with my father. This is the hardest part because we were such a huge negative effect on them and I know that if we didn't exist they would probably be more happy.

It is also possible that at some time during their life, my sister and I were a major reason in preventing my parents from separating. I cannot be sure about this suggestion since I have never discussed this with either my parents or my sister.

This student also reported her parents' marital happiness to be extremely low on a scale of 1 to 5. Another student mentioned that her parents separated recently:

As my sister and I became more mature and independent I think it was at this time my parents looked more closely at their happiness together and decided that because of their growing distance and us being at a more mature age that their separation would have less negative effects than if they had separated when we were younger and needed both parents.

It is relevant to note that, in my study of divorce, several parents also mentioned that they had waited a few years before divorcing for the sake of their children. We can only surmise here that many other parents who similarly postpone the decision to divorce actually become used to their unhappy marriage and never divorce. Others, with the passage of time, may actually revitalize their marriage. In both cases, child effect will have been a significant cause.

Strain on Parents' Marriage

On the other side of the coin, twelve students pointed out that they had put a strain on their parents' marriage. This strain generally took place as a result of the student's difficult behavior, especially during adolescence. It was, in other cases, the result of a combination of number of children and poor financial resources which forced both parents to work shift jobs and, as a consequence, such parents were never together to enjoy their relationship.

Similar students' reports actually were more often encountered in the context of another question where they were asked to evaluate their parents' marital happiness and to justify their ratings. The ratings would frequently be lower during the respondents' adolescent years. One of the explanations for the lower rating rested with the problems they were causing for their parents. Some students mentioned that their parents disagreed on how to handle the children's difficult behavior and this disagreement led to further friction between the parents. Students also reported straining parental *remarriages*:

> Eleven to fourteen [years]. As far as my mother is concerned, I feel I really affected her life in a negative way. I was very rude and rebellious toward her. I made no effort to understand her point of view. I simply blamed her for everything. I know my behavior made it more difficult for her to develop a secure marriage with her new husband. For I did not give him a chance either. I would not let him get to know me, nor I him. I realize that I made their first years together very difficult.

The parents of the following student had immigrated and were poor. They chose to work at shift jobs so that one of them would be with her at all times:

> I believe they had the best intentions for doing so and were not aware that such a decision would eventually cost their relationship with their child and more importantly their relationship with one another.

A student whose parents had immigrated from another English-speaking country felt that, as a young child, she intensified her mother's loneliness because she was difficult to pacify. Later on, as a difficult and drug-oriented teenager, she contributed to parental discord and eventual divorce. Another student explained how his disreputable behavior in high school took so much of his parents' time and attention that, as a result, not only was his younger brother neglected but his parents' marriage simply crumbled. The home atmosphere was so tense that, whenever he would step in, he created an explosive situation and his parents would end up quarrelling. In order to evade the tense home situation, his father immersed himself in his work and rarely came home. His mother became extremely lonely and depressed.

After grade eleven, I finally straightened out because I wanted to go to university as I didn't want to be poor later on. I was afraid of that above all else. My parents started relaxing and little by little my mother felt better and my father stayed home more. So in a year's time their marital happiness went up from 1 to 4.

CONCLUSIONS

The fact that only 20 percent of the students *spontaneously* mention having affected their parents (before being asked the question directly) is another indicator attesting to our society's insensitivity and ignorance of child effect. Basically, parents affect their children but, as our ideology has it, children are not meant to affect their parents. The parental role is construed and constructed as one of unidirectional effect.

But, once prompted by a specifically worded question, most students do, after further reflection, come to the conclusion that they have had an impact on their parents after all. We have reviewed the main themes perceived by students. Because these themes are suggested to them by the values of their society, it is important to look at themes which were absent or, still, which might be suggested by the values of another society with a different value system.

Basically, it is surprising that themes such as "the love I gave to my parents," or "my affection for my parents" or "the companionship I provided" were either never or only rarely mentioned. Yet, nearly all students at some point write about loving their parents. What is interesting is that students do not connect these themes to the issue of effect. If being loved by one's parents has a positive effect on a child, cannot loving one's parents and expressing that love have a positive effect on one's parents? In this context, does our society create an affectional distance between child and parents in order to insure that "individualization" takes place, that children grow up sufficiently independent? In such a context, providing parents with affection might interfere with one's growth. Yet, Boulding (1980) found, in her own study, that college students could, when asked, recall specific instances when they had, as children, given nurturance to their parents.

Implicit in the section on adolescence, although not explicitly stated, was that parents in this society have very little to do with the socialization or education of a *teenager*. In this, the students themselves probably come closer to the reality of this society than textbooks on child development lead us to believe! As teenagers with the support of a similarly-minded peer group, the students quite clearly perceived themselves as "raising" their parents. *They* were socializing their parents. Again, one cannot argue with the realism of this perception. It also fits well with the perspective advanced by several researchers to the effect that children should be considered as social actors or agents in their own right (Alanen, 1990; Peters, 1985; Thorne, 1987). What is lacking in the students' perception, however, is the possibility that this education of parents was not always necessary. That parents *had* to be changed, had to adjust is a matter of teen opinion, of cultural opinion consequently, not a sine qua non. Students were not talking about the fact that they *themselves* could have changed to suit their parents. Here one clearly sees an ideology reflected in action as opposed to a universal mandated by human nature and met in all societies of the world — as discussed in the last chapter of this book.

In this respect, it is interesting to reverse the typical direction of the socialization agent. One reads in Peterson and Rollins (1987) that "adults are social agents who have greater insight than children into the expectations, attitudes and behaviors of their culture" (p. 480). Yet, in presenting the students' viewpoint as they recalled themselves just a few years ago, it is quite obvious that adolescents view themselves as the socializers and their parents as being less well attuned than they to the expectations of *their* own culture. (See also Peters, 1985.) To follow Karl Mannheim, it is true that adolescents of each generation do provide a "fresh" view of their period, the past and even the future. But that they do so stems from the type of society they live in: one that evolves rapidly. A more stable society does not necessarily call for a "fresh" view with each generation: it calls for generational continuity of perspective.

In this same context, these students' perceptions support statements in the chapter on juvenile delinquency concerning the often all-encompassing influence of the peer group on adolescents in particular and children in general. These students' perceptions concerning the primacy of adolescence in terms of child effect are also well supported by other researchers such as Hoffman and Manis who, in 1979, had already found adolescence to be a stage more likely to produce anxiety in parents than other childhood stages, while other researchers find mothers of small children more distressed than those of adolescents (Kurdek, 1990). This discrepancy suggests that additional analyses are required, as it is possible that these studies come to different conclusions on the basis of different indicators. The prevalence of adolescence-related difficulties is also supported by Montemayor (1986) who has shown that 20 percent of parents experience difficulties with their adolescents while another 20 percent experience "intermittent relational problems."

Thus, overall, the students' perceptions of their own child effect corresponded well with the contents of earlier chapters. As well, students' perceptions were also frequently more realistic than are the theories of most child development textbooks. It is also interesting to note that students quite clearly perceived the direct role of some parental and child characteristics in promoting child effect. But the areas of parental lives which they described as having been affected were quite limited in numbers. The effects of the societal response were only alluded to indirectly and by very few students. Overall, students' psychological consciousness was much more developed than was their social or sociological consciousness or grasp of societal circumstances. The exacerbating and buffering roles of the societal response were obviously not perceived by younger students; older students (in their thirties or forties) were more likely to bring up such variables—perhaps again as a direct result of the more global perspective offered by their chronological age.

Chapter 8

The Impact of Children
on Divorced Parents

OVERVIEW

Divorce is another major area of study in which child effect has been neglected. Until now, the two major themes in divorce research have been the effect of marital disruption on children and the factors related to adjustment after divorce for adults. It is true that one can find indirect evidence of child effect in these studies. But it is only recently, especially in Hetherington's work, and mainly in the area of stepparenting and remarriage, that the possible impact of children has been directly examined, and this has been done in only a few studies (e.g., Hobart, 1988; White and Booth, 1985).

Reviews of the literature in these various areas exist, and it is not the purpose of this chapter to dwell on these aspects. Suffice it to say that studies have found several differences in children of divorce as compared to children from intact families or children of widowhood. Although statistical relationships do not necessarily mean that there is a causality, the bulk of the material nevertheless points to a detrimental effect of marital strife (Christensen and Margolin, 1988) as well as of some of the consequences of parental divorce on a majority of children, especially within the first two years post separation.

Divorce variables which contribute to negative effect on children include poverty, maladjusted custodial parent, and lack of supervision (Ambert and Saucier, 1984; Demo and Acock, 1988; Keith and Finley, 1988; Krantz, 1988). In contrast, children do better when they live with a well-balanced custodial parent, retain a supportive relation with the noncustodial parent, do not suffer from poverty, and are adequately supervised. Lack of conflict between parents is another important variable (Furstenberg et al., 1987; Maccoby et al., 1990). Moreover, the research also indicates that children's adjustment is facilitated by being in the custody of a same-sex parent (Camara and Resnick, 1988; Zill, 1988).

One can logically conclude that, if most children react negatively, at least in the short term, to their parents' separation/divorce, this negative reaction can only be detrimental to the parents as well. The reasoning here is that if children become unhappy, difficult, or maladjusted, however temporarily, as a result of their parents' divorce, their unhappiness and maladjustment is bound to impact on parents. As a result, parents will feel guilty, sad, worried, harassed, burdened, or out of control — depending on the nature of the children's reaction, on the parents' overall situation, as well as on the efficacy of the social support offered and utilized.

In this chapter, the main source of information will come from my own research on adults who had divorced, many of whom went on to remarry during the course of the study. This research was in part longitudinal: forty-nine respondents were interviewed three times while forty-nine others were interviewed twice from 1978 through 1984 (Ambert, 1989). The other 154 were seen only once in 1984. The study was also dyadic in that both ex-spouses in a divorce and both new spouses in the subsequent remarriages were interviewed. Their answers were compared in the analysis of the results. Child effect was one of the topics included in the design of the study, although it was not the main focus.

We will first present some information on the effect of children on parents' happiness and feelings of control over their lives after separation. Then we will examine child effect on divorcing adults from the following perspectives: custodial problems in general, and problems stemming from the custodial arrangements. We will then look at child effect on the noncustodial parent and on the custodial parent. Because of space considerations, we will not focus directly on child effect in remarriage (or in stepparenting). Excellent sources of information on these topics, although focusing more on child adjustment, can be found in Brand et al. (1988), Clingempeel et al. (1987), Furstenberg (1988), Hetherington (1990), and Wallerstein et al. (1988).

PARENTAL HAPPINESS AND FEELINGS OF CONTROL

I will first present a few statistics on parental happiness and feelings of control as these relate to child effect. When the respondents were interviewed the first time (1978), they were asked how satisfied they were with, among other things, their children's behavior. Their responses could range from a high of 5 indicating that they were very satisfied to a low of 1 indicating that they were totally dissatisfied. The same questions were repeated at Time 2 (1981) and at Time 3 (1984).

At Time 1, men scored a high 4.0 while women scored 2.6. Thus, within the first two years post separation, children constituted a much greater satisfaction to their fathers than to their mothers, in part because the mothers had custody (Ambert, 1982). While we will return to these figures along with parental custodial status and social class below, I will simply remark that my coded observations of the children's behavior indicated that they presented a great deal of "dissatisfiers" to mothers at that stage. My independently coded observations of children's behavior toward parents correlated with expressed parental satisfaction/dissatisfaction.

As the children aged, as the parents resolved many of the conflicts engendered by the early period of separation, as children's behavior matured, and as other older children who had been particularly difficult left home, parents' satisfaction rose. Thus, by Time 2, parents' level of satisfaction had risen and children's behavior was coded more favorably. There seemed to be a direct relation between the way children treated their custodial parent and that parent's expressed satisfaction with the children. It will be recalled here that a study discussed in an earlier chapter had found mothers of compliant children to be more satisfied with their maternal role than mothers of less cooperative children. By Time 3, both men and women were quite happy with their children's behavior, scoring 4.3 and 4.4 respectively: by then, the children were older, more settled, and many were on their own. In addition, more parents, especially fathers, had distanced themselves from their children or vice versa. Thus, reciprocal negative effect was less evident.

Another indicator of child effect which I investigated pertained to help. At Time 3, the respondents were asked whom they turned to for help. (By then, 75 percent had remarried.) Only 18.5 percent reported that they turned to their children for help and only 11.2 percent mentioned their children as one of the three categories of persons who were the most helpful to them. At that point, the children were nearly all adolescents or young adults, and could, in theory, have been important sources of help to their parents. But it is obvious that, overall, child effect on these parents did not include a great deal of help given to parents, perhaps because the developmental stages the youths had reached left them in a very self-centered mood. Or perhaps parents did not dare seek their help. Parents were still helping their children, rather than vice versa. Even household chores were primarily the responsibility of mothers rather than fathers, stepfathers or children, even when the mothers were employed (Benin and Agostinelli, 1988). Thus, as suggested in earlier chapters, child effect was still minimal in terms of helpfulness.

In fact, not only were children not seen as a major source of help, but they continued, albeit to a lesser extent, to be a source of parental concern. By Time 3, 19.5 percent of the parents still worried often about their children's future, while 33.2 percent worried "sometimes," 35 percent rarely did so, and 12 percent never did. While, as the children aged, parents worried less, nearly half of the parents were still concerned enough so that their children's future intruded in their minds in a worrisome way.

The respondents were also queried on how much they felt in control of their lives. When they chose any alternative other than total control, they were asked what aspects of their lives or whom they felt contributed to lowering their sense of control. They could mention as many aspects as they wished; then, they had to rank-order their responses. The results showed that 29.6 percent of the respondents chose their children as the first reason why they felt less in control of their lives than they wanted to be. Another 10.7 percent chose their children as the second factor contributing to diminishing their sense of control over their lives.

It should be noted that this question was asked at Time 3 when the children had already become much less of a problem than they used to be immediately after the separation. We can surmise that at the outset of the parents' separation children contribute more heavily, albeit unwittingly so, to lowering their parents' feelings of control than they do later on. If we return to the concept of parental characteristics discussed in Chapters 3 and 4, we can conclude that early separation/divorce renders parents particularly vulnerable to child effect, whether positively or negatively. It is also interesting that, in the previous chapter, students themselves had perceived divorce as an event increasing vulnerability in their own parents.

At some other point during the third interview, the parents were asked how much control they had over the children who remained at home: 21.3 percent felt that they had no control at all over their dependent children; 20.6 percent felt that they did not have enough control; 57 percent felt that they had enough control. Thus, over 40 percent of the parents felt that the control they should have over their dependent children was either absent or lacking. These statistics may be related to the previous ones and be contributory elements in the overall lowering of feeling of control over one's life.

The above statistics clearly illustrate that children play a key role (although not necessarily consciously so) in lowering or raising their parents' feelings of happiness and control over life after divorce. If we use the concept of avoidable child effect, especially as it pertains to adolescence and young adulthood, we see the emergence of the potential for redirecting certain research and policy questions in the area of divorce. Basically, the adequacy of the social resources placed at the disposal of these parents/children, and how they avail themselves of these resources, will be in great part responsible for reducing negative and avoidable child effect (as well as assorted divorce effects both on parents and children).

CUSTODIAL PROBLEMS

One of the main problems that separated and divorced parents face is the continuing battle over child custody (Luepnitz, 1982). Although most children are placed in their mother's custody, many fathers contest it or threaten to contest it as time goes by. In addition, a minority of parents share custody and, here as well, there is a wide variety of alternatives. Moreover, many children use the threat of changing custody in order to obtain concessions from their custodial parent. The following custodial father is such an example and remarks that he would like to have a little girl, in addition to his new baby son, from his remarriage to compensate for the insecurity brought about by his sixteen-year-old daughter and fifteen-year-old son from his previous marriage. He has had custody of his daughter on a sporadic basis only:

> Maybe it's unavoidable in a divorce situation that you lose a child or two because they have more loopholes that allow them to slip out of your sphere of influence, they have ready-made excuses like adopted children; if they can't get along with their parents they can always blame their adoption. My daughter can always look to her mother if she doesn't agree with me.

A custodial mother, for her part, explains that her life has been made very difficult, even after she remarried, because her ex-husband "has been in and out of courts for custody." She feels that she cannot parent adequately because of the constant threat of having the children removed from her custody or opting to live with their father, who is an unstable man. Another example involved a custodial father who had sought and won his sons' custody as a revenge on his wife. He showed great irritation at the time of the first interview because his ex-wife had tried to have the order revoked. Later on, she had to go to court to obtain more liberal visiting rights. As he fought her every inch of the way, she eventually remarried and decided to have children again to make up for the children she had lost. She subsequently had twins, and by the following interview, it was very obvious that her ex-husband was greatly irritated at her again. This time, he complained during his interview that she was not seeing her sons often enough. In her own interview, the mother put it this way:

> Before, my ex-husband was annoyed because I was fighting to have access to my children. When I stopped, he turned around and started accusing me of not seeing my children often enough. It is a case of a double whammy.

The following noncustodial father and his new wife were actively planning to gain his children's custody:

The problem will be their mother. We'll have to restrict access to once a week or so, otherwise she'll be here begging for money for herself instead of working, and criticizing everything my wife does. We'll have to be very firm with her. Really, she's just a big child. My oldest is more reasonable than she is.

(*Thirty-three-year-old remarried father, three children aged seven, eight and ten, with an ex-wife on welfare; although she is remarried, her husband is unemployed. She is her new husband's fourth wife.*)

While custodial problems affect parents more acutely during the onset of their separation or divorce, in many families these problems are perpetuated under one form or another. Adults who have children and divorce subsequently are very much affected by the presence of their children, and one of the first child effects appears in the area of custodial arrangements.

CUSTODIAL ARRANGEMENTS

As seen above, the very *presence* of children creates many difficulties between the ex-spouses after a divorce. For other ex-couples, the presence of the children forces them to forget about each other as ex-spouses and, rather, focus on their coparental responsibilities. Indeed, researchers and clinicians generally agree that it is important for ex-spouses to cooperate as parents (Ahrons, 1979, 1980; Rosenthal and Keshet, 1981). A remarried custodial mother explains her situation:

What is most important is that neither parent tries to put down the other. We make a point of complimenting each other in front of them. . . . When you have a structure like this the children feel very safe. They have ground rules, they know where they are at and they can't play mind games.

An ex-couple has split the custody of their children, the girls with the mother and the boys with the father. The latter tells this researcher:

> I make it a point to involve her [ex-wife] in everything that is decided about the children, even for the boys who live here. . . . The way I've got it arranged, the children have *two* parents, can't take sides, we're not using them and they're not using us. . . . I have raised them [the boys] to love their mother; it's very important in their development and I've found that *I* am a better man for it.

His ex-wife, who is also remarried, fully concurs with his assessment of their arrangement:

> He didn't take our daughters because they prefer to stay with me and because he was told that girls need their mother more than their father. . . . [He] always makes certain that our sons phone me. . . . Sometimes when the children need to make a decision, he asks them what *I* said first. He never contradicts me.

Custodial arrangements impact on the parents, not only because they have to continue seeing each other when they might well prefer not to do so (Ambert, 1989), but because the sharing of children forces them to alter their role toward each other: they have to think of the ex-spouse first of all as the parent of their children. This is often very difficult to accomplish because it means putting aside mutual antagonisms, yearnings, and regrets. It is not surprising if, instead of coparenting, most ex-couples engage in what has been termed "parallel parenting" (Furstenberg, 1987).

Moreover, when custodial problems arise, custodial arrangements have to be readjusted, thus requiring a never ending adaptation process on the part of one parent or the other. Because women generally have custody of their children, they are likely to be more affected than men in this respect as children are at times encouraged by the father to switch residence and even allegiance. Such mothers may feel particularly rejected and defeated. Their sense of loss is compounded by a new set of financial circumstances: they often find themselves paying for a larger house or apartment than they need after one or all children leave. And the first thing the fathers generally do is to cut off child payments which were actually helping to maintain the housing situation.

On the other side, when the children make the switch from one parent to the other in midstream, the new custodial parent may have to undergo a change of life style and seek larger accommodations. His or her new spouse suddenly has to adjust to having full-time stepchildren and, if children had been born in the remarriage, additional adaptations are required to integrate half-siblings.

NONCUSTODIAL PARENT

While much of the impact of child care, child rearing, and related financial responsibilities lies with the custodial parent, the other parent, often referred to as the "visiting parent," has a unique set of problems. The main one perhaps resides in the erosion of the parent-child relationship. American statistics indicate that only 33 percent of fathers still see their children regularly after two years of divorce (Arendell, 1986). Percentages were higher in my Canadian study, in part because Toronto residents tend to relocate within the area, while Americans experience more geographic mobility and are thus less able to see their children. It may also be that circumstances allow Canadian parents to be more committed to their parental role after divorce than are their American counterparts.

Children become disenchanted with the absent and often neglecting parent, while the absent parent feels abandoned and exploited. The rift is particularly marked when teenagers become more distant, as they do not wish to miss out on their weekend activities with their friends. As the following father explains it:

> They have been coming over about once every third week-end in the past six months. . . . Their mother. . . . claims that they feel cut off from their friends and family when they come to visit, as if I wasn't their family. . . . Two weeks ago they came over but I had to drive them to a babysitting job they said they couldn't miss. . . . [much later in the interview] So I am paying for these two girls who see me less and less. Not that I have strings attached to support payments, but I am their *father* and I would like for them to love me.

The absent parent comes to be seen as the external member of the family or as nonfamily. Often, the father helplessly watches as his children's behavior deteriorates and his role as an outsider prevents him from having any influence on the situation. The following father has a son with a drug-related juvenile record and his daughter is frequently truant from home and school:

> I can't have a meaningful conversation with them, or try to straighten them out because they wouldn't listen or they would complain to their mother and she would prevent me from seeing them. I can always take her to court but you must appreciate what a headache this is. . . . In addition my ex-wife never had much discipline. . . . they go as they please and she blames me. So long as the children know that *I* am to blame, they're not going to put their act together. . . . I hurt for them but as an onlooker.

A noncustodial mother who had a daughter and a son in her remarriage realized that her oldest son from her previous marriage was visiting her only reluctantly. She tried to make him understand that she loved him as much and that *he* should also take some responsibility in maintaining their mother-son relationship. After years of being rejected, she now states:

> No, I can't say that I love him as much as the other two *now* because he has made himself scarce for me and when you have three children you worry less about each one in particular and even less about one who has never encouraged your love. I think children are raised to take parents for granted in this country and they grow up thinking in terms of unconditional love, you know that philosophy. Well, I don't agree. It's unrealistic, everything on earth is conditional.

Many fathers stop or reduce support payments as a direct result of feelings of rejection (see also Seltzer et al., 1989). As one father said, "I don't see them enough to say that they think of me as their father, so I don't see why I should have to support someone else's children." Similar statements were often made during the six-year study. Some were excuses for their unacceptable desertion of their families, but others were a reflection of the effect of feelings of rejection, of helplessness, and of loss of hope.

> In a way, I'd rather see them more often but I had been away from them for so many years and their mother has brought them up so differently that I feel like an outsider.

Taking refuge in the child born of the remarriage is thus an outlet which looms large in the lives of many noncustodial parents. The new child acquires a meaning that the other children do not have and never had. This new child then has a particularly great effect on the parents:

> I have a baby boy of my own here with another one on the way and sometimes I feel it is pointless to maintain a relationship with my daughter. . . . If I didn't see her I'd be blamed for it and she'd say that I had abandoned her and my other children might [later] think the same when they grow up. It's a difficult situation because I can't say that I am attached to her, she doesn't feel to me like my child the way my boy does and the other will. It's hard to explain why.

This father had separated when the daughter in question was not yet born. Another father also has a new baby boy:

> At my age it's another fresh start. My older son is at Yale. . . . my daughter visits infrequently and it used to upset me considerably but now that I have a baby I accept it so much better. The baby has provided me with a secure feeling; he is here and not about to leave; he is the symbol of family life. My wife's [little] daughter is a very pleasant child who needs a father and she is a sharp contrast to my daughter. These two children have healed the wounds. . . .

These parents are very conscious of some of the effects that children born of a remarriage have on them. It should be noted parenthetically that when researchers talk of the effect of remarriage on children, they generally refer to children of divorce whose parents remarry and may or may not have other children. But the children *from* the remarriage are not studied. It is true that such children belong to an intact marriage and as such are probably grouped along with children of first marriages. Are there differences between the two groups of children? We do not know. Nor do we know the differential impact on parents of children born from remarriages. The data herein presented indicate that children of remarriage *do* affect their parents differently, at least in certain areas. Considering the fact that nearly half of the women who remarry while still in their childbearing years have a child in that remarriage (Wineberg, 1990), one can immediately appreciate the relevance of this research topic.

CUSTODIAL PARENT

The custodial parent, generally a mother, often becomes a de facto solo parent with all the incumbent responsibilities. A majority are employed, many are on welfare, and a great proportion find their role incompatible with their own personal needs. For many, the children are a source of comfort and company. For others, as illustrated in the statistics presented earlier, the children constitute their major source of problems — in great part because society does not offer an appropriate structure for these parents, especially financially and in terms of day care and after school care facilities.

The following mother had a very difficult adolescent daughter when I first interviewed her in 1978. After the girl left for a premature marriage, life with the other children became more bearable, as the mother explained it in her 1984 interview:

> Life was so difficult when she was around that I'd rather forget about her and when she comes she fights with the others and her husband had made a pass at my other daughter. . . . I just wish she moved away. . . . There ought to be a law protecting parents against children like that. It seems that the whole world belongs to children.

Discipline and behavioral problems loom large in many families, especially between mothers and teenage sons (Hetherington, 1989). As the following mother put it:

I am getting better but I am still very bitter and I have so much trouble with my son. He doesn't listen to anyone, he picks up fights, he gets picked on, he was suspended from school the other month, and so on.

In a study published elsewhere (Ambert, 1982), I found that custodial fathers held an advantage over custodial mothers both in terms of the satisfaction they experienced from their children's behavior and in terms of how well the children behaved toward them. Moreover, when I divided the custodial mothers by socioeconomic status, I found that the lower-SES mothers were the most disadvantaged of the custodial parents. Not only were they sorely dissatisfied with their children's behavior (low score of 1.5), but their children's behavior in general, and toward the mothers in particular, was the most problematic of all categories of children.

I concluded that "the fathers as males seemed to command authority and respect from their children quasi-automatically, when they had their custody . . . The mothers, by contrast . . . had to prove themselves . . ." (Ambert, 1982: 82). Moreover, "Children of lower-SES mothers, inherit the low social status of the mother and often end up at the bottom of the totem pole in [the] school system . . . [this] leads them to posit rejecting acts toward their mother, who becomes the scapegoat for their frustration" (p. 81). These lower-SES mothers received no help from the fathers, lived in neighborhoods with a high delinquency rate, and basically had very little control over their children. Their lives were entirely at the mercy of financial and child-related problems.

In contrast, mothers with a sufficient income, and especially those with a higher level of education, were more in control of their familial lives. They were less negatively affected by their children: they were less vulnerable. Elevated social class was an important determining characteristic of child effect in that it acted as a protective factor for both mothers and children. In many cases of divorce, it was even more protective of mothers than of children. It is thus regrettable that, on the one hand, studies of divorce in general rarely take social class into consideration. It is also regrettable that child effect and social class are not studied conjointly.

Custodial mothers often felt helpless and resented the fact that their ex-husband was failing in his fatherly role (Maccoby et al., 1990). The requisites of raising children alone placed severe limitations on the mothers' own development:

> As a single parent one has responsibilities that are incompatible with career achievement. One can't be both a devoted single parent and a very successful person at work. Something has to give. . . . Yes, I would still have my children's custody if I had to do it over, of course, but I'd rather not have to do it over. It was a duty, not a choice. Nobody chooses to be a single parent.

Another woman put it this way after she had remarried:

> When I was first married and after we separated, any problem my child would have was my fault. My [current] husband doesn't see it this way and neither do I. My children create their own problems, perhaps to get back at us for being divorced. . . .

She added that the problems created by their respective ex-spouses have contributed to uniting them as a new couple, while "the problems with the children tend to be divisive if we aren't careful."

While interviewing the mother of three teenage daughters, aged thirteen, sixteen and seventeen, I became the inadvertant observer of a family scenario which was more revealing of certain family processes than any interview material could be. The mother was just telling me that her daughters had "a lot of friends and their friends get into all sorts of trouble. So far I'm lucky but they're a constant concern . . ." when the interview was interrupted by a plain-clothes policewoman ringing the doorbell. The latter informed the mother that the daughters were throwing huge parties during her weekend absences and the neighbors had lodged several complaints about noise, drunk and doped teenagers, as well as vandalism. Windows had been smashed and tires slashed. The police had been called in. My respondent protested that her daughters "wouldn't get involved in anything like that" but the police officer was firm and pointed out that charges might be brought against them. The episode lasted about fifteen minutes, and the interview resumed as if nothing had occurred as the mother chose to ignore the incident. Later on, she added that she was proud of her daughters because they were "sociable and socially successful."

It should be added that the girls' father had complained bitterly during his own interview about the life style the snobbish mother was leading and how his daughters were growing into "materialistic, dumb, boy-crazy blonds." It had been obvious during her interviews that money and social appearances were of paramount importance in this woman's life. She dated men only when they had money ("he's loaded") and unconsciously encouraged her daughters to do the same. Moreover, she was obviously overwhelmed by her daughters and had lost control over the situation, but defended herself by pretending that nothing was wrong, as she wanted her daughters to be, above all else, "socially successful." In addition, she herself wanted to remain free during weekends to date. The unsupervised girls were taking advantage of the situation, and were allowing their boyfriends to run their lives — and the neighborhood — during their mother's absence.

Another mother with a different set of values would have been much more negatively affected by these daughters' behavior. This case is a good example of what was meant in Chapter 4 by situations where child effect on parents is either minimal or nonexistent. In this instance, the individualistic mother simply chose to ignore child behaviors that were not yet costly to her. Since she was not very committed to parenting, since certain areas of her life were of paramount importance to her (money, career, well-to-do men), and since her children were irrelevant to these areas, she could to some extent compartmentalize her life so that negative child effect did not intrude — except in her neighbors' lives!

In another household, with five difficult children still at home at the time of the first interview, a mother on welfare was bodily bruised and appallingly swollen when I met her. I was able to draw her out to the point where she admitted being beaten by her oldest son, then sixteen (Ambert, 1989). But she never complained to anyone about the abuse because the boy worked and helped her financially. When I returned for another interview three years later, the young man had been incarcerated for assault (on someone else).

She was a far happier woman by then as her two most difficult and out-of-control children had left.

A woman in a very similar situation had seen her children leave to get married or co-habit between the first and the third interviews. She felt that, although her children had been "trouble," it had been her lack of money "which has been my biggest problem because with some money I could have changed some things, have moved, have been less tired and bought more things to keep my children off the street." Another mother echoed a similar problem by saying that divorce itself was not a catastrophe. Being poor was the catastrophe. Thus, for these custodial mothers with too little education, few job skills, and too many children, the combination of these characteristics was catastrophic. Not only were they sad victims of negative child effect, but of poverty and lack of marketable skills (see also Weitzman, 1985, 1988). Many of the characteristics (such as being poor) which made them particularly vulnerable to stress and child effect were actually caused by negative societal responses or characteristics, as set out in Chapter 3.

Other custodial parents, however, were thankful for the presence of their children after their separation/divorce. Although surprisingly few parents actually verbalized such feelings, the ones who did pointed out that their children provided a structure for their lives: "If I didn't have the children with me I might spend all my time self-destructively at singles' bars and the likes, but with them here I can't afford this and it is for the best." Others pointed out that the children were good company, provided them with moral support "when I am down," gave them a goal, and forced them to "cope rather than mope." Custodial fathers reported such benefits more often than custodial mothers, in spite of the fact that there were fewer custodial fathers in the study. It is instructive that results showed custodial fathers to be in better mental health than noncustodial fathers. And, as we have seen, custodial fathers were also experiencing fewer problems with their children than custodial mothers (Ambert, 1982, 1984). It should be added that all but one of these fathers had actively sought custody of their children, while most custodial mothers were simply granted custody or had had no say in the matter in cases of desertion. Thus, it is possible that custodial fathers who are "seekers" (Mendes, 1976) seek custody when they predict that the situation will be under their control and beneficial for them to some extent.

In comparison, few mothers have the option of weighing the pros and the cons of custody, as it is something which simply happens to them. They often have less control over it than custodial fathers. It is not a socially acceptable act on a mother's part to refuse custody of her children, even if she knows that she is not the better parent. Fathers, however, are given more latitude in this respect so that the father-children "fit" has a greater chance of being correct for custodial fathers than for custodial mothers. It has also been noted that fathers seek custody of their children more frequently when they have sons (Ambert, 1989; Ferri, 1976; Grief, 1985). We have seen earlier that same-sex parent-child custodial arrangements are more beneficial to children; they are also more beneficial to parents, but this latter point has not been sufficiently emphasized in the literature (exc. Hetherington, 1989).

CONCLUSIONS

I have chosen to let divorced adults with children speak for themselves. I often found it surprising how many such adults spontaneously offered comments indicating that they were negatively affected by children in a situation of divorce. My surprise stems from the fact that parents are generally loath to admit that their children have or create problems, and do not believe that complaining about one's children is socially acceptable. This attitude stems in great part from this society's construction of children as passive recipients and of parents as all powerful agents in their children's lives. Consequently, a parent who complains is seen as a parent who has failed in his or her role. Parents, especially mothers, find it emotionally unbearable to be so judged.

My educated guess is that divorced parents may more readily perceive child effect than never-divorced parents or, for that matter, than other adults (see Introduction). I would suggest that this results from the fact that divorce is a very powerful, marking passage in the lives of most persons, and it forces them to confront or reevaluate some realities within a different perspective. This may lead them to perceive certain phenomena, such as child effect, more clearly than other parents. Having suffered the problems of divorce, they may be more willing than others to discuss a topic which is not generally considered socially acceptable.

It is also interesting that many of the divorcing adults who had no children spontaneously commented on how much more difficult their situation would have been with children. Basically, the statistical results of the study showed that childless adults who divorce benefit from not having the two major causes of post-separation strife between ex-spouses: children and money (Hetherington et al., 1982; Richards, 1982). These were the two battlegrounds for divorced *parents*. By contrast, among the childless, even money was of lesser importance between them as it was not related to children and, without children, less money was needed.

Thus, it was one of the key overall results of my study that individuals who recover the most easily after divorce generally had no children (although there were several exceptions, mainly among custodial fathers by choice) and were financially independent from their ex-spouses. In contrast, children immediately brought economic dependence of one spouse with resulting conflicts or, often, dependence on the welfare system with consequent losses in self-esteem and control over one's life.

Moreover, the childless ex-spouses could start all over again without having to maintain ties with each other if they so chose, while the ex-couples with children often felt tied down to each other at a time when they wanted to be free of each other. Children were indeed the key determining factor in the relationship between ex-spouses (Ambert, 1988a; Ahrons and Wallisch, 1986; Bloom and Kindle, 1985; Clingempeel, 1981; Goetting, 1980; Kurdek and Blisk, 1983; Rosenthal and Keshet, 1981), and even in the relationship with ex-in-laws (Ambert, 1988b).

Most divorced adults with children were faced by far greater constraints than childless adults. It was more difficult for them to have a "successful" divorce because, in order to achieve this goal, they had to overcome far more problems, whether emotionally, socially, or financially. Divorced parents also had less time for leisure and social pursuits, were less free to go out, and were often lonelier.

In addition, divorced parents had to cope with the emotional and behavioral upheavals which often occur in children within the first two years post-separation. Of course, this problem was especially acute for custodial parents (generally mothers), as these parents at the same time often suffered the backlash effect of poverty and of neglect on the part of the absent parent. Indeed, studies show that failure to support children and to maintain ties with them has serious negative consequences for the children themselves (Furstenberg et al., 1987; Hetherington et al., 1983; McLanahan, 1985). Thus, not only do divorced parents have to adjust to their new situation, but they have to make additional adjustments for the sake of their children's emotional well-being.

The results of this chapter constitute only one small example of the research which still needs to be carried out in the field of divorce, this time by shifting the focus to child effect on parents rather than on the effect of divorce on children and adults. This research can easily be extended into the area of remarriage, especially when a stepparenting situation exists (Ahrons and Wallisch, 1988; Clingempeel et al., 1987; Furstenberg, 1987; Ganong and Coleman, 1987b; Hetherington, 1987).

We have seen that the variables of sex and socioeconomic status were important determining factors in child effect in divorce. This flows well from the theoretical paradigm of parental characteristics described in Chapter 3 where parents' sex and social class are presented as two of the key variables that may determine to what extent parents are affected by their children and whether the effect is more likely to be positive or negative. We have also seen how certain child characteristics (difficult behavior, adolescence) contributed to negative child effect, as predicted in Chapters 3 and 4. In situations of parental conflict and divorce, children are, on the one hand, greatly affected, generally negatively, and often only temporarily. But, on the other hand, these same children are key agents affecting and even controlling their parents' lives.

I have also mentioned the fact that some of the negative characteristics of parents which made them particularly vulnerable to child effect were actually direct results of societal characteristics, as spelled out in Chapter 3. I am especially thinking of poverty here, of having to be on welfare, and of the lack of support these parents receive from many school systems and neighborhoods. As well, one could add that the negative peer group culture often fostered among adolescents constituted another barrier and even source of vulnerability for these parents, although it could have constituted a source of comfort for the children.

Consequently, the situation of divorce is one which can benefit from an analysis informed by the framework presented in this book. On the one hand, child effect in divorce is a relatively unique approach in the research and it can complement the focus on the effect of divorce on children. On the other hand, divorced individuals are rarely studied from a perspective which brings into focus the entire social structure as a set of contributory variables in their adjustment or simply in their overall experience. Social causes of divorce have been widely debated. What need to be examined are the social causes of stress and failures *after* the divorce, including society's failure to offer more services to such parents and children.

Chapter 9

Mothering Children Who Have Severe Chronic Illnesses

OVERVIEW

In the past two decades a new and complex form of parenthood has evolved. It consists of raising children who have survived catastrophic illnesses, conditions, and injuries. Their survival is due to recent advances in medical knowledge and biotechnological developments which in turn have led to improved treatments and technical devices (Burr et al., 1983; Schreiner et al., 1987). Because there is no known cure for their underlying conditions, some of these children remain dependent on life-support technology such as respirators and kidney dialysis machines. In addition to physiological problems, many also have serious motor impairments, sensory losses, developmental delays, and/or emotional problems.

Given the complexity of their needs, technology-dependent children require long-term care by very skilled caregivers. Until very recently, children with complex chronic healthcare needs were raised in institutions at extremely high costs. However, in North America at the present time, most of these children are living at home with their families. This shift in the site of long-term caregiving has occurred in a context of fiscal restraint in which money has been diverted from chronic to acute care medicine (Newman, 1983:16-17). It has been made possible by refinements in biotechnological devices and treatment protocols and it reflects the wide-

This chapter was written by Patricia McKeever, a faculty member in the Graduate School of Nursing at the University of Toronto.

spread assumption that institutions are detrimental to children's development (Aday et al., 1988; Frates et al., 1985).

In most parts of the Western world, homecare for chronically ill or disabled people usually is the responsibility of female relatives (Anderson and Elfert, 1989; Fraser, 1987; Goodman, 1986). The fact that women are family caregivers reflects cultural expectations about gender, family relationships and domestic labor. In addition, in times of fiscal restraint, women take up the economic "slack" by performing the tasks and services that are cut back by the market (Sokoloff, 1980:131). The economic contribution of women to caregiving in the home remains largely unrecognized (Anderson and Elfert, 1989), even though the formal healthcare system greatly depends on women's informal extra-market labor (Graham, 1985; Land, 1978; Stacey, 1985).

Cultural beliefs about child rearing compound the unequal division of labor for mothers and fathers regarding the care of chronically ill children. Despite that fact that it is now the statistical norm for mothers of young children to work outside the home, the care of chronically ill children is still almost exclusively their responsibility (Lamb, 1983; Parke, 1986; Schilling et al., 1985).

When children are technology-dependent, their care is complex, sophisticated, and labor intensive. In addition to nurturing disabled children, their caregivers carry out life-sustaining procedures on a daily basis, maintain equipment, and coordinate and negotiate needed professional services. Cessation of this care would cause harm and could result in the child's death within minutes, hours, or days (Thomas, 1986).

According to Sara Ruddick, maternal work is determined by three demands: preserving children's lives, fostering their development, and ensuring that they are socially acceptable. Conceptually and historically, preservation is preeminent of these demands in that the prolonged fragility of children essentially creates and defines maternal work. Preserving the lives of children is the central, constitutive, invariant aim of maternal practice and the commitment to achieving that aim constitutes maternal activity (Ruddick, 1989: 17-19). From this flows unavoidable child effect, as discussed in Chapter 4.

Most mothers enjoy a sense of well-being when their children flourish and experience distress when they are unwell or unhappy. Ultimately, all mothers are beholden to the workings of "nature" whose indifference, so poignantly evident in illness, death, and damage to children, can frustrate their best preservative efforts (Ruddick, 1989:29-34). Most technology-dependent children are extremely vulnerable physically; preserving their lives is fraught with uncertainty. It is very unusual in many ways because machines replace or augment such vital physiological functions as breathing, eating and urinating; and monitoring systems replace cries or words as indicators of distress.

REVIEW OF THE LITERATURE

The experience of raising technology-dependent children at home is too recent a phenomenon to have been described in any detail in the literature. However, numerous studies about parenting chronically ill or disabled children indicate that the experience is stressful and that the impact on mothers seems to be particularly profound (Graham, 1985). Despite the fact that most researchers focused on intrapsychic and intrafamily relationships when studying the effects of these children on their families, it was possible to glean from their findings the following picture of what this maternity is like.

The Maternal Experience

Children's chronic illnesses and disabilities affect almost every aspect of the day-to-day mother-child relationship (Gallagher et al., 1983). The repetitive tasks that are inherent in caregiving often resemble housework more than child care because they are ". . . physically taxing, mentally exhausting and dispiritingly monotonous" (Baldwin and Glendinning, 1983:41).

For example, feeding chronically ill or disabled children is frequently time consuming, technically difficult, and emotionally draining. Many cannot eat independently; moreover, swallowing, chewing or digesting food can be problematic. Others are anorexic, have restricted food preferences or have behavior problems associated with eating (Luiselli et al., 1985; Palmer and Horn, 1978). Disabled children may also suffer from prolonged bowel and bladder incontinence causing much more laundry and cleaning for their mothers (Bradshaw and Lawton, 1978; Kazak and Clark, 1986).

These mothers also confront unusual dilemmas in relation to disciplining and expressing affection for their children. In some situations, physical contact can cause damage or pain. In a recent study, mothers of children with extremely fragile bones expressed how distressing it was not being able to cuddle, spank or play roughly with their children. They also worried that bones broken accidentally would be interpreted by professionals as signs of abuse (Deatrick et al., 1988).

Many researchers have reported that these children have more behavior problems and can be more demanding to be with than healthy children (Kazak and Marvin, 1984; Pless and Pinkerton, 1975; Tinkleman et al., 1976; Travis, 1976). They are also at higher risk for such secondary afflictions as emotional and school adjustment problems (Breslau, 1985; Cadman et al., 1987; Nolan and Pless, 1986). Even as infants, these children may be less rewarding to care for in that they are often irritable, less responsive, smile infrequently, and develop slowly (Field, 1983, in Blacher, 1984).

As a consequence of the fact that disabled children are often isolated and stigmatized in this society, their mothers must provide unusual amounts of companionship and stimulation. They also have been reported to help their children find and maintain friendships (Cadman et al., 1987; Kazak and Clark, 1986; Madiros, 1982; Voysey, 1975). This task becomes increasingly difficult as children approach and reach adolescence (Deatrick et al., 1988).

The precautions and taboos that govern the social actions of the mothers of disabled children are often subtle. For example, mothers in Roskies' study (1972:141) dressed their limb-deficient children attractively because they feared that play clothes would be interpreted as a sign of maternal neglect. Mothers in another study reported that they had learned that disabled children's disobedience and social mistakes are often attributed to faulty mothering (Voysey, 1975:83). Unlike the mothers of healthy children, these mothers have no ritualistic norms to follow and even the most basic expectations about child rearing are called into question (Darling, 1983; Glendinning, 1983; Madiros, 1982). In the absence of acceptable norms, they learn to treat their children's embarrassing behaviors and symptoms as routine events (McCubbin and Patterson, 1983; Voysey, 1975: 87-89).

Most disabilities and some chronic illnesses curtail the social and physical mobility of both the child and the mother. They tend to avoid situations in which they would feel stigmatized; the child's physical problems and dependence on equipment make leaving the house difficult. This problem was quantified by Butler et al. (1985) who found that 45 percent of mothers in his study had never travelled with their disabled children on public transportation; a further 33 percent experienced considerable difficulty when they did so. Mothers' mobility is also severely limited by the difficulty they have finding babysitters willing and able to care for these children at affordable costs (Wilkins, 1979, in Philp and Duckworth, 1982).

In addition to the activities and restrictions described above, mothers of disabled children routinely perform highly specialized tasks that are usually carried out by professionals such as nurses, therapists, and teachers. They develop a degree of competence in carrying out these skills that is comparable with that of the professionals (Deatrick et al., 1988; Schreiner et al., 1987; Thomas, 1986). In the course of administering treatments, mothers inflict pain or discomfort and repeatedly observe their children in distress (Travis, 1976:85). The vigilance and monitoring demanded by many chronic childhood conditions can be onerous, leading to months and years of disturbed sleep and little time for leisure activities (Anderson and Spain, 1977; Gregory, 1976; Goodman, 1986).

Like most female domestic labor, caring for disabled children is done in isolation (McRobbie, 1982). This isolation is compounded by the demands and stigmatizing properties of their children's conditions. Loneliness and little ongoing emotional and material support from extended family members or friends have been reported extensively (Aday and Wegener, 1988; Glendinning, 1983; Madiros, 1982).

Although no longitudinal studies have been conducted with mothers of chronically ill children, many of the most difficult aspects seem to be related to time. The tasks involved in caregiving are in themselves extremely time consuming. Less obvious is the fact that, unlike healthy children who are raised to be independent, severely disabled children often remain dependent on maternal care indefinitely. Because the work associated with caring for these children usually increases as they grow and/or their conditions deteriorate, their mothers' labor becomes more onerous as they age themselves (Wikler, 1983).

Mothers of disabled children do not seem to have a sense of their children's lives as wholes. They live from day to day (Voysey, 1975:198), and view the future with a mixture of fear and hope. Worry about the child's prognosis and long-term care vitally shapes this form of maternity. These children require social and medical services, but services are disjointed and do not have life-span perspectives (Damrosch and Perry, 1989; Wikler, 1983). Normal childhood developmental milestones usually are inappropriate for chronically-ill children; yet their failure to achieve them is another cause for recurrent maternal distress (Wikler, 1981).

Although researchers have focused almost exclusively on the stress and negative effects of caregiving on the mother-child relationship, I would be remiss if I neglected to mention that family caregiving also has been described as satisfying and rewarding (Callahan, 1988; Colerick and George, 1986; Kinney and Stephens, 1989). Gottlieb (1989) recently argued that women caring for elderly relatives derive companionship, affection and a sense of meaning from the caregiving role. Similarly, mothers of ventilated children have reported their appreciation that their families had been reestablished; they had more control over their children's care, and their children's emotional states had improved at home (Aday et al., 1988). When the alternative is institutionalization, most families clearly consider homecare much less noxious (Callahan, 1988).

Family Relationships

Although they have been included in very few studies, siblings of disabled children seem to behave in ways that place unique demands on mothers. They have been said to demonstrate jealousy, resentment, increased anxiety, lower self-esteem, aggressiveness, decreased school performance, frequent illnesses, and depression (Brett, 1988; McKeever, 1982; Seligman, 1987; Wikler, 1983). On the other hand, some research suggests that these siblings may be easier to raise because they are mature and altruistic as a result of their experiences related to the ill child (Simeonsson and McHale, 1981). They may be ostracized by their friends and face misunderstanding in school (Seligman, 1987). Research findings also indicate that, to protect the family's image, mothers invest considerable energy managing the nature and amount of illness-related information that often goes to neighbors, relatives, teachers and friends via siblings (McKeever, 1982).

Parents of disabled children do not have higher divorce rates than the population at large. Significant numbers of parents have reported that the child's health problem has strengthened the marital relationship (Beglerter et al., 1976; Gath, 1977; Martin, 1975; Sabbeth and Leventhal, 1984; Silbert et al., 1982). Sprey (1979:143) suggested that these findings may reflect a situation in which conflicts engendered by the child are defined as less costly than divorce or separation. Fathers have low levels of participation in caring for disabled children (Lamb, 1983; Parke, 1986; Roskies, 1972); however, their incomes are crucial. These mothers are also very unlikely to remarry should their marriages end (Travis, 1976). Thus, it seems that mothers of disabled children have a vested interest in working hard to maintain their marriages. They have more to lose and less to gain if the marriage fails than do mothers of healthy children.

Relationships with Professionals

Anderson and Elfert (1989) argued that the concept of maternal competence structures the ways in which women make sense of their children's chronic illnesses. They also highlighted the fact that maternal competence is an ideological category derived from the social context. Because judgment rests with those considered experts, the evaluations of health professionals, especially physicians, serve to sanction and legitimize the dominant ideologies about women as mothers and caregivers. By virtue of their education and high social status, physicians are extremely powerful in relation to low-status, unpaid, caregiving mothers (Graham, 1983).

Most mothers have neither prior experience with nor a workable belief system about disabled children; hence they perceive professional advice to be preemptively important. However, because professionals and mothers live in completely different worlds related to childhood disability, the experts' prescriptive advice is rarely relevant to mothers' social and personal experiences with their children (Strong, 1979; Voysey, 1975:175).

Mothers of chronically ill children have many more encounters with professionals than mothers of healthy children. They are the ones who always accompany the children to various appointments and accompany them during hospitalizations (Breslau, 1985). Professionals also assess, treat or help care for many technology-dependent children in their homes (Schriener et al., 1987; Thomas, 1986). Relating to and coordinating the activities of these people is very time consuming and demands considerable interpersonal skill on the part of mothers.

The privacy of the mother-child relationship is invaded and subjected to ongoing professional scrutiny. Consequently, as Voysey (1975:161) argues, these mothers are ". . . more than normally held accountable to the official morality of childrearing while their experience is less than normally manageable within its terms." In relating to professionals over the years, the child's problem gradually comes to be conceptualized in terms of how well the mother has "accepted" it. In some ways, as seen in Chapters 5 and 6, the mother becomes the primary patient (Roskies, 1972; Strong, 1979) and treatment failures are attributed to her inadequacies (Hewitt, 1976).

Several researchers have reported the difficulties mothers have getting and retaining the professional help and support services their children require throughout their lives (Birenbaum, 1970; Schreiner et al., 1987; Strong, 1979; Thomas, 1986). Some of these endeavors require mothers to exaggerate their children's problems to get help while others demand that they minimize them to gain acceptance (Birenbaum, 1970; Voysey, 1975).

After extensive observations of mothers' encounters with health professionals, Strong (1979:40) concluded that professionals assume that all mothers of disabled children want to care for their children and that they will do so with a "wholly natural competence." He noted that, as mothers, the women were viewed as "authorities of unblemished character." Relative to professionals, however, they had no authority. Hence, the idealization that they were naturally loving and able was counterposed by an equivalent exaggeration of their medical ignorance (p. 70).

Physicians commonly advise parents to raise disabled or chronically ill children as if they were "normal." Although normalization may seem to be a straightforward process, it is in fact dynamic and complex. In a qualitative study, Anderson (1981) identified the adjustments mothers make to normalize their experiences, accept disease processes and carry out therapeutic regimens. Normalization is a very arduous process when children have severe disabilities and when support services are difficult or impossible to obtain.

The Costs of Caregiving

Comprehensive analyses of the economic costs of raising disabled children have been very limited but available data suggest that illness-related costs frequently reduce disposable income to the extent that many families endure chronic financial strain (Baldwin and Glendinning, 1983). It is also evident that children in low-income families have a disproportionate incidence of chronic health problems (Butler et al., 1985).

Raising disabled children involves many start-up and ongoing costs due to extra transportation requirements, therapeutic diets, special clothing, household help, babysitting, medications, and supplies. Often equipment must be purchased and structural changes must be made to houses (Butler et al., 1985).

Incomes frequently fall when wages are lost due to time off to accompany the child to appointments, during crisis periods or when the child is hospitalized. Taking part in training programs to learn necessary homecare procedures is expensive in terms of both time and money. They may take days or weeks but they usually necessitate absence from paid employment (Foster and Hoskins, 1981; Giovannoni, 1984; Wateska et al., 1980).

Hidden costs to caregivers, such as being unable to enter or having to leave the work force, or working at less demanding jobs, have been overlooked by most researchers. However, several studies indicate that these mothers are much less likely to work outside the home than mothers of nondisabled children. The differences in labor force participation increase as disabled children get older but remain dependent. Women interviewed in these studies did not work due to chronic fatigue, the child's frequent "illnesses," the lack of suitable child care and the inflexibility of employers.

The findings of one British study concluded that, in comparison to working mothers of healthy children, working mothers of disabled children earned less money throughout their working lives and their salaries increased more slowly. In addition, they worked under poorer conditions and received fewer employee benefits (Baldwin and Glendinning, 1983). In summary, although poorly explored, it seems that the experience of mothering disabled children occurs in a context of chronic financial strain and diminished resources.

In addition to financial consequences, there are physical and emotional health consequences. Given the relentless physical and emotionally taxing work these women do, it is not surprising that they have little time or energy for themselves. Many never have vacations and rarely engage in leisure activities (Anderson and Spain, 1977; Gregory, 1976). Although current understanding is rudimentary, studies suggest that occupations demanding constant vigilance and carrying high levels of responsibility for the lives of others are extremely physically and psychologically stressful (Elliott and Eisdorfer, 1982:111).

Researchers rarely have asked caregivers about their own physical health; hence, very little is known about the physical consequences for women of prolonged caregiving experiences. However, in a few studies, caregiving mothers have reported chronic fatigue, headaches, and menstrual problems (Romans-Clarkson et al., 1987; Roskies, 1972). Symptoms of psychological distress such as depression, anxiety, and irritability have been reported much more frequently (Breslau et al., 1982; Gayton et al., 1977). Damrosch and Perry (1989) described most mothers in their study as sad and burdened. They tended to blame themselves for their children's problems and felt self-conscious in public. Mothers of disabled children in two other studies had low levels of maternal competence and diminished confidence in their ability to care for their children (Cummings et al., 1966; Kazak and Marvin, 1984).

RESEARCH APPROACH

Because virtually nothing is known about what it is like to raise chronically ill, technology-dependent children, I recently initiated a longitudinal, exploratory study. Using Ruddick's conceptualization of maternal work, I will focus on findings that highlight the work these mothers do to preserve their children's lives, foster their physical development and enhance their social acceptability. I will then discuss the impact this type of maternity has on their feelings of competence.

In the first phase, a sample of twenty-five mothers of technology-dependent children agreed to participate in an intensive, open-ended interview. The interviews were conducted over six months. The yearly incidence of children becoming technology-dependent is relatively low. Hence, this sample represented almost the entire population of mothers of children who became technology-dependent in a Metropolitan area in a six-month period.

These mothers constituted a demographically heterogeneous group. A variety of cultural and religious backgrounds were represented and about one-third of the women were immigrants. Most of the women had completed secondary school and eleven had some post secondary education. They ranged in age from twenty-four to forty-six years with a mean age of twenty-nine years. All except one were married and living with the father of the chronically ill child.

At the time of the interview, nine women were working part-time or full-time outside the home in traditionally female-dominated positions. They lived in families whose mean 1989 income was $44,000. More than half of the women reported family incomes that were lower than the current Canadian average. In order to be close to the hospital where the children were treated, the majority lived in a very expensive, large urban center.

The children in this study ranged in age from six months to thirteen years; had severe disabling conditions; and depended on continuous or routine procedures involving technological devices that augmented, replaced or facilitated normal physiological functioning. They had been cared for at home by their mothers for at least two but not more than six months. Fifteen were male and ten were female. Fourteen had between one and four siblings and eleven were only children. Their health problems and the technological devices on which they depended are illustrated in Table 1. All of the children had been catastrophically ill and many had very rare or severe conditions.

Table 1

Childrens' Health Problems and The Technology they Require

Child's Health Problem	N*	Medical Technology
Neurological Damage/ Disease	2	Suction machine, oxygen, food pump
Congenital physical abnormalities	2	Suction, food pump, heart monitor
Gastrointestinal damage/ disease	3	Total parenteral nutrition (Feeding through vein)
End stage kidney disease	4	Dialysis machine (replaces kidney function)
Conditions requiring tracheotomy	4	Oxygen, suction, respiratory and heart monitor
Severe lung disease	2	Oxygen, compressor for inhalation of medications

* 2 children have multiple problems and
are counted in two categories

RESULTS

Although this was a heterogeneous sample of women, their experiences of mothering technology-dependent children were remarkably similar. Their complete accounts portray this maternity much more comprehensively than can be represented here. In keeping with the major themes of this book, I will describe how technology-

dependent children affect their mothers' lives. I will illustrate how
threats to maternal competence are inherent in the work they do to
preserve their children's lives, foster their development, and strive
for social acceptability. I will then discuss the impact of this experience on women's physical health and psychological well-being.

Preserving Fragile Lives

Even though most U.S. and Canadian children are protected relatively effectively from a medical-technological perspective, Ruddick (1989) argues that the preservation of children's lives still constitutes the central aim of maternal work. The mothers I interviewed
were engaged in extremely complex preservative work because
their children's lives were continuously in jeopardy. Powerful
threats to feelings of maternal competence clearly were part of this
experience.

For most women, preservative work begins in pregnancy, in that
behaviors are adjusted to protect the developing fetus. One young
woman described her efforts to protect her unborn child:

> I went to prenatal classes and did everything I was supposed to
> do during pregnancy. I didn't smoke or drink and I only al-
> lowed myself one cup of decaffeinated coffee per day. I had
> two ultrasound tests and everything was fine. I was going to
> have a beautiful natural childbirth . . . it didn't turn out that
> way.

For mothers such as this one who gave birth prematurely or to children with congenital anomalies, questions of maternal competence
were raised during the diagnostic process. Virtually all women recalled physicians' attempts to reassure them that they were not responsible for their infants' conditions and that they should not feel
guilty.

However, the comfort in these statements was seriously undermined by contradictory, detailed questioning about their behaviors
during pregnancy. All had been asked repeatedly about their nutri-
tional intake, smoking, and alcohol and drug ingestion. They had
also been asked about their work histories and work environments.
This seemed to leave the mothers with a lingering sense that they,

by virtue of their behavior during pregnancy, were responsible for their children's problems. The biological competence of many women was also undermined because they had had infants with genetic defects, previous or subsequent miscarriages or stillbirths, fertility problems, delivery by Caesarian section, or premature delivery. Many were convinced that their bodies were "defective."

Prior to bringing their technology-dependent children home from the hospital, all mothers had undergone teaching programs to learn the procedures required to care for them. They literally learned how to keep their children alive. As reflected in the following quote, many recalled extreme anxiety and fear associated with learning such complex procedures as tracheotomy caring and kidney dialysis:

> Learning was terrifying. The doctors and nurses have experience so they know it's safe to send children home to have dialysis but you don't have that knowledge so you're very worried and um . . . scared half to death . . . .

Despite this fear and anxiety, they all felt they had no other option but to learn what was required of them and said they would have learned to do anything to be able to take their children home. For example, a former teacher who had two children with progressive degenerative kidney disease said that she ". . . wasn't cut out to be a nurse, but you have no choice. I'm not at all medically-minded. I love to teach children but even as far as bandaging cuts and bruises, I wish I didn't have to."

At the time of the interviews, the children had been living at home for at least two months. The mothers had mastered the technical procedures and seemed undaunted by the equipment. As one mother noted, the stress related to the technology was different at home: "It's not really the machine itself that's upsetting now — it's the stress of knowing it's keeping your child alive." Although the procedures had become routine, the children's precarious conditions made it impossible for their mothers to take their physiological stability for granted. They all experienced great anxiety when they noticed worrisome symptoms or when they had to deal with emergencies. Despite the fact that one child had stopped breathing many times, his mother said, "My heart still stops a million times whenever he stops breathing."

Preserving the lives of technology-dependent children involves constant vigilance. As the mother of a tracheotomized infant explained:

> Having her home is nothing like I thought it would be . . . With all the monitors I'm tense all the time—listening for them. When I go downstairs to throw in some laundry I make my five year old stand beside her and watch her. I can't really even see my basement unless I take her with me.

The work also included restraining and inflicting pain on children, many of whom lacked the capacity or were too young to understand the need for the discomfort. Mothers said that they felt like they were "torturing" or "stabbing" their children in the course of suctioning them or inserting tubes. They worried that the children hated them for doing the treatments.

Mothers must also create a hospital-like environment. For example, equipment must be maintained and supplies kept in stock. Most houses needed to be meticulously clean to prevent infections or breathing problems in the children. Cigarette smoke exacerbates breathing problems so the mothers who smoked only did so outside or in their basements.

All of this complex preservative work was very time consuming and labor intensive and it was carried out almost exclusively by the mothers—even when they were sick themselves. One mother expressed her frustration with the amount of work involved: "There's so much care required—you're never allowed to just be the mom; you're everything but the mother you wanted to be." Some husbands and occasionally grandmothers helped with the child's care; but only one father routinely assumed responsibility for doing the procedures.

The nature of the children's problems necessitated that the mothers work closely with professionals. Although they had acquired professional expertise in many ways, maternal competence was threatened repeatedly in these relationships. Health professionals gave conflicting messages. They clearly expected mothers to be able and willing to care for very ill children at home. As one mother explained,

> It's almost like the doctors see me as a martyr . . . "Oh Virgin Mary — take him home — you can deal with it." I feel like saying "No, no, I'm a stupid little woman who can't deal with things — keep him in hospital — please."

Despite the fact that few of these women had any previous medical or nursing background, they were expected to understand medical terminology, to give detailed histories and "to know the child best." On the other hand, they were expected to follow orders and accept professional interpretations without question.

As illustrated with this mother's words, all of the women had at times felt "stupid" with professionals: "Just because they think the child is retarded, they think the mother is too. Until I learned what everything meant I always felt stupid with professionals — I still do a lot of the time." These feelings were exaggerated in women whose first language was not English, each of whom had been forced to improve her language skills while under enormous stress.

Finally, despite many threats to their competence, all of the women had developed considerable expertise and self-confidence regarding their children's care. With time and experience, virtually all of them acted as advocates for their children and did not hesitate to criticize care given by professionals.

Fostering Growth in Children Who Fail to Thrive

In addition to protecting and preserving children, mothers are expected to nurture them and foster their emotional and physical development (Ruddick, 1989). Despite their mothers' valiant efforts, technology-dependent children do not thrive in the usual sense. All of the children were visibly different and many were extremely or multiply disabled. All mothers talked about how painful this aspect of maternity was for them and how difficult it was to maintain a sense of competence. The words of a mother of two seriously ill children represent the feelings of all the mothers I interviewed:

> We go to church Sunday and Monday is a bad day for me. I
> see these other children flourishing and mine just don't. I feel
> like a real failure. That's really what I struggle with. I feel
> people think I don't know how to be a mother—that's such a
> deep hurt I can't describe it.

With these children, the nurturing work was often frustrating and
disappointing, especially related to feeding. Before they had been
diagnosed, many infants did not grow at a satisfactory rate. Their
mothers recalled how very difficult the babies were to feed. Their
feelings of competence were unwittingly undermined by physicians
who repeatedly asked them details about how they were feeding the
infant.

Many women had been told that their milk was inadequate or
insufficient. This was very stressful for mothers: "I was told at first
that I didn't have enough milk for her and that's why she was losing
weight, I felt like the worst mother in the world for stopping breast-
feeding." Another stopped pumping her breasts to feed her baby in
the Intensive Care Unit due to feelings of inadequacy and embarrassment when she observed that "other mothers were bringing in
bottles full and I could only fill up little jars."

Very few of the older children could eat normally and many had
major dietary restrictions. As one mother resignedly said, "If a
child doesn't grow, you can't make him. He really looks like a
starved child. I know people stare at me and wonder what I do to
him." Another mother maintained that she kept asking the physician,

> Don't I feed them enough broccoli; aren't they getting enough
> iron? I give them vitamins plus, plus. I don't know why it's
> me . . . people look at me and ask "Don't you feed them right
> or dress them warm enough . . ." you honestly feel that it's all
> your fault and people look at you as if it's all your fault.

In contrast, children who were fed through a vein or tube had become much healthier looking as a result of their improved nutri-
tional states. Although this pleased their mothers, the abnormality
of this feeding method continued to trouble them. For many se-

verely disabled children, eating by mouth had been the only relatively "normal" activity the child could engage in: "Although she
didn't eat well it was the only normal thing she did. I would rather
sit for three hours feeding her with a demitasse spoon than hook her
up to the pump."

These children were also difficult to nurture in a more general
sense. Many were slow to develop, relatively unresponsive or extremely irritable. Mothers described experiences like the following
one:

> I was a wreck for two years. The only way I could stop the
> crying was to bounce on a big green gymnastics ball. I had to
> bounce with her. So I bounced on that ball all day long with
> her in my arms, holding her very tightly . . . half the time I
> even fed her bouncing up and down, up and down.

Mothers expressed how painful it was to compare their children to
normal children. Most had, in fact, developed strategies to avoid
situations where comparisons would be made. Instead of keeping
records of normal developmental milestones, many mothers kept
detailed medical notes related to the child's progress. Professionals
typically had advised mothers to raise these children as "normally
as possible." The difficulty in following such advice was highlighted by many mothers in such statements:

> Within a very short time I knew there was absolutely nothing
> normal about her. She couldn't breastfeed, she was obviously
> blind, she was having seizures and all she did was cry. She
> cried for two years day and night—I'm not exaggerating.

Finally, mothers reported the enormous difficulty they had procur-
ing appropriate social and educational services for these children. In
summary, fostering and nurturing these children was very difficult,
frustrating, and time consuming.

Enhancing Social Acceptability

All societies require that mothers shape their children's development in "acceptable" ways. Most mothers want their children to

behave in ways that will ensure that they will be "delightedly appreciated" by others (Ruddick, 1989:21). For mothers of children who are technology-dependent, meeting these expectations is fraught with difficulty.

Discipline, for example, poses complex challenges for mothers whose children stop breathing whenever they cry, or whose every movement causes discomfort. It is also often hard to differentiate misbehavior from effects of the disease or the treatment and to establish reasonable limits for these children. They are also socially different from their non-disabled peers in many ways. Their appearances and behaviors commonly attract whispers, stares and questions. One mother, worried about her son's future, stated: "It's sad when a 30-pound child has a seizure but it's repulsive when a 200 pound man has one."

Severely disabled children often cannot offer rewards to adults such as verbal expressions of love or gratitude. For a mother whose toddler had nearly drowned, the worst thing was the fact that he had suffered brain damage to the extent that he no longer had a "personality."

Many mothers talked about how friends and relatives stopped visiting them after the child returned home. The distress this caused is obvious in this woman's remarks: "We call our house the plague house: nobody visits us anymore. I don't want much, I would just like to show off my baby. I wish people would drop by and say, 'Isn't she cute!'" All talked about the multifaceted loneliness that was part of this maternity. People did not want to hear about their experiences and only four women had confidantes other than their husbands or mothers.

Finally, these mothers had children who generated fear in friends, relatives and some health professionals. People were afraid to touch, hold or care for the child in case something might happen. Some mothers reported that they had friends and relatives who would not look at the child or observe treatments because they found it too upsetting. Perhaps to counteract the many socially aversive aspects of these children, all mothers made enormous efforts to dress them well and cared for them meticulously.

Overall Impact of Caregiving on Women

In describing their lives in general terms, the mothers of technology-dependent children said that their lives were like roller coasters, nightmares, infernos, traps, and mental prisons. Many felt as if their own lives were "on hold" or "suspended." In that the children's needs were ongoing, multiple and complex, these mothers rarely relaxed or engaged in leisure activities. Only one mother had had a vacation of any kind since the child had been at home. Finally, these women said they were tired. They rarely or never got uninterrupted sleep, and 60 percent of them had had five hours or less sleep per night for months or years.

Seventy-five percent of the women in this study were obese and a few were extremely thin. The majority suffered from headaches and backaches at least weekly. Many said they were worried about themselves because they noticed they were aging quickly, were not in good health and often felt depressed. They also worried about who would care for their children if they died or became incapacitated.

Virtually all mothers maintained that they had become much more aggressive and assertive with health professionals and in their personal and marital relationships. Many had contacted politicians for the first time in their lives to lobby for better services for their children. They recognized that some professionals, relatives and friends did not approve of these personality changes but most added that they "really didn't care anymore."

It is important to note that every mother stressed the positive aspects of caring for these children. They described how their values changed, how they worried less about things that now seemed insignificant and how they appreciated good health. They all also derived pleasure from these children — from their laughter, smiles, courage, perseverance, or contentment. They all experienced joy when a dismal prognosis turned out to be wrong or when children showed signs of progress. Finally, almost every mother had seen a child she considered to be "worse" than her own and hence could and did consider herself "lucky."

CONCLUSIONS

Through intensive, qualitative interviews, mothers of technology-dependent children described a radically different experience of motherhood. The seriously damaged children made extraordinary demands on their mothers' efforts to preserve their lives, foster their growth and enhance their social acceptability.

It was clear that the mothers' identities were linked with the well-being of their children and that they worked hard to sustain feelings of maternal competence. Caring for these children at home demanded tremendous personal sacrifice on their parts. In that most of these women had little social, familial or institutional support, it is obvious that the distribution of responsibility for caring for these children at home is inequitable.

Women's abilities to determine their own and their children's lives depends on economic and social policies over which they have minimal control (Ruddick, 1989:35). Social policies reflect society's values related to the division of domestic labor and the raising of children. It is at the micro level that social policy and the values of the "experts" converge to affect the lives of individual mothers. Competition for scarce resources is central to the establishment of public policy. If program and policy changes affecting technology-dependent children are to be achieved, advocates must work hard to raise public awareness. Since women provide most caring services, it is a feminist demand to secure for caretakers the autonomy, economic benefits and political power they need for themselves and their work (Ruddick, 1989:46).

Chapter 10

Children's Active Role
in Mother's Premenstrual Syndrome

We have just seen in the previous chapter how mothers are affected by the care required by their chronically ill children. In this chapter, we will focus on a different type of child effect; one where it is the mother who has the "medical" problem.

When I first began gathering research material for this chapter, I was struck by how little literature there is on the way in which children actively influence the patterning of illness behavior in other family members. This is true not merely for the social sciences, but for popular literature as well. Rarely do we find accounts of how children proactively "manage" their parents' illness behavior patterns. Indeed, for the most part, children are seen as playing little or no agentic role in the meaning construction processes which mold and regulate health and illness behavior among family members (Bahr, 1989:274).

The idea that children have some agency in determining the course of illness and illness role behavior among adult family members may seem anomalous to many. It is difficult for many of us to entertain the notion that children, particularly small children, have the kind of legitimate power in families to influence the etiology and expression of illness in other family members, particularly their parents, and perhaps even more particularly, their mothers. That bias may account for the paucity of literature examining the socializing role children play in the illness dynamic.

Studies of family illness which do focus on children look either at

---

This chapter was written by Marion Pirie, a practicing psychotherapist as well as a researcher.

the impact of family structure (or illness) on a child's health (or coping mechanisms) or how families cope with a child's illness or physical limitation. Thaxton (1985), for example, looks at the effects of abuse on the health of a child. Even the large number of studies of disabled children (where a broader focus on family dynamics would seem warranted) tend not to utilize a "family-level" or systemically oriented analysis either (Foster and Berger, 1985: 742).

In the psychohistory literature, however, deMause (1982) has documented instances of role reversals at different periods in history where children have taken on a predominantly nurturing role, and their parents have become overly dependent on them. Similarly, in the general social-psychological literature, Lopez (1986: 508) cites research on parent/child role reversals occurring during the adolescent separation stage.

In the more clinically oriented literature on psychosomatic families, Minuchin et al.'s classic studies of anorexia nervosa and diabetes mellitus in children similarly recognize the proactive role children play in engaging the whole family in their own "symptom" management (1978). What may be said about these studies, however, *is that they still focus on the illness of the child, and not on how children play a role in sustaining the illness behavior of their parents.*

Only recently, in the "Adult Children of Alcoholics" literature has the proactive, "enabling" behavior of children in the maintenance of adult illness patterning been explored with any consistency (Black, 1981; Steinglass, 1987). Claudia Black's 1981 study of ACOA families stands out as an exemplary model of illness socializing activities among children.

In her study of children of alcoholics, Black (1981:49-64) interviewed a number of adult children of alcoholics and her book draws a vivid portraiture of how these adult children reinforced or enabled their parents' addictive behaviors. Her subjects reported, through a series of retrospective accounts, highly patterned behavior where children engaged in meaning construction processes in which denial of their parents' condition was mutually constructed and reinforced. Similarly, these adult children of alcoholics recalled placating, nurturing, and withdrawal behaviors which reinforced a highly rigid dynamic that facilitated their parents' alcoholism. Indeed, Black's behavioral classifications have served as a very useful and timely model for my own study.

In this chapter, I examine the unique role children play in the patterning of a different kind of illness role: the premenstrual syndrome. In what follows, I demonstrate through in-depth interviews the very active part children play in configuring and reinforcing the premenstrual syndrome illness role adopted by their mothers. My theoretical framework is General Systems Theory. That model, which emphasizes a systemic-interactional concept of illness behavior in families, is a helpful theoretical point of departure here. As Minuchin et al. (1978), Satir (1983) and others adopting a systemic model of illness have pointed out, the management of illness patterns in families is never one where individuals simply cope with their maladies, while others look on. Rather, all family members interact to "make sense of" and to organize behavior around the illness state. From this perspective, we can reexamine the premise that children are merely passive victims or silent observers of parents' illness and look at how children play active roles both in legitimating and organizing premenstrual syndrome illness role behavior.

My central argument is this: PMS women lack an adult social context within which illness behavior associated with premenstrual distress may be explored on a continuing basis, and subsequently legitimated as a valid illness role. The mother/child dyad, therefore, provides a key meaningful and supportive context within which PMS symptoms may be validated as "real," and legitimated as acceptable behavior. Children play a key part in this meaning construction process, at least among educated, middle-class families.

THE PREMENSTRUAL SYNDROME ILLNESS ROLE

Before discussing the methodology and results, it is necessary to provide some information on the aetiology of PMS. In fact it is precisely because of the ambiguities and confusion surrounding PMS in the medical profession that women seek validating contexts within their primary groups. The mother/child dyadic formations discussed in this chapter have evolved as a direct result of the fact that the medical model of PMS has been inconsistent in its definition and treatment of the syndrome.

There are particularly ambiguous and often negative connotations attached to PMS. Until very recently, doctors told women that premenstrual distress was "all in their heads." Today, women are being told that PMS is either a serious hormonal disruption necessitating hormone replacement therapy, a vitamin deficiency, or a psychiatric disorder requiring prolonged and intense psychotherapeutic interventions (American Psychiatric Association, 1987). Despite a plethora of medically based research, PMS still has no clearly established cause and no universally effective cure (Abplanalp, 1983; Rausch and Janowsky, 1983; Allen, 1984; Witt and Masterson-Michael, 1983). While cyclicity of certain symptom clusters is said to determine the presence of PMS, many doctors argue that even cyclicity itself can not be accurately determined in most women (Allen, 1984). In short, the definition, cause, and treatment of PMS remain as elusive as they did a decade ago. As a result, the women interviewed for this study found no appropriate medical context within which they could validate their experience of premenstrual distress. Accordingly, these subjects turned to their families for validation of their premenstrual experience, and their children played a key role in providing a reality bestowing context.

METHODOLOGY

The data discussed here are taken from twenty in-depth interviews with women suffering from premenstrual syndrome symptomatology. Twelve of these interviews derive from early research on professionalism and illness reporting (Pirie, 1988). Those interviews took place from September to December, 1987, and were conducted in the homes of the women involved. Eight further interviews were conducted during the month of January, 1990, with women who have sought counselling for premenstrual stress in a clinical setting. These interviews took place in the setting in which the author works: a Women's Health Center in a large metropolitan city.

All subjects interviewed were married, had at least one child under the age of fifteen, were middle-class and Canadian born and raised. The average age was thirty-four.

The interviews were open ended and women were asked to reflect upon their premenstrual stress experience. Questions about children were interpolated with general questions about the family dynamics. A typical question focusing specifically on the mother/child dyad was "How would your child describe you during your premenstrual phase?" Other more general questions were as follows: "What was happening in your family life when you decided you had premenstrual syndrome symptoms?" "Could you describe a typical week when you are premenstrual?" "Where do you seek nurturing and support during your PMS time?"

Given the size of this sample and its exclusive focus on premenstrual syndrome sufferers who are middle-class and have children, no broad interpretations may be made with respect to women's health and illness patterns in general, or to any universal role children may play in sustaining these patterns. Rather, the findings discussed here are meant to serve as a heuristic device from which further research can flow.

RESULTS

Spousal Interactions

When I first started interviewing and counselling women with PMS, one very strong need stood out: the need to be validated. As one woman put it when she first read about PMS, "now I know what this thing is . . . there is something out there I can put my finger on!" At the same time, these women received little reinforcement or validation from their husbands. Without exception, the women I interviewed described their husbands as, at best, "confused," and, at worst, hostile to their premenstrual complaints.

> One of the big things about PMS is that you don't want to go around where everyone is continually sluffing you off; that can make me furious. When they do that around here [in her family], I really blow up and say, "I don't care what [you think] it is; it's still a goddam problem you gotta help me with!"

Women who preferred nongenital forms of sexual intimacy during the premenstrual phase often found husbands unsympathetic and blaming. While some subjects "put up with sex just to avoid tensions," most became sexually distant, and husbands responded with emotional distance. Among many of the women interviewed, sexual tensions were prominent and troublesome and withdrawal from all but the most instrumental forms of spousal interaction was a standard coping mechanism.

Lacking spousal support, these women turned to their children to provide not only nurturing and intimacy needs, but the forum for exploring the meaning and legitimacy of distressing premenstrual changes.

Mother/Child Interactions

It is important at this point to speculate on how this role patterning began. As with the institutionalization of any role, the interaction between mother and child involved mutually reinforced behavioral cues which then became habitualized as role sets or role patterns. With respect to parent-child role patterning, we tend to assume that it is largely the parent who provides the initial behavioral stimuli, and who largely controls or structures the subsequent interaction. Retrospective accounts suggest that this was not exclusively the case in these households.

Many mothers talked about "turning" or "looking" to their children for nurturing and understanding. In that sense, it could be argued that the mothers largely initiated the interaction, and children learned their respective part in the illness drama. However, children also seemed to initiate these interactional sequences. One mother described her children taking it upon themselves to circle "bad days" on the calendar and she responded to these cues or flags by adopting the illness role. In other instances, children were reported to cue their mother by alluding to subtle changes in her behavior. Once the illness label "PMS behavior" was applied, the role patterning became institutionalized. As put by one mother, "It's hard to tell who notices [her PMS phase] first . . ."

These examples of circular effect suggest that we cannot assume that role patterning between parents and children necessarily develops along unilinear lines where a parent teaches or cues her children to respond to her in specific ways. Rather, the patterning that occurred here could be characterized as developing in a much more reciprocal manner with neither parent nor child acting exclusively in providing the initial stimulus for the sequencing of behavior or its subsequent structuring. In other words, children took very active roles as agents, as well as recipients, of illness socialization patterning.

The following typologies describe the differential roles children played in this dynamic of legitimating and structuring their mother's PMS behavior. I have entitled such child roles as: "The Monitor," "The Reflector or Mirror," "The Alternator," and "The Enabler/Nurturer."

The Monitor Role

One of the more interesting findings with regard to PMS has to do with the fact that symptoms are often reported regardless of whether or not the subject is ascertained to be entering the premenstrual phase or not. In an elegant study, Diane Ruble (1977) attempted to delineate the difference between objective physiological changes and the subject's own belief systems. Subjects were led by experimenters to believe that the exact date of their menstrual cycle could be predicted based upon some physiological measures, including an electroencephalogram.

While all subjects were tested at a stage in their cycle which would correspond to the beginning of the premenstrual phase, two groups were randomly told that menstruation was either due in one or two days or a week to ten days. A third group was given no information about the expected date. Subjects were then given a standard premenstrual symptom indicator chart to complete. Ruble found that cyclic differences in symptoms were reported by women who only *believed* they were premenstrual or intermenstrual. Accordingly, many PMS sufferers may rely as much on external, social cues, as they do on internal physiological changes, to signal the onset of the premenstrual phase and ensuing illness behavior patterning. In my sample, children played a significant role in providing those cues.

The women I interviewed revealed that children played a major part in constructing the "belief system" which led their mothers to enter into the illness behavior they labelled their PMS phase. The role children played in this respect would be best typified as that of "the monitor."

Two women I interviewed referred to a situation where a teenage daughter in one case, and a preschool son in another, actually took it upon themselves to circle the days on the kitchen calendar when "mommy's bad days" were expected.

In other households, it was often the school-aged children who took it upon themselves to circle the calendar days denoting what they anticipated as the upcoming premenstrual phases. This circling of the calendar was generally endorsed (certainly not resisted) by all family members, and served as a signal, not necessarily that "mother is going to be a bitch for the next week" (although this was one form of discourse arising in other contexts), but as a signal to begin to reorganize family patterns of interaction. As family members referred to the premenstrual phase flagged on the calendar, new adaptive behaviors were put into motion. For example, older children would take greater responsibility for meals, fathers would volunteer to drive the children to school that week, mothers would not plan large social gatherings.

Another woman, comparing her premenstrual distress with that of her own mother, told me that her two adolescent children "announce" to their father (and anyone who might be present at the time) that their mother is "premenstrual." "Now, in fact, it is announced to everyone. This would never happen in my own family (of origin); it's really changed from something hidden to something that is kind of open now."

When asked how they felt about this kind of "flagging" behavior on the part of their children, these mothers were far from embarrassed, and appeared to be grateful that someone was "looking out for them," as one respondent put it. In a very important sense, the monitoring function not only signalled, but validated the symptoms. In the absence of any other legitimating social context, the circling of the calendar days is a way of giving substance to the symptoms, as providing an external reference point for this vague, indeterminate condition which many of these women felt may still be "all in the head."

Another key characteristic of the monitoring role is the fact that children often initiated and helped structure or configure the illness behavior rather than simply reinforce a pattern already begun by the mother. One woman reported an uncanny ability on the part of her preschool children to intuit her PMS phase:

> I don't usually prepare my kids ahead of time; like I won't talk to them two days before, so they just know. Often they know before I really know . . . But sometimes, I don't feel I'm really entering the premenstrual phase until my kids point it out. Other times, they just seem to know without me telling them to stay away. By now, it's hard to tell who notices first.

Here, the signalling of the premenstrual phase by children was mutually constructed through conjoint interaction between mother and child. Again, the child played not a passive role, but an agentic and reciprocal role in the meaning construction process. Sometimes this process was initiated by the mother, at other times, the child initiated the process. Regardless of the stimulus for this dynamic, the illness behavior became quickly patterned through conjoint interaction processes.

Surprisingly, preschool children played a more influential role than older children in this monitoring/signalling process. At first, one may suspect that small children, lacking the linguistic and conceptual capacities of older children, do not have the intuitive "radar" to perceive subtle shifts in their mother's behavior, or to respond to such questions as "Is mommy being cross today?" This was very definitely not the case as reported by the women in this study. Small children, rather, seemed exceptionally "tuned in" to their mothers' behavior, and as will be discussed later, played a more substantial "mirroring" role than did their older counterparts.

One subject, in particular, described recognizing entering her own premenstrual phase, not through directly seeking confirmation of cues from her children, but through recognizing shifts in the behavior of her two preschool children. "I know when I'm premenstrual because I get more edgy with my kids. For one thing, they keep repeating questions, over and over again. . . .'' She goes on to say later that

> One thing that happens to me [during the premenstrual phase] is that I kind of opt out, stop paying attention to things, so I've come to recognize that when the kids are getting to me, I'm probably coming on to my PMS phase . . .

In this case, the children, perhaps intuitively responding to this shift in their mother's interactional patterns, flag her symptoms through a shift in their own behavior — namely by becoming more persistent in repeating questions. Notably, this pattern had to repeat itself a number of times before the mother became aware of the "flag."

These examples illustrate the recursive, circular nature of family dynamics in meaning construction processes. A typical pattern is as follows: early tentative explorations of meaning are presented for validation (often through questions like, "Am I being too cross today?" or, even, a child asking their mother "What's wrong?"). These questions about perceived shifts in behavior and demeanor then trigger interactional processes which link those perceptions to a meaningful "cause," namely "mommy's bad days." In effect, we have a closed system where *generalized* or non-illness-specific shifts in behavior (for example, an increase in general irritability) go through an attribution process where they are labelled as *premenstrual* behavior, and the validation process is complete.

The Mirror and Alternator Roles

Closely related to the "Monitor Role" are those of the Mirror and the Alternator roles. These patterns generally seemed to occur once the flagging function had become highly patterned and "institutionalized" as part of the illness behavior dynamic.

I asked respondents the following questions in order to tease out any possible patterning: how did their behavior change during their premenstrual phase and how did their children's behavior change? As a further supplementary question, respondents were asked to describe how their children might describe them during their premenstrual phase.

The interaction that described children's behavioral changes as reflective of their mothers was coded as "mirror" role. When a respondent described herself as "moody and quiet" and similarly described her children as becoming more quiet and insular or adopting more withdrawing behavior, I coded that dynamic as the child's "mirror role." The same held true for aggressive, conflict-laden behavior. For example, one respondent reported the following of her six-and-a-half and two-and-a-half-year olds: "[When premenstrual] I change drastically. I yell; I make a mountain out of a molehill . . . don't want physical contact, I sleep more, the house is messy." In describing her children's behavior, she said

> They basically reflect my own behavior. The volume gets louder (on both counts), I yell to make them stay away from me; they yell back. They make loud, annoying sounds to get attention. They yell at each other, and generally slam doors and bang things around.

A thirteen-year old responded to her mother's "outbursts" and "mood swings" by yelling back and telling her to "control your hormones!"

Even more striking among these patterns was the role of the "alternator." Here, the children entered into the illness dynamic by adopting behavior which was the alternate of that expressed by their mothers. If the mothers appeared withdrawn, the children demanded more attention. If mothers were more affectively labile, their children appeared calmer than usual. For example, one subject who described herself as much *more* in control, and "interacting quite well with my kids," described her five-year old and two-and-a-half-year old as being "more whiney, bored, complaining, moody." Similarly, another woman who reported feeling much more irritable, critical and "picky, like really on my kids a lot" during her premenstrual phase, at the same time described her six-year-old daughter as being quite solicitous. The daughter in this dyad would ask her mother if she was "feeling okay?" would "withdraw a bit," "become a bit quieter" and willing to entertain herself more.

Typically, children in the alternator role acted out aggressively when their mothers distanced themselves, withdrew and became nurturing when mothers became more argumentative, and would even "get upset if [the mothers] pay full attention to them." Sensitive to their mothers' shift in behavior, these children, rather than imitating or responding in kind, adopted an opposite stance as an adaptive strategy. This adaptive strategy, however, had the effect of escalating the opposite behaviors in the mother. These behaviors, moreover, were attributed not to generalized mother/child dyadic conflict, but to PMS.

To be sure, one could argue that these roles played by the children represent their own coping mechanisms. But to conceptualize them as such overlooks the generative, proactive properties of the dynamic which occurred. Both roles provided these mothers with an indirect reinforcement and, therefore, source of validation for their experience of premenstrual changes.

The alternator role differed from the mirror role in one important respect, however. For children in the mirror role, their mothers' behavior was seen for what it is. When children mirrored their mother's behavior, respondents reported that their children would be likely to describe their mothers in terms congruent with their behavior, or, "accurately" as it were. When mothers reported acting aggressively, they also reported that their children would see them or their behavior for what it was. Children who mirrored their mothers' aggressive behavior would, according to their mothers, have no ambivalence about describing them as "mean, angry, screaming." But children who were described as adopting an alternating role were reported by respondents to be more confused and troubled about what was going on. One respondent reported that her child would describe her as "spazzed out . . . having a cow" during her premenstrual phase. Others reported that their children would respond with such phrases as "Mommy doesn't love me any more," "I don't understand her," and "Sometimes she scares me."

In other words, the mirroring role for these children and their mothers seemed to be a way of confirming for the children what was happening with their mothers. The alternating role, on the other hand, may have been a way of "testing out reality" for the children. Whatever the characteristic of the behavior enacted by the child, mirroring or alternating, the result was the same: a highly patterned illness dynamic between the mother and the child, which served to validate for the mother the concreteness or "objective reality" of her PMS symptoms.

The Enabler/Nurturer Role

The final role enacted by the child was that of the Enabler/Nurturer. The choice to use the term "enabler" was based on the alcoholic family treatment model where other family members are seen to enable or foster (often unwittingly) the undesirable addictive behavior of the alcoholic. In this usage, the term "enabler" connotes something of a value judgement in that the child is seen to reinforce (however unintentionally) crippling, addictive behavior in the parents. A similar process occurs with respect to children of PMS mothers and the moral implications should be discussed here, as well.

PMS, while a far different condition from alcoholism, also involves certain value-laden judgments in this society. Women today are being urged to challenge the PMS label because of the many negative connotations attached to the idea of women being "victims of raging hormonal imbalances." The "wellness model" encouraged in the women's health movement urges women not to invalidate their experiences of premenstrual distress, but to challenge the passive, victim role associated with those hormonal changes. The argument put forth by the women's health movement is that only by feeling empowered and in control of premenstrual changes will women feel able to participate fully in society. From the perspective of the wellness model, anyone, however well intentioned, who encourages women to adopt the cloak of "illness" rather than "wellness" and to embrace passivity rather than empowerment may be seen as "enabling" behavior which is essentially undesirable and, in the long term, deleterious for women. Again, the intent here is not to pass judgment on behavior, but to demonstrate how the nurturing behavior enacted by these children can, nevertheless, be seen as "enabling" or validating the social assumptions and postures of passivity traditionally associated with PMS.

One respondent, for example, stated

They always look after me, and, in a sense, I think they kind of shamed [her husband] into following suit. The kids let me go to bed, and understand when I am having a blue day. We even stop going skiing, and no one minds.

Another reported her three-year old providing justification for her increased irritability. This respondent speculated that her daughter would describe her in her premenstrual phase as "Mommy got up on the wrong side of bed today; Mommy must be tired, she isn't listening to me." While the three-year old was providing justification, the older child in this family further reinforced the illness role by becoming more demonstrative and solicitous, according to the mother.

Others reported that with their children they can "finally relax."

With the kids, I can just kind of be myself . . . they kind of accept that I'm not myself and don't make a whole lot of judgments . . . like if I want to stay home from work. I no longer feel compelled to push myself so hard.

Children, particularly preschool children, tended to adopt the enabler role. Unlike the mirror or alternator roles where children acted independently of their mother's request for a certain kind of behavior, the enablers often responded directly to their mother's request for nurturing. Preschool children love to be cuddled and hugged and returned this kind of demonstrativeness to their mothers without question, or confusion. As put by one respondent:

I can ask them [her children] for hugs. They know it's a time when I really need some nurturing and they have no expectations. So I think they become extra affectionate then . . . they just kind of know when I need some hugs.

Listening to these statements, it became increasingly obvious that the children played a surrogate spousal role. While this dynamic had the positive effect of allowing the mother her unique, nongenital, intimacy needs during her premenstrual phase, because many women avoided genital sexuality with their spouses during their premenstrual phase, certain spousal tensions around intimacy needs often remained unresolved.

Whatever value judgment may be made with regard to the connotations of "enabler" versus "nurturer," the result of this role was the same: it reinforced for these women, a (largely medically oriented) belief that premenstrual changes warrant a somewhat passive, succumbing posture, where issues are avoided and challenges remain unmet.

For women, there is a delicate and fine line between "taking care of one's needs" and "meeting life's challenges head-on" in a patriarchal system where, undeniably, women have to fight harder for equitable access to society's valued resources. It is not my intent to debate this issue in this chapter. Rather, my point here is merely to delineate a socializing pattern which potentially reinforces rather than challenges passivity in women. That children participate actively in this socializing process makes it no less deleterious to the overall well-being of women in a partriarchal system.

CONCLUSIONS

It should be stated at the outset that this is an exploratory study designed to offer a new perspective as well as to stimulate research within a perspective that has been somewhat neglected in the literature. No broad, sweeping generalizations are intended. Nevertheless, this material clearly reveals that children can play a key role in structuring the illness behavior of their mothers, in this instance, behavior associated with the premenstrual syndrome. These children, moreover, were not psychically damaged by overly neurotic, dependent mothers, seeking to regress into a childlike state. Neither did these children appear to attempt to manipulate their mothers for some sort of secondary gain of their own.

Some may argue that inappropriate intimacy needs are displaced onto these children by their mothers during the premenstrual phase, but I did not detect any indication of pathology in this regard. If anything, the bonding that occurred between the mother and her children was reported as a particularly close and affectionate time. What was an unfortunate consequence of this dynamic was the detouring of issues relating to the spousal dyad.

Similarly, while the circling of days on the calendar by children certainly flagged the illness dynamic, these interactions, too, often provided closeness. Such activities were sometimes treated as a joke, and served the function of channelling family tensions, of giving family members a chance to discuss feelings in a non-threatening atmosphere. Again, while the behavior described in this study sustained a socially undesirable illness role, it is important to point out that, at the primary group level, such behavior was, in many cases, quite functional.

Having said this, however, I do not wish to imply that the patterning of the premenstrual syndrome illness role is, in any ultimate sense, healthy or positive for the family, or the symptom carrier herself. As mentioned earlier, the discourse around menstruation still harkens back to a mid-Victorian image of women as helpless victims of raging hormones, and that discourse has not changed appreciably today. However well-intentioned family members are with respect to managing illness, they are bound to the larger social discourses which configure vocabularies of illness. For women, that vocabulary is uncompromisingly deleterious with respect to menstrual disorders. Until we challenge that discourse in the larger society, women with PMS will continue to feel confused, frightened, and isolated, particularly in their relationship with adult men, for whom, as Barbara Ehrenreich and Deirdre English (1986:285) have put so directly, "menstruation is a perennial source of alarm." At the same time, female children who participate in this dynamic will acquire through the osmotic process of reciprocal socialization, the same attitudes towards their bodies as those exhibited by their mothers. Ultimately, the daughter/mother dyad, circumscribed as it is by the larger social order, will continue to promote female dependency, fear, guilt, and a general sense of incompetence with respect to premenstrual distress. Moreover, it will do so intergenerationally as the same dyad will perpetuate in another generation the configuration of the absent husband figure followed in this study. It is therefore crucial that we explore this dynamic more fully if we are to reconstruct a more positive discourse around women who experience premenstrual distress.

My purpose in writing this chapter is to suggest that children play a highly active role as socialization agents of their mother's PMS illness behavior. More generally, children necessarily play a part in the configuration of meaning surrounding their parents' illnesses, particularly those of mothers who rely so strongly on primary relationships for forging identities and validating experiences. But children are part of culture and society, and will, in that regard and to a significant extent, reinforce the dominant values of patriarchy and the medical discourses deriving from that societal system. What is at issue here is the theoretical premise that children need to be conceptualized in their agentic, active capacities as socialization actors. In order to exploit this new perspective in useful ways, we need to develop a more systemic paradigm of family health, and a renewed effort to legitimate qualitative research in family health.

Chapter 11

Two Case Studies of Interracial Mothers and Daughters

In this chapter, we investigate the life adjustments forced upon two mothers whose daughters are of a different race than themselves. The two mothers present a complete reversal of racial status: one is a member of a visible minority and has a white child; the other is white and has visible-minority children. Consequently, their life experiences are complementary and, from different perspectives, mirror social intolerance toward minority group members and interracial families. It is from this vantage point that we will look at child effect.

Studies in interethnic relations rarely focus on interracial families, apart from studies on such marriages. Moreover, children and parents of different races have been studied mainly within the context of interracial adoption. The focus of these studies is on the children's identity development and the potential problems for such children of having been interracially adopted (e.g., Feigelman and Silverman, 1984). This research does not address the effect that interracial adoptions may have on the *parents* (an exception is Simon and Altstein, 1981), perhaps as a result of the literature's emphasis on child socialization and child development. Moreover, even within references to biological interracial families, the emphasis is either on spouses' marital adjustment or on the effect that the situation may have on the children. This focus once more disregards the effect on a parent of having a child of another race.

This chapter was written by Saroj Chawla and Anne-Marie Ambert. Saroj Chawla is a faculty member in the Department of Sociology at York University.

Interracial families *in themselves* are not scientifically interesting. What makes them interesting sociologically, however, is the double fact that they constitute a deviance from the general norm of racial homogamy and because our societies are heavily stratified along racial and ethnic lines, in addition to class lines. Thus, it is logical to conclude that such families' life experiences must be different from those of racially homogeneous families. Moreover, in North America, there is a great deal of overlap between class and race lines, as a disproportionate number of nonwhites are found among the disadvantaged groups. Belonging to visible minorities is tantamount to a stigma and results in lower life opportunities, whether this is reflected in poverty, higher child death rate, lower life expectancy, lower educational level, higher unemployment, higher criminality or higher rates of victimization. In addition, visible minorities are subject to polite discrimination and even social ostracism from the majority groups.

Nevertheless, in our ethnically pluralistic cities (Adams, 1989), there exists a substantial degree of status ambiguity (Curtis and Scott, 1979; Curtis et al., 1988; Jeffries and Ransford, 1980). For instance, a dark person could be a doctor, an engineer, or a professor — all higher status occupations. Dark children may attend a private school. The dominant perception of the white population, however, equates dark complexion with deprived economic and cultural status, including low intellectual and scholastic ability.

This status ambiguity creates status dissonance for the affected children and adults. The parents are affected by the societal reaction to mixed marriages (Wilson, 1981b) and adoptions, while the children, caught in the middle, are also affected. Under these circumstances, child-teacher interaction and child-peer interaction become critical for the children involved. For the adults, parent-teacher relations, relations with children's peers, and social reactions to their interracial families might bring them face to face with subtle and not so subtle forms of prejudice.

This chapter analyzes the experiences of two interracial sets of mothers/daughters in terms of situational ethnicity (Okamura, 1981; Wilson, 1984) and status dissonance (Rosenberg and Simmons, 1971; Rosenberg and Pearlin, 1978). The situational ethnicity approach assumes the interplay of the objective (or structural) and the subjective (or cognitive) dimensions of ethnicity. In the context of this chapter, the objective dimension is the dichotomous message — white superior and dark inferior — which is conveyed to the individual.

The objective or structural dimension imposes constraints upon the options of individual actors within social situations as a consequence of the dichotomous perception of the ethno-class structure. For example, a light child from an interracial family might decide to define herself as white (the cognitive dimension). Such a self-definition, however, if it is to be accepted by others, necessitates that his/her peers and teachers do not gain the knowledge of his/her minority family background (the structural dimension).

Wallman (1979) suggests that there is a process of ethnic identity construction involving a dynamic negotiation between the actor and different ethnic groups. He concludes that, depending on the perception of the individual actors and the constraints and opportunities of the context in which they act, ethnicity may be an essential resource, an utter irrelevance, or a crippling liability. Within the limits imposed by the structure of society, the ethnic categories relevant in a classroom situation might not be the same as those in a family setting.

Another concept already mentioned and which is helpful in understanding the situation is that of status dissonance. It is defined as the discrepancy between the individuals' cognition of their social characteristics and the response of the interacting person or persons to these social characteristics (Krause, 1983; Rosenberg and Simmons, 1971). Individual characteristics are abilities as well as professional, academic, and occupational qualifications. The collective characteristic is the value attached by society to a person's or a group's general property, for example, skin color. For instance, a black lawyer representing his company in a court is assumed to be the assistant, while his white assistant might be assumed to be the lawyer. While adults can handle such status dissonance by asserting their professional qualifications or privileged status, most children facing such dissonance in the classroom or playground are vulnerable.

Status dissonance can also be discussed in terms of the theory of status characteristics and expectation states (Berger et al., 1972;

Cohen, 1982; Cohen and Roper, 1972). According to this theory, color is only one of a number of diffuse status characteristics all having the capacity to affect the prestige and power order of inter-personal relations. Research has shown that black children in pre-dominantly white schools score lower in self-esteem, and are likely to realize that their race places them at the bottom of the ethnic stratification order in their society (Krause, 1983; Rosenberg and Simmons, 1971). Other characteristics, such as low economic sta-tus and having divorced or separated parents, have a compounding negative effect upon such children's interaction with teachers and schoolmates.

Hallinan (1982) and Hughes and Demo (1989) show that visible minority children encounter discomforting experiences in the school system and the playgrounds. Teachers might expect a visible minority child to perform at a lower level in quality and quantity. The child might accept the teacher's evaluation of him/her as less capable and therefore fulfill these very expectations of inferiority. Without parental intervention, the pattern of low performance may be set.

In such cases, the parents have two options: (1) to restrain them-selves from intervening in the school system and let the child fend for him/herself, or (2) to empathize with the child and intervene to create a more positive environment for learning. Interventionist strategies (Aguilera and Messick, 1982) involve understanding and defining the problem as well as planning and executing interven-tion. A short account of the interracial experiences of two mothers (one white and one a visible minority) of three girls will illustrate the prejudice and discrimination which the two mothers and their daughters encounter, and the steps the mothers feel compelled to undertake to resolve them.

THE APPROACH

The two mothers simply discussed the problems they and their children encountered in the areas of relations with teachers, rela-tions with their daughters' peers, social reactions to their "rain-bow" family units, and their children's reaction to the mothers' race. The authors recorded the conversation.

The daughters are thirteen in the case of the "white" daughter and eleven and sixteen, respectively, in the case of the "brown" daughters. The white daughter is the result of an interracial marriage which ended in divorce. The mother belongs to a visible minority group. The brown daughters, who belong to two different races themselves, are the result of two adoptions by their white mother. Both mothers can be considered to be single parents. In terms of social class, both mothers are highly educated; the caucasian one is economically advantaged. All three girls are intellectually "gifted" and/or do very well scholastically. All three are psychologically normal and are involved in a wide range of extracurricular activities. Thus, apart from being highly educated, the two families studied herein are deviant in only one major area that is not widely accepted socially: their interracial configuration.

RESULTS

The first key theme to emerge from the discussions is that both mothers try to protect their children from, and try to compensate for, the minority group status which results in acts of both overt and subtle (Feagin, 1987) discrimination against their children or themselves. This identical result is quite striking when one considers that the mothers themselves belong to two poles in terms of majority-minority group status. The white mother has to protect her daughters because of *their* visible minority status while the dark mother protects her daughter from her *own* visible minority status.

School

Visible-Minority Mother

She avoids face-to-face contacts with her white daughter's teachers because such contacts have resulted, in grade two, in a deterioration of the teacher's attitude and behavior toward the little girl. She phones teachers instead. (She has a British accent.)

White Mother

She makes a point of meeting her daughters' teachers, or of being *seen* by the teachers, as soon as possible when the girls go to a new school or when they have a teacher who is new to their school. Failure to do this resulted, two years ago, in several problems for her younger daughter.

The white girl had, until her mother's appearance for the parent-teacher interview, enjoyed an excellent relationship with her teacher. Although the child was labelled "gifted" and had straight A's in English, the teacher began criticizing the child's English to the mother during the interview: "She's probably acquired so many bad habits that it's probably hard to change her" she said, with a long, reproachful glance to the mother. The mother has no doubt that the teacher saw her as "an ignorant and poor colored woman." The mother's racial appearance robbed the daughter of the high intellectual status she had previously enjoyed with the teacher. After the interview, not only did her marks plummet on her subsequent report cards, but the teacher became very sarcastic and more or less called the child stupid. The teacher also began expressing disbelief whenever the child talked of her trips (each summer, the mother returns to her native country to work in psychiatry).

A parallel but reversed scenario took place in the case of the white mother when her "light black" younger daughter transferred to a new school for grade four. The teacher began complaining aloud that she could not read the mother's handwriting whenever the mother sent a note when the child had to be absent from school. At one point, the teacher even threw the letter around the classroom, greatly embarrassing the already shy little girl. The child came home several times relating that the teacher had refused to believe her during "show and tell" sessions, especially when she talked about trips abroad.

Finally, the child received the worst report card of her brief life: straight B's. The mother was certain that the teacher was in a quandary: the child was obviously doing very well . . . but she was colored. The two adjectives, colored and bright, did not seem to fit together in this teacher's mind. The mother took the child's note-books and compiled the marks she had received in tests and on a daily basis: A's would have been in order. The mother appeared for the parent-teacher interview and the teacher was unpleasantly shocked. She, however, regained her composure but never looked the mother in the eyes and never once smiled at her. (The mother had overheard her joke and laugh with the two previous sets of parents.) In order to control her outrage, the mother nudged the discussion around to the fact that she wanted to plan her daughter's homework for their forthcoming three-week trip to Hawaii.

The teacher never thereafter questioned the child's veracity; the child's grades *went up*, the teacher began complimenting her as deserved, and she stopped criticizing the mother's handwriting in front of the entire class.

The minority mother feels that she has to stay away from her daughter's teachers, lest she lower the girl's academic status. The minority mother de facto cannot be involved in her child's educa-tion at school. The white mother feels that she has to insure that her daughter's status is normalized, and that the quickest way to achieve this is to raise the child's status by simply "showing my face around."

The minority mother lives in a neighborhood known, rightly or wrongly, for the poverty and criminality of a proportion of its in-habitants. Many single mothers dwell in these government-subsi-dized housing projects. The school her daughter initially attended in that area was rather tough. One day, an older boy saw the mother/daughter pair near the school. When he thought that the mother had left, he pulled the little girl by her hair and tripped her. The mother then met with a sympathetic teacher who admitted that "these things [racial incidents] were going on." The mother went to see the principal with the teacher. "He immediately asked, 'Mrs. X., are you a single parent?' as if being a single parent was associated with my race." Then, "Is she your only child?" — "Yes" — "You are overprotective." — "Are you telling me that it's all right for my child to come to school and be beaten up?" — "Yes." The previ-ously sympathetic teacher did not utter a word during this inter-change. The mother had to transfer her daughter to another school some distance away where racism is neither practiced nor tolerated by the school authorities.

"Devious Means"

"You can't lead a normal life; you have to resort to devious means to give a normal life to your children," says the minority-group mother.

Visible-Minority Mother

Because she is neither affluent nor white, she uses her educational level as a "shield." "I told the principal I was a university student to show that I was a 'somebody,' an intelligent person—which he was denying my right to be because of his obvious presumptions about my race. I even started 'bragging' about my marks at university to put me on a more equal footing with the other mothers, yet bragging goes completely against the grain of my culture. It forces me to deny my cultural heritage."

White Mother

"I do make certain, although in a subtle way, that teachers and principals know what I do for a living. But I have to be careful not to overdo it. Rather, I'll wear expensive clothes when I go to school." Although she laughs at these tactics, the white mother's experience is that they work. They allow her children to be treated fairly or, at the very least, to be given a better chance of being treated fairly. At least they are not treated both as "poor and colored."

The white mother has very rapidly realized that her own social standing is greatly diminished when she is with her daughters in situations where she is *unknown*: with service people, store clerks, people on the street, emergency room personnel, and the like. "People immediately assume that I am married to a black man—in fact, this is the first question my children are asked—and being allegedly married to a devalued minority group person means that there must be something wrong with me." And she has to make up for this loss of status in order to function socially at the level she is accustomed to.

Both women have to use status compensation strategies (such as materialism in one case and boasting in the other) which they deplore and go against their value system. Both mothers find the situation unfair and are quite cynical about it. The minority-group mother, however, suffers more than the other because *she* is the status-lowering person and cannot escape her own status. The white mother generally survives unscathed, but not pleased, sheltered by her professional status, her race, and her relative affluence.

Children's Peers

Visible-Minority Mother

Her white daughter does not want her to go near her friends at school. When her daughter goes to a party, the mother does not go in the parents' home as previous experiences of doing so have cost the daughter her friends. The girl rejects potential friends who have a dark complexion.

White Mother

Her daughters do not mind at all when she comes to school. When the younger child goes to a party, the mother meets the (white) parents. The daughters, however, find it a nuisance because the children unavoidably ask them if their father is black or "why is your mother white and you're brown?" Both have friends of all races.

The white daughter has no peer problems, except when her peers see her darker mother. As her daughter was going on a school trip, the children saw the mother for the first time: "Your mummy is a Paki!" The children called the girl "Paki" (a derogatory, racist term in Canada) several times thereafter. Whatever racial problems the girl suffers from have been linked to her mother's presence.

The other two girls, both darker, have experienced direct racial discrimination. The older was also called "Paki" and baited. The school principal stepped in quickly after the girl was forced by her mother to complain that her "civil rights were violated." The younger one is occasionally called "blackie," but in a joking manner. She has, however, experienced occasions when, in grade one, white children would refuse to hold her hand for a game, saying that she was "dirty." And in grade four, a white boy refused to dance with her during a gym class for the same reason. When they first meet her, children often tell her that she looks like Tina Turner or Michael Jackson. Such behaviors, however, diminish by grades five or six. Nevertheless, the younger girl has become very sensitive and fears rejection by peers, although not by adults. She is especially shy when encountering new children, as she never knows how they will react to her. Such a situation has deprived her of "agency" and of a sense of control in her relationships. The mother believes that the child's personality has been radically changed by her first overt and covert experiences with racial discrimination.

Children's Racial Identity

White Child

The girl identifies as white and works very hard at rejecting any element from her mother's background. She refuses to talk to her maternal grandparents who are even darker (because of sun exposure) than her own mother. She would never have wanted a black doll. She idealizes her absent white father, even though he has never shown any interest in her nor contributed to her support.

Visible-Minority Children

Both girls identify as "brown" — as they are. The older identifies as Native racially, but as a Canadian culturally. The younger used to identify as "brown" but now identifies as black as a direct result of peer pressure. She adores both her black dolls and her white dolls and finds black babies "cuter" than white babies.

Perhaps as a result of their own victimization, the two "brown" children have a lot of sympathy for the poor, AIDS-victims, and visible-minority persons. The older girl, when thirteen, used to say that "the kids I really feel sorry for at school are the blacks . . . The other kids just don't like them." The younger girl gets frustrated by the high rate of black criminality that is evident on the six o'clock news: "Oh, no, not another black." She also expresses verbal support for black activists who make passionate but constructive speeches. She will even raise her fist in support. But she disagrees with black activists "who hate white people."

She sees absolutely no contradiction in having a white mother. Around age nine, both children expressed the wish that they were white, but mainly because they would be better accepted socially. Both have found and still find it a "nuisance" to have to explain why their mother is white. Otherwise, they seem comfortable with their race and have a reasonably high self-esteem, though they probably have lower achievement goals due to the lack of a sufficient pool of role models among their racial groups. The younger girl is an excellent ballet student, but has passed up an opportunity to audition for the National Ballet School because she was convinced that "brown" children would not be accepted. "Have you ever seen a black white swan in Swan Lake?"

Effect on the Mothers

The visible minority mother feels rejected by her "flesh and blood." At times, she even resents the child's rejection of her race. The mother has had to struggle financially to complete her education. She always wears the same clothes and has deprived herself in order to provide her daughter with books and ballet, jazz, and tap lessons. "Ballet is a white, middle-class, Western phenomenon. I like it, but at the same time, by wanting to give her the best of the middle-class culture, I have given her the ammunition to reject me."

Both mothers have become very race conscious: The white mother after the adoption of the first child (that is, after witnessing others' reactions), and the minority mother since her white daughter has begun attending primary school. Before, she was never very self-conscious about her own race and easily brushed off the minor racial incidents that are part of the fabric of the daily life of a visible-minority person.

The minority mother, a graduate student, tries to do better than the whites in school in order to be perceived as equal to them. Ten years ago, such thoughts would never have entered her mind. They arose because of the built-in at home racial difference. "I am representing my people. 'Hey, look, we can do it.'" She would want her daughter to be more militant but, because the daughter is white and passes as white, she has no need for militancy.

The minority mother is concerned that, if her child developed psychological problems, she could not easily seek help for her. She recalls that, during a period when she was under a great deal of stress, she asked her doctor for a few prescription sleeping pills. "I explained to him that I was tense and I told him that once I had even taken my daughter by the shoulders and shaken her up." (The girl was already in school, and was not an infant.) The doctor immediately reported to the Children's Aid Society that she was abusing her child and a social worker paid her a formal visit. The social worker soon realized that nothing abnormal was going on and agreed with the mother that this had been a case of racial discrimination. Nevertheless, the mother was thoroughly humiliated by the incident.

The white mother, on the other hand, wanting to have a better grasp of her younger child's aptitudes, had her tested by a school psychologist: she wanted to make certain that she was not placing undue educational demands on the child. The experience was pleasant, the child generally enjoyed it, but the psychologist detected a dip in self-esteem in terms of body image. She suggested to the mother that the child's self-description of "brown" should be corrected "because all the children will define her as black anyway. There will be a gap between the child's perception of herself and other people's perception as a result of which she will be treated differently than she expects and this will create psychological problems." The well-meaning psychologist gave the mother several articles on interracial adoption—though the mother had read this literature long ago!

The white mother felt deprived when her children were both small, because no strangers—other than casting agents for child models — would compliment her on their attractiveness. Yet, by all standards, both girls were unusually attractive, even beautiful, when little. People would stare at them, and might reluctantly say, "Oh, what nice *hair* you have" or "Oh, what nice *eyes* she has," as if trying very hard to find something to compliment or, perhaps, trying very hard to avoid concluding that the children were pretty. Was this done to punish the mother? At times people would point at one of the children and exclaim incredulously, "Is *that* your child?" in the same tone of voice they would use to wonder about a dog's breed — and that is probably putting it mildly.

This mother also found a very large difference between people's attitudes depending on the geographic (and thus cultural) location. For instance, a contrast was made between Hawaii and Tahiti. The younger girl prefers Tahiti because "I got so much attention over there," as interracial mingling is more tolerated by French-speaking persons. She actually looks Tahitian and fit right in. Whites and Tahitians alike never stopped commenting on how pretty she was. In contrast, the more anglicized Polynesians of Hawaii looked at the mother/child duo with the same suspicion that whites generally do in the rest of the U.S. and in some parts of Canada. The mother has actually curtailed her traveling in the U.S. because of the children. "It's not too good in Canada, but it's worse in the States. I actually am less free as to where I go when I travel with one of them. I have to choose my destinations carefully."

Both mothers agree that their race or that of their children lowers their own social status, no matter what their achievements are. The minority mother feels that her category of single parent "is of a lower class category" than that of the other mother who is white. She suffers from a double stigma: she is both "colored" and a single parent.

The white mother has noted *repeated* instances where she is less well treated when accompanied by one of her daughters. Basically, the common theme is that her social status, when measured against her buying potential, is lowered. The minority mother, in contrast, finds herself permanently in that position.

DISCUSSION AND CONCLUSIONS

The two case studies presented here are highly racially integrated families: they are in fact interracially composed. Each member lives in close proximity and intimacy with a member of another race. Studies of intermarriage and interracial families do not generally address matters of racism; rather, they address matters of demographics, marital stability, happiness, and children's adjustment in general. Little is actually known about acts of discrimination directed against them by the members of the racial group which is most prevalent in their neighborhood. Indeed, unless a neighborhood is completely integrated, at least one member of an interracial family lives among people racially dissimilar to him or her (Simon and Altstein, 1981:10).

We will first discuss the applicability of the concepts of situational ethnicity, status dissonance, and interventionist strategies to the two case studies. Though both case studies are examples of interracial families, and the problems they encounter are similar, the strategies they pursue, while parallel are different. The white mother has to make herself visible, whereas the dark mother has to remain invisible.

The white mother, when accompanied by her brown daughters, suffers a status decrement, as people assume that the daughters must be the result of a marriage with a minority person. The daughters experience status dissonance when in the classroom: it is assumed that they came from an economically deprived background; white children refuse to play or dance with them; teachers embarrass and ridicule the girls. The girls' self-esteem and confidence are affected by such incidents.

The daughters perceive their mother as an asset or an essential resource (Wallman, 1979). The white mother is able to fight the low ethnic status imposed on her daughters by superimposing her white ethnic status as well as her professional and economic status. She protects her daughters by status compensation strategies and intervention in the teacher-student relationship, though such strategies and intervention are against her value system. She especially questions the fact that, were she also a minority person, she and her children would be more defenseless.

The visible minority mother encounters a more complex situation because of the manner in which the daughter defines her ethnicity. The daughter is not only white in complexion, she also cognitively chooses to identify herself as white. Such a choice is congruent with American data which show that interracial children, if light enough, may choose to be white (Wilson, 1981a, 1981b). For the white daughter, the mother is a liability, as her appearance at the school and playground creates status diminution and status dissonance for the child. The mother's university education is the only status characteristic that she can employ to compensate for her ethnic status. Such a strategy is not very effective, and her intervention in the school system is perceived as overprotection.

The dark mother has to protect her white daughter from her visible minority status. Such protection amounts to a denial of her own existence. Such denial is a recurring phenomenon for her. The daughter's rejection of her mother is extended to include the mother's parents (who are darker than the mother).

Several research questions come to mind as one reads this chapter. Some are more general questions while others focus specifically on child effect. To begin with, do children who are members of an interracial family tend to marry across racial lines more often than peers of their own race do? If the answer is positive, does this stem from geographic opportunity, because of a greater familiarity with the other race, or because of prejudice? For instance, the minority mother is certain that her daughter will "marry white," or, at least, will try very hard to achieve this because she rejects her mother's racial background. The white mother sees a half-and-half chance of marriage happening in either direction, more a matter of geographic opportunity for her children than of actual racial preference on their part. And last, but not least, are there variations on these themes according to social class or educational level?

On another front, these case studies point to problematic parent-child relationships, at best, at some stage in these families' life cycle. Yet, we have no studies in which the children who are of a different race than their parents have themselves become adults and even parents. For instance, the white mother in this study asked the minority mother if she had discussed with her white daughter the possibility that her children may turn out to be dark. In view of the teenager's emerging rejection of her mother's race, how will she react if her own children are darker than she herself is? Would such young adults choose not to have children? Or will they react less warmly to a child who is darker than expected? Still, will there be a favorable reversal in attitude and, if so, at what age and under what circumstances? How do the racial problems transmitted across such color lines change with each generation?

Strictly from the point of view of child effect, we would want to know how the parent/adult child relationship develops in comparison to uniracial families? How does the grandparent/grandchildren relationship develop (Simon and Altstein, 1981)? How do people socialize themselves in anticipation of such possibilities? For instance, the white mother is already looking forward to grandmotherhood. She has accepted as very likely that at least one of her daughters will marry a visible-minority person. If this were to happen, what about the quality of the affinal relationship?

Again, in this double case study, one sees quite clearly how both child effect and parental effect are related to child and parental characteristics — in this instance, race, social class, perhaps age. Moreover, several characteristics of the societal response, as described in Chapter 3, come into play. Not only is the overall prejudice and discrimination a factor, but so is the quality of the response on the part of the school system and the peer group. These two elements of the societal characteristics increase *negative* child effect here because they are clearly deficient and even detrimental.

Basically, this study has only begun to explore a few of the questions which could be researched. Nevertheless, we have, in this chapter, raised additional questions pertaining to child effect and have done so in combination with another field of inquiry (interracial families) which is itself rarely encountered in the literature. The exploration of esoteric topics is not the purpose of this book per se. Rather, the topics explored herein are all unusual for the simple reason that they are rarely approached in the sociology and psychology literature and, when they are, they are not studied from the vantage point of child effect.

Chapter 12

Mother-Blaming
in a Recent Hemingway Biography

The first chapters of this book have shown that an uncritical acceptance of the concepts of child socialization and the family system, as depicted in the traditional male-oriented literature, has led to the view that children are nonactors in a social sense, and that parents are overwhelmingly influential in terms of child and adult development. In the clinical literature itself, mother-blaming has been, for several decades, a taken-for-granted etiological explanation of emotional problems, not only in young children but in adults who have left the parental nest a long time ago.

The clinical literature depicts the first five years of a child's life as if it were a map offering a grand tour of the child's future life. In turn, this clinical literature and practice of Freudian influence have had a tremendous impact on the public consciousness in past decades. As a result, both adults and children have assimilated the belief in parental, especially maternal, fault when clinical or even delinquent symptoms erupt. These points have been discussed at great length in our chapters on delinquency and emotional problems. The literary world, a product of its century, certainly has not failed to find a convenient and fashionable analytical instrument in this ideological orientation. Biography, as a literary genre, frequently has recourse to a well-known author's childhood as a source of explanation for some aspects of his or her literary output. A recent case in point is the justifiably acclaimed *Hemingway* by historian and literary biographer, Kenneth S. Lynn (1987). In the first fifty pages of the impressive 700-page tome, Hemingway's mother is firmly entrenched as the villain at the root of her creative son's mental instability.

LYNN'S GRACE HEMINGWAY

Lynn begins his analysis by presenting Hemingway's inter-generational background, both on his father's side and his mother's side. First, it should be recalled that Hemingway was born in 1899, eighteen months after his sister Marcelline. Within a few years he and Marcelline were joined by three other sisters, and, at age fifteen, Hemingway's only brother was born when their mother was forty-two. Lynn describes how both grandmothers had been unusual women for their time. His paternal grandmother, Adelaide Hemingway, had studied at Wheaton College while his maternal grandmother, Caroline Hancock Hall, "held the reigns of power in her marriage to Ernest Hall" (p. 31). From these descriptions, one gets the fleeting impression that the grandmothers are presented to highlight the sad plight of the two grandfathers. Indeed, both grandfathers, Hemingway and Hall, were educated men but of comparatively weak character.

In turn, the family pattern of strong-willed women married to "henpecked" husbands was replicated in Hemingway's own parents. His father was a doctor whose income was relatively modest. His mother, Grace, who had been a "tomboy" as a child, had elected to go to New York for voice lessons before marrying Clarence Hemingway, a fairly bold course of action in her day. She was, as was her mother before her, an able organizer, an active woman, and an emerging feminist, all the while obviously devoted to the education of her four daughters and two sons.

As described by Lynn, both sets of grandparents and the two parents showed a rigidity of behavior and inhibitions that are less frequently encountered today among persons of their educational level. This personality profile, however, seems fairly typical of the Victorian era if one judges the case on the basis of biographies of other artists and historical figures. Lynn makes it amply obvious that Grace Hemingway did not handle her son's sexual identity and development in a modern manner, that is, according to today's standards. From a sociological and developmental perspective, however, it is impossible to judge whether these maternal idiosyncrasies had any nefarious repercussions later on in Hemingway's life because, by the time Hemingway had become an adult, too many other historical and personal events of possibly greater import to him had taken place.

These cautionary caveats nothwithstanding, Grace Hemingway is depicted by Lynn as a more powerful and irremediable molder of personality than one could reasonably expect her to be. Even some of Hemingway's *specific* personality traits are traced back to his early relationship with his mother (before age three). For instance, after describing the little boy nursing freely up to six months (this was in 1899), loving to look at books and magazines with his mother who was teaching him names of birds, one suddenly reads at the end of this nearly bucolic description: "At some point, though, in his edenic infancy he awakened to an understanding of the situation in which his mother had placed him. A quarter of a century later, Ernest Hemingway would become known for his habit of beguiling friends" while at the same time "pillorying their habits" in his fiction (p. 43).

This statement is the more puzzling since it is not at all clear what situation his mother had placed him in, nor is it clear how a situation so vaguely alluded to could translate directly into such specific character traits as backstabbing and vindictiveness *some twenty years later or more.* Lynn's conclusions are even more scientifically far-fetched when one considers that they are reached while he is in the process of describing what actually seems to be an ideal mother-infant situation. At the same time, one is also puzzled by the fact that Lynn does not find *positive* traits that might have emerged as a result of the obviously positive aspects of the mother-infant relationship. For, if Lynn is to thusly trace the root of the negative, logically, he should be expected to seek the positive as well. However, he does not do this.

Similarly, Lynn attributes Hemingway's inability to fall asleep at night directly to maternal treatment, and this even has sexual overtones which may appear gratuitous to a modern researcher: "That Hemingway's black sweats and waking nightmares were a legacy of what his mother did to him can be extrapolated more easily from the story called 'Now I Lay Me' . . . for the mother . . . looms up in his symbolic searching imagination as a destroyer of male sexuality" (p. 46). An alternative explanation, for the depiction of the mother in this story may well reside in the fact that Hemingway was simply following a multitude of literary precedents. Hemingway was, after all, a product of his environment, including the literary one, in which mothers were ritualistically immolated on the altar of mother-blaming.

Despite this sleeping disorder, Hemingway is nevertheless described by Lynn as a rather typical adolescent, even model in many respects, with no obvious behavioral problems. His adolescence is actually very tame and in no way predicts his future adult turbulence. It is true that, as a young adult, he disappoints his parents, particularly his mother, as he refuses college and embarks on a rather bohemian life style. But such parental disappointment should perhaps be more appropriately analyzed as a result of child effect for, at that point, Hemingway had long since left behind the first three years of his life that were allegedly to mark him forever.

At one point, having had enough of this bohemian behavior, his mother writes him a letter on the following theme:

> A mother's love seems to me like a bank. Each child that is born to her enters the world with a large and prosperous bank account, seemingly inexhaustible. For the first five years he draws and draws—physical labor and pain—loss of sleep—watching and soothing, waiting upon . . . (p. 117)

Lynn calls this letter "a rejection slip with a vengeance." Yet, this may be a very biased interpretation: A feminist researcher in particular, or any researcher who focuses on reciprocal effects, would certainly find room to disagree. After all, Hemingway was no longer a child at that stage, nor was he living with his parents any longer. It is true that, later on in the book, the biographer characterizes Hemingway as not detached enough from his mother to recognize that, after all, "she had done her best to be a good mother, that she had not meant to harm her son and that she, too, had been tossed about by psychological impulses she did not understand" (p. 260). In spite of itself, this disclaimer once more proclaims Grace's guilt!

OTHER HEMINGWAY BIOGRAPHIES

Since Lynn acknowledges his debt to previous biographies, I undertook a content analysis of these works. Both Bernice Kert's *The Hemingway Women* (1983) and Marcelline Hemingway Sanford's *At the Hemingways* (1961) contained some overlapping material concerning Hemingway's childhood and, of particular relevance here, concerning his mother. But the analysis offered by these two women has a drastically different flavor than Lynn's.

First, while Lynn expounds at great length on the fact that Ernest and his older sister were, as infants, often dressed alike — as girls — neither of the other biographies lingers on the situation. Neither sees this early infancy dress code, as Lynn did, to be at the root of Hemingway's sexual identity problems. Actually, it was quite popular in the years surrounding Hemingway's birth to dress little boys as "girls," and this included growing their hair long down the neck. The Hemingway manner of dressing represents nothing peculiar for this time. I have pictures of my own father similarly dressed in Europe circa 1904. This was the fashion of the day and had little effect in itself on these children's later adult sexuality.

Second, Grace Hemingway comes out as a lively, sociable, hardworking, liberal woman who was also an *affectionate* mother and who, along with her husband, offered her children a vast and rich array of life experiences and a lot of "fun." Gone is the rather Victorian impression of her that one gets from Lynn's biography. Actually, the Hemingway family life is more modern than Victorian, and although the children are raised strictly, they are not inhibited or repressed. The family life has its full share of humor, laughter, nature, and the children are made to *participate* rather than be subservient. "Grace believed that in a large family it was important for a parent to have time alone with each child" (Kert, 1983:38) — a very modern point of view, one might add.

Kert sensibly adds that "Ernest's later hostility toward his mother might have been due in part to the rapid displacement he suffered after the birth of the younger siblings — two in less than five years" (p. 29). This assessment, albeit more charitable than Lynn's, should, however, have applied more urgently to the older sister, Marcelline, who was displaced even more frequently. Yet, in her own autobiography, the latter does not evidence any mother-blaming, although it is known that, as an adult, she never got on well with her famous brother. It is true that her own autobiography is an attempt to sanitize the Hemingway family life and to exonerate her mother. But one could just as well have expected her to write a "Mommy Dearest" type of account instead. Yet, Marcelline was not the only Hemingway daughter to view her mother fairly positively.

Rather than deriding Grace's activities and viewing them as examples of a spoiled, domineering woman, Kert points out that both Hemingway *sons* were "ambivalent about their mother's musical activities." Yet, the daughters, whom she interviewed, "perhaps not surprisingly, perceived her as a successful woman who enjoyed her success" (p. 34). Basically, it seems that Grace Hemingway's daughters were more liberated than her sons in terms of gender roles ideology. Nevertheless, what I want to draw out here is that, by comparison, Lynn's portrayal of Grace Hemingway seems suffused with a masculinist narrow-mindedness and simplistic condemnation.

Whatever poor "mother-son fit" existed, it is clear in both books, and even in Lynn's, that it surfaced only *after* Hemingway had left his family, that is, in his late teens. Based upon all *observers'* and biographers' descriptions, Ernest had a happy, well adjusted childhood—surprisingly so when considering the turbulence of his adult years. Michael Reynolds, in his *The Young Hemingway* (1986), similarly fails to uncover abnormal mother-child patterns when Hemingway was small.

CRITICAL EVALUATION

Lynn thanks several doctors (p. 597) "for medical and/or psychiatric instruction," which may in fact account for the rather strident mother-blaming tone. Had he consulted research-oriented psychiatrists and developmental psychologists, he would have learned that the way in which a child reacts to a parent's actions greatly depends on the child's own personality and that, in turn, the parent tailors his/her own actions in response to a child's reaction (Belsky, Robins and Gamble, 1984; Lerner and Busch-Rossnagel, 1981).

Surely, the Hemingway family was not immune to reciprocal parent-child effect.

But, above all, even if one admits that Grace Hemingway was a
"rigid" mother (albeit a liberal one for her time, allowing her children to dance, bathe in the nude at the lake, and permitting Ernest to
hold boxing matches in her music room), it requires an act of faith
to leap to the conclusion that she molded her son into what he was
to become. This line of reasoning has shades of the tired old joke
that "my mother made me into a homosexual." Most sons treated
as Hemingway was did not grow up to become either as disturbed or
as creative as he became. It is doubtful, moreover, that she was
very different from other mothers of her social class at the turn of
the century. Considering the fact that she gave birth to and raised a
son who was to become a famed writer who would lead a tumultuous life and then tragically end it, if one follows the mother-blaming model, one should expect Grace Hemingway to have been a
more disturbed and *deviant* mother than she was, or, perhaps, a
more rejecting one than she was during her son's young years.

The second error of this psychological historiography resides in
the omission of the role of Hemingway's *father* in his son's life — as
well as in his other children's lives. Admittedly, Dr. Hemingway
was "henpecked" (however ridiculous such an adjective is when
one takes into consideration all those *women* who are dominated by
their own husbands — a situation to which one has yet to attach a
pejorative label). But Clarence Hemingway had a loving and devoted relationship with his children. It is possible that witnessing
the moral humiliations their father suffered at the hand of his wife —
albeit exaggerated in Lynn's book — could have had a detrimental
effect on the children, especially in terms of their own expectations
concerning their future marital lives. Yet, beyond this, the father
had some positive impact on his son (vitality, sense of discovery,
curiosity, love of nature), as did the mother.

But the most objectionable lacuna in Lynn's analysis is the failure to link Hemingway's problems to his *father's mental health*,
rather than to any particular method of treatment *either* parent exer-
cised toward their children. Lynn does mention that Hemingway's
father likely suffered from manic depression (p. 36). Indeed, he
quotes Ernest's older sister, Marcelline, who described their fa-

ther's mood as changing drastically from one minute to the next. The clinical profile is unmistakable. When one adds to this the fact that Ernest's father committed suicide in 1928, the "diagnosis" is even more plausible, as clinical depression is a major cause of an estimated 60 percent of suicides.

Moreover, one of Hemingway's younger sisters, Ursula, probably his favorite sibling, terminated her life in 1966 after learning that she had cancer (p. 56). His much younger brother, Leicester, also committed suicide in 1982. Finally, we know that Hemingway himself committed suicide in 1961 because of depression.

It is difficult to understand how this family history is not taken into consideration in determining the etiology of Hemingway's psychiatric disorders. It is actually ignored at a time when more and more evidence points to a biochemical genetic link in the causation of such disorders as schizophrenia and manic depression. Moreover, one year earlier than Lynn, another biographer, Michael Reynolds, quite clearly established a link between Clarence Hemingway's depression and Ernest's own mental state. As Reynolds describes the situation, the father had not been well emotionally since 1909. His wife was certainly aware of his emotional lability (which could well explain why she took on a more powerful role in their domestic life — as a compensatory mechanism, rather than a pathological trait) and, by 1919, so were Ernest's sisters. Reynolds adds, "Later Ernest would say that his father had been caught in a trap only partially of his own making. What he did not want to discuss was the possibility that the trap had been biological" (p. 83).

When Hemingway took his own life (with a rifle propped up in his mouth) in 1961, he exhibited many of the same symptoms as his father's before his own suicide: "erratic high blood pressure, insomnia, paranoia, severe depression. Like his father, he kept meticulous lists . . ." (Reynolds, pp. 85-86). While, as we have seen earlier, Lynn attributes Hemingway's insomnia to maternal treatment (although one can never tell what the specific treatment was), Reynolds attributes it to simple heredity: both Marcelline and Ursula were insomniacs. In addition, to complete this ill-fated family history, one of Marcelline's children had a nervous breakdown at a relatively young age.

Moreover, while Ernest's relationship with his mother becomes overtly problematic mainly after his return from the war in 1919, his relationship with his father became more distant at the much earlier age of twelve. This was a result of the fact that the father was becoming more morose and included his son less often in the activities they had previously shared. These activities, because of their nature and Ernest's own temperament, had probably been more important to the young Hemingway than the activities initiated by his mother. This was a gradual loss which "he could not understand . . . . Ernest tried even harder to gain his affection" (Reynolds, p. 102). In other words, not only has Lynn resorted to convenient mother-blaming in his biography, but he has also failed, in typical fashion, to include the father as a parent. This exclusion is the more biasing, not only because of the obvious heredity connection via the father, but because the father-son tie had been close and was seriously weakened while Hemingway was still a child.

It may not be too presumptuous to say that, whomever the mother he would have had, Hemingway would have grown into the disturbed and creative man he became. Admittedly, such a conclusion is not as exciting biographically as the mother-blaming theory is. A biographer left with this relatively less complex scientific theory has a less novel-like—less fashionable—explanation to provide. The castrating, domineering mother is a popular theme in psychiatry and biography. It has great appeal, especially to men. But it does not follow from this that it is the appropriate explanation. Feminist researchers would certainly qualify it as unscientific and even bordering on the "hysterical"—an epithet until now largely reserved for women in the psychiatric literature.

It seems that, in terms of a theory of embeddedness (Lerner and Lerner, 1987), there was a relatively poor mother-son "fit" between Hemingway and his mother *after his adolescent years*, after his personality had already taken a turn in a different direction. She held expectations which her son did not go on to fulfill and he led a life she certainly disapproved of. Therefore, according to this theory, the demands she placed on him were more detrimental than would have been the case had the personality fit between mother and son been more congruent. The most that one can conclude is that this relatively poor fit created additional problems for

Hemingway, as it did for both his father and his mother, and provided Hemingway with a convenient excuse to "hate" his mother, the "bitch." There was no precursor sign of Hemingway's adult attitude toward his mother while he was a child. But whatever theory one espouses, the tragically self-perpetuating family history (on the *father* side, after all) of depression and suicide cannot be accounted for by the quirks, whatever they may have been, of this liberal, strong-willed, Victorian-era mother.

In addition, neither Lynn himself nor the other biographers fail to note the great impact on Hemingway of his first love rejection at age twenty, immediately after the war. Thus, by age twenty, Hemingway was already both a war and a romantic casualty—neither of which had had anything to do, in terms of causality, with his mother or, for that matter, his entire preceding life.

Following Agnes' rejection, "he set about collecting a pride of mostly older women" (Reynolds, p. 61). Hemingway came of age and simultaneously experienced crucial and all-encompassing situations which may have been more important in determining his adult personality than had his entire childhood. For, indeed, his behavior became very different thereafter. There was a sharp break between what had been and what was to be. Basically, the brutal war, this love rejection, and the disappearance of the environment he had known during his childhood were certainly potent determinants of his adult behavior. In sharp contrast, Lynn's mother-blaming theory posits a developmental model whereby the *adult* is immediately molded by and wedded to the first years of life. This model assumes a static quality to life, a lack of adult development, and totally and unrealistically ignores later influences on personality development. This theory is anathema to more recent psychological and sociological research.

In fact, one can even wonder if, in Hemingway's case, his first years, because largely "normal," had not been relatively inconsequential. With hindsight based on his adult personality, one could easily assume that, had his first years been perturbed, he would have been a distraught teenager (and he was not), and he would have written about his childhood (whereas he did not). One could certainly have recourse to a theory of repression (repressing the mother) to explain this silence, as Lynn does. But one could also posit that the author, with a predilection for the unusual, had not noticed much about his early childhood as he had been relatively happy and very active. One could also posit that he did not want to trample literarily on what had been perhaps the happiest and the least perturbed chapter in his entire life.

POSTSCRIPT

Literary works are written by persons who are themselves a product of their environment, although one of their characteristics is that they often rebel against that very same environment. Kenneth Lynn as a biographer went to traditional sources (clinical) in order to seek the roots of Hemingway's genius and tumultuous life. Our cultural environment currently interprets adult disorders as reflections of childhood traumas. Since the mother is the prime caretaker, she becomes an easy target for whatever ails her children, even after they reach adulthood (Caplan and Hall-McCorquodale, 1985a,b). Lynn's biography certainly fell for these cultural traps, and because his work has received a great deal of acclaim in literary circles, it serves to perpetuate antiquated theories which are both deleterious and biased. In this respect, this biography lacks creativity and stacks up the old rhetoric deck.

I have presented a critique of this literary work in a book on child effect so as to illustrate how clinical theories are slow to change even after more up-to-date research pointing to alternative explanations has been carried out. As was discussed earlier in this book, when a child "goes wrong," parents unavoidably ask themselves, "What have *I* done wrong?" even if they have done nothing wrong. Actually, I suspect that it is the more caring (thus least guilty) parents who ask this question. In the case of Hemingway's mother, it is biographers who ask the question for her . . . and answer it along the lines of current cultural constructs.

Chapter 13

Additional Considerations and Conclusions

In this book, I have chosen to include topics which have been especially neglected in the literature on family relations, specifically the area of child effect. We have investigated, at some length, juvenile delinquency, emotionally disturbed, "difficult," and chronically ill children, and the role of the child in maternal PMS, divorce, and interracial families. This included results from five empirical studies, and a critique of the mother-blaming genre in some literary biographies.

I have left out the effect on parents of child autism, learning disabilities, physical handicaps, cerebral palsy, and developmental delay, as these areas have received some attention in their respective literatures from the perspective of child effect. Moreover, textbooks on these subjects generally offer some material on child effect. Thus, I saw these important areas as being in less urgent need of reexamination and critique than some of the other areas included herein. In the sections below, we will focus on immigrant parents, adoptive parents, and the cross-cultural perspective in order to present additional research questions and hypotheses. This will be followed by the examination of a topic which is suffused with ideological overtones: parental gratification. Finally, general conclusions will be presented.

IMMIGRANT PARENTS

One area which could not be covered at all in this book is the effect on immigrant parents of raising their children in North America. This topic could not be adequately reviewed for the simple reason that it suffers from a complete lack of research. Although family texts broach the topic of ethnicity (e.g., Wilkinson, 1987), they do not do so from the perspective of child effect. There are several aspects of the condition of immigrant parents which make them particularly susceptible to child effect, as well as subject to certain forms of child effect which other parents neither benefit nor suffer from.

For one, not only do these parents generally see their children become rapidly more proficient than themselves in the use of the English language — via the school system — but their children necessarily adopt attitudes, values and a behavorial repertoire which may be alien to their parents and even against their own value system. In order to adapt to what is *their* country, children of immigrants have no choice but to socialize themselves to the North American ways. In so doing, they often unwittingly create a cultural gulf between themselves and their parents. This was illustrated to some extent in Chapter 7. Immigrant parents, compared to other parents, are often less knowledgeable about the child socialization goals of the host society and this places them at a disadvantage with their children. In comparison, other parents "have greater control over environmental contingencies than children" (Peterson and Rollins, 1987:480). For immigrant parents, the situation may well be reversed in that their children may acquire more such control.

There is a great deal of literature dealing with the assimilation and adaptation of immigrants and with the generational gaps that often occur. Studies also show that adaptation is more difficult for those who do not know the host language, who come from rural backgrounds and settle in large cities, are of lower-educational level, and who are poor. In light of this information, many research questions could be addressed within the framework of our analysis. For instance, such parental characteristics as sex, age, rural versus urban origins, educational level, occupational status, religion, and racial visibility could be utilized to see which types of parents are most susceptible to being influenced, including being helped, by their children. Do older or younger, rural or urban parents learn more about new ways of living through their children? In other words, which type of parents are more likely to undergo the process of secondary socialization with the help of their children? Which types of parents *change* some of their ways of thinking and of behaving as a direct result of their children's influence? Which parents resist the most? Which parents are most *negatively* affected by their Americanized children's attitudes and behavior? And which *areas* of the parents' lives are most changed and affected? Is it just a superficial change in terms of language or a deeper one concerning values?

In turn, we can also ask what types of children of immigrants produce change in their parents? Boys or girls; smaller children or adolescents; children who do well in school or children who do less well? Who are the most successful at contributing to parental resocialization? Which types of children can do so with the least negative impact on their parents? Certain children reject their parents "as bearers of alien cultures" (Nye, 1958:70). Are there characteristics which differentiate children who can accommodate both sets of cultures from rejecting children? Which combinations of parent/child characteristics produce the most pain in immigrant parents? The most rewards? The most gratification?

Following our model, we can look at the societal response to immigration (including refugee status), individual immigrants, or groups of immigrants, and see how it can buffer negative child effect (as well as negative parental effect) and can contribute to maintaining a high level of familial integration. For instance, will social rejection of immigrant parents and/or their children, especially if they belong to a visible minority, exacerbate negative child effect or foster supportive child effect? Will it contribute to family integration? How do school classes in English as a Second Language (ESL) contribute to the process and in which direction? What role does the peer group play? For instance, during adolescence a child may place the importance of the peer group over that of the family. This may be a particularly difficult situation for Asian parents, for whom such a phenomenon does not normally exist, as their cultures view the family as preeminent. Do immigrant parents fare better in terms of child effect when they become established in a neighborhood populated largely by people like themselves or better in an integrated neighborhood? The neighborhood, with its social networks, could serve as a preventive to child effect aimed at parental assimilation or as an incentive to such effect.

These few questions combining child, parents, and societal response characteristics clearly indicate how relatively little we know about this vast area of potential research. The social conditions of currently large waves of immigrants and refugees from developing countries, who are often members of visible minorities, would demand that we investigate these questions in greater depth. But families of immigrants are generally left out of sociological and psychological studies and surveys because they are "unrepresentative," "difficult to reach," "too few," and because of the language barrier. The number of such families in most states and provinces is still relatively low; as a result, they are often dropped out of surveys because their numbers are too small. Thus, we only get to learn of them in scholarly journals dealing with ethnic relations, but certainly not from the perspective of child effect.

Basically, North American sociology of the family is largely one developed around English-speaking Christian and Jewish caucasians, with a sprinkling of material on black families and, more recently, on Chicano families. In Canada, the multicultural ethnic mosaic has encouraged a somewhat less narrow focus. Nevertheless, literature on the large French element is generally in French and unavailable to the rest of the North American monolingual English-speaking scholarly community. In summary, immigrant families have received little attention in the literature. Their dynamics have not been studied, especially as they adapt or fail to adapt to their host society. Thus, the children are not studied in conjunction with the parents, and the field of child effect is particularly barren at this intersection.

ADOPTIVE PARENTS

Another area where relatively little knowledge exists concerns the effect of being an adoptive, as opposed to a biological, *parent*. There is some recent literature which discusses the stigma of being an adoptive parent, mainly because of the implication of sterility or inability to carry a child to full-term. There is, of course, a vast literature, mainly genetic and psychological, focusing on the nature versus nurture dialogue, where, for instance, twins reared separately are studied to see if they become more similar to their adoptive parents or inherit traits, such as schizophrenia and alcoholism, from their natural parents. There has also been quite a bit of research on adopted children themselves. One of the results is that adopted children were found to be disproportionately represented in populations of children treated for emotional problems. In view of the fact that *some* adopted children have difficulties with their status, is it not possible that some parents also have problems because of these same difficulties?

For instance, children often encounter prejudice among their peers when they reveal that they are adopted. A twelve-year-old girl received this reaction from a classmate: "Oh, no, you're adopted! You, poor, poor thing. You don't have real parents." And she shrieked while covering her mouth with her hands, to the bewilderment of the adopted girl, who then told her mother, "You can imagine that this did not make me feel very good." Another girl has been asked about her "faked" mother. And, of course, the mother feels very sorry for her child and has to explain to her that adoption is not common enough for people to be used to it and they don't understand it. And so on. The negative peer effect on the child affects the parents.

Other parents are saddened when their own parents prefer grandchildren who are of their "own blood." Or parents become upset when a teacher says, "Of course, your child is difficult, but you never know what you get when you adopt them." Or, another points out, "Well, I understand, you can't quite love them as much as if they were your own." Or the case where a new acquaintance insists upon asking, "What about children of your *'own'*?" In other words, the social response is irresponsible, to say the least.

Another aspect to consider is the new open-record policy and the fact that older adopted children can search for their biological parents and receive help from welfare agencies in this enterprise. However "liberal" one may want to be on this issue, the fact is that this situation probably gives rise to a great deal of anxiety, perhaps even insecurity, anger and resentment, in adoptive parents. But this matter is not studied because adoptive parents are "not supposed" to feel like this—it is not an "in" attitude. How *are* parents affected by the fact that in another year their child may have found their "natural" mother? And what about in later years? Much has been written on this process by adoptees. What about the adoptive parents as well as the other children, whether biological or adopted?

As mentioned earlier, there are studies which have found that adopted children have *higher* rates of *treated* emotional problems than biological children (Bohman, 1971; Lifshitz et al., 1975; Reece and Levin, 1968; Senior and Himadi, 1985; Work and Anderson, 1971). Some possible explanations which have been advanced include: the children's difficulties coping with adoptive status; defective foster home care before adoption; incompatibility between adoptive parents and children; inappropriate parental coping and expectations; and the possibility that adoptive parents may be more anxious about their children's mental health and may be more willing to seek treatment as soon as they notice the slightest problem. It should be pointed out, however, that the bulk of this literature is clinical and the theoretical orientation definitely emphasizes continuity of deviance, rather than change, throughout a child's lifespan. It emphasizes parental role in the development of children's problems. Additionally, much of that literature is old and research methods were often lax. Nevertheless, at the very least, such studies and the explanations proffered indicate that research of child effect on adoptive parents would be highly appropriate.

In this respect, a comparison of parents whose children are adopted, nonadopted and a mixture of the two would be especially important (Grotevant et al., 1988, for a clinical sample). Age and sex of the child, desire of the child to locate natural parents, their reasons for doing so, and child's attitude and attachment to parents would be a few child characteristics of importance. Parental and societal support characteristics could be taken from Chapter 3. An added societal characteristic here would be the attitude of family and friends towards the child as an adopted child. Thus, while a reasonable amount of research has been carried out on the effect of being adopted on children, the counterpart does not exist for parents. How are these parents affected by their children's reactions to them? By their children's acceptance of their status? Or rejection of their status?

CROSS-CULTURAL PERSPECTIVE

One subject we briefly addressed in the first section of this book, as well as in the conclusion of the chapter on students' perceptions, is the fact that child effect differs greatly from culture to culture. This is especially so when substantial cultural differences exist from society to society.

To begin with, some of the child and parent characteristics presented in Chapter 3 do not apply universally: they were intended to fit the North American context. For instance, in agrarian societies where a large number of children, preferably male, is the ideal, the *personal* characteristics of the *individual* children may matter much less than their sheer number, or their demographic characteristics such as age, sex, and birth order. There was a suggestion of the occurrence of this phenomenon in large North American families as reported in students' own perceptions (Chapter 7). Because parents are too busy to respond to the idiosyncrasies of individual children who are often taken care of by older siblings or by an entire kin group with a homogeneous set of values, children in agrarian societies are brought up more uniformly; distinctions of personality are not deemed important beyond their ability to provide food, become a hunter or a herder, and reproduce themselves as they grow older.

The very important stages in child development outlined in Western theories may not even apply in many of these societies. For example, the processes of individuation, of separation from family, and of independence from parents, are largely Western phenomena and theories. For instance, Braconnier and Marcelli (1979:326) state the following, as if it were an article of faith: "If the child experiences the adults' world as a source of security and support, one of his first moves during his emerging adolescence is to attempt to distance himself from that world, urged onwards in this by the onset of sexual maturity." In many countries and subgroups of the Pacific, Asia, Africa, and Latin America, adolescents simply pass into the adults' ranks, and a human being is not a separate entity from his/her family (see Matthiasson, 1974). In fact, the person is a continuation of the familial line, and ancestors are part of everyday life. Individualism, understood as one being psychologically apart from the family or kin group, is an aberrant behavior and not a normal trait in these societies. Interdependency, familism, and group consensus are the traits which *normal* individuals in such societies nurture. Western psychology offers as universals features which are specific to a particular regional culture.

Thus, certain "stages" in human development which, in Western societies, bring conflict between parent and child, and which affect both parents and children, do not exist in other societies: negative child effect is thus minimized. As Skolnick (1980) has pointed out, many of our social practices, especially the fact that our society is age-graded, may be responsible for many of the developmental characteristics which psychologists believe to be universal. Thus, other social practices give rise to a different developmental pattern.

Similarly, certain Western concepts used to describe problematic family situations might, in other cultural contexts, be describing a normal state of affairs (Weisner, 1984). I am thinking here of the term "family enmeshment," coined by Minuchin (1974), which describes families in which the members are so involved with each other that they lose their individuality and independence. It is actually the concepts of individuality and independence which might be quite detrimental to both families and individual family members in other societies. This is just one instance which illustrates the lack of universal application of Western psychology and sociology, as well as the potentially different child and parental effects. It has also been argued that, even within our own society, ethnic and class differences are actually cultural differences: white, middle-class standards of parenting and of child development, thus of child effect, may be inappropriate for other groups (Ogbu, 1985, 1987).

Similarly, it is probable that most of the parental characteristics we have discussed, with the exception of sex and age, may have little relevance in rural, agrarian or gatherer societies where everyone is first and foremost a member of a kin group, and where children are cared for by a network of caregivers, including parents, uncles, aunts, cousins, and grandparents. In such societies, many of the parents' and children's needs met by the parent/child system in our society are met by the kin and village system (Lewis et al., 1984). Because these cultures are internally homogeneous, all parents hold similar beliefs concerning children and one's place in the kin system; animism and familism may take precedence over concepts such as personal happiness, marital satisfaction, and personality. Under such circumstances, other parental characteristics of the Western type may be totally irrelevant.

The characteristics of the societal support may also be entirely different. Wars may be the key variable which guides child effect. Malnutrition, disease, and droughts may be aspects of the environment which will determine whether one will have children, as well as determining how many, if any, will survive to young adulthood. In such drastic environmental and political contexts, societal support of the North American type becomes a moot question when the global environment is so deterministic. At that point, the overall political situation as well as the international reaction to war and famine may be the salient deterministic characteristics of child effect. For instance, as this book is written, civil war in Ethiopia, combined with recurrent droughts, leads to the starvation of thousands of Tigreans and Eritreans. Only a sustained and coordinated international effort could save these parents and children.

In other agrarian societies with less drastic environments, the presence of a mother's sister who can share in child rearing may be a key alleviating variable in a mother's welfare. The ability to provide a dowry for a daughter and to contract a suitable match for a son may have a far greater "child effect" on these parents than any other aspect of child or parent characteristics and the societal support category, for that matter.

Cultural encroachment occurs as both Western and Eastern ways of life, whether capitalistic or socialistic, eradicate local institutions and traditions without appropriate replacement, and begin to alter the balance of rather uniform, predictable, largely positive, and nonindividual child effects. As a society becomes colonized or conquered, adolescents and young adult children may abandon the village as they are conscripted into the military or go to seek their fortune elsewhere, leaving their parents to experience a generation gap for perhaps the first time in the long history of these societies. These parents will miss out on the feeling of *continuity* through their children, a feeling which they have provided for their own parents. They will be deprived of their children's labor, even though the children may return periodically with money and new material possessions, which in turn may further erode traditions.

The areas of parental lives which can be affected by children are also different from culture to culture. For instance, in a relatively stable and homogeneous society, it is unlikely that parents' beliefs and attitudes will be affected by their children, who simply inherit the same patterns as their parents. Parental personality is probably much less vulnerable to child effect, if at all, rooted as it is in the larger kin system. An irritating child can easily be cared for by a grandparent or an older sibling. Similarly, community relations will mediate child effect when there is a sufficient number of children or no children at all. The community will be supportive of the adult who becomes a parent. The *mere presence* of children will give status to the adults and will contribute to binding them more closely to their community. It is also important to point out that there are areas of parental lives which exist in these societies but not in ours, such as the relationship with ancestors (which should be facilitated by the presence of children).

In spite of cross-cultural differences, the model presented in this book is applicable provided one keeps in mind that the categories have to be redefined and adapted to the type of society one may be studying. I propose here a universalism of child effect, with the understanding that in some societies child effect may mean the effect of the mere *presence* of children rather than the effect of *individual* children. It is impossible to subscribe to a universalism of child and human development *as developed by Western theorists*, according to Western values and ideologies. Our conceptualizations would certainly appear utterly foolish to a society living on an island in Indonesia, in a relatively untouched rural area in Latin America or Africa, or even in Inuit societies on our own continent (Munroe et al., 1981). For instance, it should be recalled that today's concept of adolescence as a period of "storm and stress" originated with the psychologist G. Stanley Hall (1904) who was to greatly influence Freud. Even such early anthropological studies as those of Margaret Mead in 1928, showing that adolescence is not universally existent or a period of turmoil, failed to counteract our society's perception of adolescence.

In an earlier chapter, we proposed a distinction between unavoidable and avoidable child effect. It was suggested that, while unavoidable child effect knows no national boundary, the context within which it operates will differ significantly from society to society (and within a society, from one cultural group to another). For instance, in some groups, a baby may be fed relatively continuously, upon demand, while in another adjacent group, babies are fed according to a schedule. Both arrangements, however dissimilar, fulfill an unavoidable, natural need: that of food. Both arrangements, as well, will impact differently on the parents' lives, as their schedules and even their health may be affected differently.

It was also suggested that, in contrast, avoidable child effect is generally a cultural product. That is, it is created by a society's values and norms. Basically, avoidable child effect is a social construct with a powerful reality. By the same token, it may be entirely nonexistent in another society. A graphic example here would be the "necessity" for middle-class parents to provide artistic and/or sports experience for their children in the form of music, dance, skating, and skiing lessons, to name only a few. These "necessities" of our middle-class North American culture have quite an array of effects on parents who have to pay for them, do without certain other luxuries to afford them, drive children to these lessons, and spend their time, and who may be consequently more tired, more fulfilled (or less), more proud and so on. Such middle-class, North American necessities are totally immaterial to a very poor neighborhood populated by groups of recent immigrants with a different culture. Thus, these "necessities" are avoidable, as they are not necessary at all for many children across the world. The effect on parents, consequently, is avoidable.

IDEOLOGICAL QUESTIONS: PARENTAL GRATIFICATION

The literature on child socialization and general parent-child relations has still another focus which has yet to be questioned as purely ideological. It resides in this belief: it is the role (duty) of parents to gratify their children's emotional needs so that children will grow into emotionally stable persons with a healthy level of self-esteem. The validity of this statement is not questioned. Common sense and

scientific knowledge clearly indicate that children who are neglected, rejected, emotionally abused, or on whom parents place
excessive or inconsistent demands are more at risk than other children of developing problems while they are still young or of suffering the sequels of such emotional sterility when they reach adulthood.

Similarly, parents who expect small children to gratify their own
needs for love and companionship tend to be immature, have lacked
love themselves and may not be able to give it. Such parents are at a
high risk of physically abusing their small children when the latter
disturb them too much, are sick, or when the parents suffer a rejection from someone else.

The above paragraphs are accepted as nonideological and empirically valid. (It is not my intent to review that literature as most
textbooks do the task more than adequately.) All else, however,
that has been said as to what constitutes the proper way of being a
parent is of questionable validity and may be merely ideological,
that is, purely a matter of beliefs. The double question asked here in
terms of parental gratification is:

Why should parents of older, dependent children (eleven to
eighteen) not *expect* some gratification out of having children?
Why should these same parents not be entitled to *demand*
some gratification out of having children?

By "gratification," we mean a sense of personal pleasure, a feeling of being emotionally fulfilled as parents by one's children, a
sense that one's children appreciate what one does for them, at least
more than once a year (on Mothers' or Fathers' Day). Of course,
parental gratification will mean something different for each parent,
depending on the personalities involved, so that only a ball park
definition is needed here. For instance, some parents may feel very
gratified if their child is the most "popular" teenager at school:
such is their value system. Other parents will feel very rewarded if
their teenager has a part-time job and promises to do well financially as an adult. Still others will be gratified if their child is
streetwise and can put up a good fight and show that he is "all
boy." Finally, other parents are gratified when their child is la-

belled "gifted" or when the child gets the best marks in his or her
grade.

There is generally nothing wrong with these modes of parental
gratification . . . provided the parental motivations are not pathological or are not imposing on the children a sense of value which is
not conducive to the building of a healthy personality and of a
healthy society. Instances of the latter would include: a child cheats
to get the best marks and this is overlooked by parents who value
achievement over honesty; a boy or girl is popular because he/she
has a flashy car, clothes, and can have unsupervised parties at
home; a child is aggressive and uses his fists to solve problems or
even to provoke problems; a part-time teenage worker neglects her
studies to earn money to buy electronic equipment or endangers her
health pursuing that goal.

In the industrialized and technological world of today, children
remain dependent upon their parents longer than in other societies
and longer than in the nontechnologized past. The main reason for
this is that children have to be schooled and trained to hold the jobs
which our society has to offer and needs to have filled. Consequently, adolescents (a universal biological category of young people who are developing sexually and are completing their physical
growth) are transformed into teenagers. Teenagers are a category of
people, between thirteen and nineteen, who, in our culture, are supposed to differentiate themselves from their parents, learn to be
independent, go to school, and hopefully have a good time. They
are also expected to be rebellious, go through a "phase" of parental
rejection, all the while remaining under the responsibility of their
parents for their protection. Teenage years are expected to be "tumultuous," "a search for one's identity," "conflictual," and "full
of risks," for the adolescents. They are years when the "peer
group" becomes "more important" than the parents. Often, in the
lower class and among certain subgroups, teenagers are expected to
earn their living and, in the case of girls, even to get married or
have babies.

But, in terms of middle-class ideology, there is obviously a clear-
cut dichotomy in the division of labor here: parents who support
children on one side and said children who generally would rather
be with other children than with their parents. Or, put another way,

there are parents whose main purpose in these young persons' lives is to support them and teenagers whose main purpose for being with their parents is to be supported. Fortunately, not all parents or all teenagers follow this ideology. Indeed, many parents expect their teenagers to contribute to their own maintenance, and many teenagers do so. Moreover, many families with teenagers experience a great deal of closeness and sharing. But, overall, in terms of ideology, middle-class society has definitely constructed a situation of imbalance and intergenerational separation. Even in terms of exchange theory, the imbalance is very tilted: the parents give and the teenagers receive. What is in it for the parents, one may ask?

Fortunately, most parents have been well-conditioned and believe that this is the way things unavoidably have to be. It is their "duty." Writing about mothers, Elaine Heffner (1978) pointed out that no one "suggests that it is permissible for her to consider herself, or indicate that she is as important as the child" (p. 27). This applies to both parents, and she adds that parents in our society are not allowed to exhibit negative feelings concerning their role or their children. Parents are socialized to believe that they owe everything to their children. If they do perceive an imbalance, they will rationalize it away: "it will pass"; "it's a phase"; "they will outgrow it." Such parents are at a *waiting* stage: waiting for the "phase" (one phase after another for *ten* years — a very long "phase" . . .) to go away, waiting for the teenager to come back to his senses, waiting for her to be a responsible adult. Such *parents' own lives are suspended* while their teenagers go through their series of phases, some minor, some major, some positive, some negative — but most negative ones are avoidable as they are dictated by the cultural context.

Even parents who have demanding and difficult teenagers are expected to derive satisfaction from their role. At the very least, they should "accept their lot." They should "stand by" their child who, in another society, would be considered an adult. Should it then be surprising if parents are generally relieved when their children are on their own? In the past, the "empty-nest syndrome" involved expectations of loneliness and purposelessness by parents who found themselves alone. More recent studies clearly indicate that such parents may have suffered from an overflowing nest before and the new state of their nest suits them just fine. In the recent past, one parent, the mother, was meant to have no other purpose in life but to be a housewife and mother. She may indeed have keenly felt the loss of her central and core role when her children left. But today's parents are usually both employed, have an enormous amount of financial responsibilities (one of the largest is the maintenance of their adolescent children), have more complicated personal lives (higher divorce/remarriage/stepparenting rates), have many extra familial "distractions," and can look to post-parenthood and still be in a state of good health for many years to come.

The imbalance against parents may be reflected in the drastic decline in the birth rate in this century. As children's schooling has extended, as urbanization has outpaced rural life, as adolescents have become teenagers, and as experts have told parents that all this is quite normal, couples have had fewer and fewer children. The *use* of children has diminished. The *value* of children has decreased. The *costs* of children have increased. Why, otherwise, would more people choose not to have children and most others choose to have only one or two? If children were as useful and as gratifying as they were or *could* be, people would have them in greater numbers. If children were not so costly, more people would have them or have more of them.

Our society is more egocentric, individualistic, and hedonistic than in the past century. Such characteristics can also explain why adults prefer to minimize child encumbrance. But the vicious circle can only keep spinning if one encourages teenagers to be egocentric as opposed to family-oriented. If one encourages teenagers to receive from their parents with no reciprocity involved, these teenagers will grow into additional individualistic persons who, later on, will not want to be responsible for children either nor perhaps even for their aging parents. Teenagers do look back occasionally and see the life their parents had — and reject such a life for *themselves*; paradoxically, *they* were its chief beneficiaries.

If raising children was not so emotionally draining and isolating, and if it was less costly economically, more adults would have more children. Adults have a great *need* for gratification; yet, they see that parenthood may supply very little of it. The perceived imbalance leads adults to other forms of gratification instead of parenthood. A career, travelling, hobbies, a single life style are such sources of alternate gratification. Consequently, unless we have an influx of very young immigrants who will have large numbers of children, we will have, in twenty to thirty years, a severe imbalance in the ratio of children and then young adults to seniors.

Allowing parents the *right* to seek emotional gratification, *as parents*, from their adolescent children whom they have to support may encourage parents in their role, and may even encourage others to have more than one child. Whatever the fertility outcome is, such policies would certainly make parents' lives more fair and equitable. Of course, such a simple statement does require the entire restructuring of our society . . . a task that is easier said than done.

In many current societies, and fifty years ago in most Western societies, adolescents were young adults with rights but with duties. They probably gave as much to their parents as they received; both parties reciprocated. Each had a need for the other—whether economic and/or emotional. Adolescents were not dependents. In contrast, *teenagers* are dependents. But so long as they are, why can't those who pay their way have the pleasure of their cooperation, their help, their smile, their at least occasional company, and, why not—their gratitude? The relationship would be reciprocal, interdependent rather than dependent, and obligated with immediate returns for one's emotional investment for both parties involved.

IN CONCLUSION

In this last chapter, topics rarely discussed, or rarely discussed from certain perspectives, have been presented to encourage alternate forms of research paradigms as well as to stimulate research questions in the areas. The field of child effect is an emerging one but it is not emerging equally throughout the entire spectrum of sociological research; in other words, certain areas, such as juvenile delinquency, are even more neglected than others.

Moreover, I have purposely raised certain topics (such as parental gratification) which are suffused with ideological overtones. Being the "devil's advocate" can be a useful consciousness-raising device for a researcher. Basically, our North American, Western ways of thinking prevent us from exploring their universal applicability. What is good for us is not necessarily applicable to other cultures. But, more importantly, what is applicable to other cultures *could* be a useful instrument with which to initiate change or a reversal in our research directions, with certain implications for social policy regarding families.

The study of child effect from the triple causative perspective of child, parents, and societal reaction characteristics is a useful analytical model. It follows in the footsteps of those who study families within an ecological perspective (Bronfenbrenner, 1979, 1987) as well as a "parental empowerment" ideology (Zigler and Berman, 1983). It opens the door to research hypotheses and questions that have not been studied, as well as to a reevaluation of certain developmental theories. And it does so cross-culturally, provided one keeps in mind that the model presented herein has to be adapted to each society where it would be applied.

Throughout our various discussions, we have, whether implicitly or explicitly, highlighted the fact that definitions and theories of childhood, child development, and family life are *social constructs*. That is, they change when sociohistorical circumstances change (Meyer, 1988). Human nature, including the nature of children and of their relationship with their parents, is not a static phenomenon of universal applicability. Each culture constructs human nature somewhat differently. Each society constrains, shapes, and defines human nature as befits its own context. It is thus not surprising that we are currently questioning certain tenets of psychology and sociology. Both disciplines have been shaped within a particular cultural context and are evolving along with the society that has nurtured them. The study of child effect probably would have been unacceptable three decades ago. But various social forces, including changing roles of parents, of children, of the sexes, technological impact, feminism, and new developmental models are allowing for the emergence of this "new" area of research.

The study of child effect as one key element of family sociology and of human (child and adult) development promises to redirect the unidirectional causality models generally found and to initiate research that studies not only one direction of effect but reciprocal and feedback effects as well. This in no way implies that research on parental effect on children should be abandoned. What it means simply is that child effect is a legitimate area of research, as valid as the other, and that the two combined will offer a more complete and less biased perspective on the family.

References

Abplanalp, Judith. 1983. "Premenstrual syndrome: A selective review." In Lifting the Curse of Menstruation, ed. by Sharon Golub. New York: The Haworth Press, Inc.

Abraham, Barbara, Shirley S. Feldman, and Sharon C. Nash. 1978. "Sex role self-concept and sex role attitudes: Enduring personality characteristics or adaptation to changing life situations." Developmental Psychology 14:393-400.

Adams, Michael. 1989. "Canada's new ethnic and racial reality." Canadian Speeches 3:14-22.

Aday, Luann, Marlene J. Aitken, and Donna H. Wegener. 1988. Pediatric Home Care: Results of a National Evaluation of Programs for Ventilator Assisted Children. Chicago: Pluribus Press Inc.

Aday, Luann, and Donna H. Wegener. 1988. "Home care for ventilator-assisted children: Implications for the children, their families and health policy." Children's Health Care 17:112-119.

Adler, Patricia, Peter Adler, Spencer Cahill, and Nancy Mandell (eds.). 1986, 1988, 1990. Sociological Studies of Child Development, Vols. 1, 2, and 3. Greenwich, CT: JAI Press.

Affleck, Glenn, Howard Tennen, Jonelle Rowe, Beth Roscher, and Linda Walker. 1989. "Effects of formal support on mothers' adaptation to the hospital-to-home transition of high-risk infants: The benefits and costs of helping." Child Development 60:488-501.

Agnew, Robert, 1985. "Social control theory and delinquency: A longitudinal test." Criminology 23:47-61.

Agnew, Robert, and Sandra Huguley. 1989. "Adolescent violence toward parents." Journal of Marriage and the Family 51:699-711.

Aguilera, Donna C., and Janice M. Messick. 1982. Crisis Intervention: Theory and Methodology. Toronto: C.V. Mosby.

Ahrons, Constance R. 1979. "The binuclear family: Two households, one family." Alternative Lifestyles 2:499-541.

Ahrons, Constance R., and Lynn Wallisch. 1986. "The relationship between former spouses." In Close Relationships: Development, Dynamics and Deterioration, ed. by Steven Duck and David Pearlman. Beverly Hills, CA: Sage.

Ahrons, Constance R., and Lynn Wallisch. 1988. "Parenting in the binuclear family: Relationships between biological and stepparents." In Remarriage and Stepparenting, ed. by Kay Pasley and Marilyn Ihinger-Tallman. New York: Guilford Press.

Aickhorn, Angrist. 1969. Delinquency and Child Guidance. New York: International Universities Press.

Ainslie, Ricardo C. 1985. The Psychology of Twinship. Lincoln, NB: University of Nebraska Press.

Alanen, Leena. 1990. "Growing up in the modern family: Rethinking socialization of the family and childhood." In Sociological Studies of Child Development, Vol. 3, ed. by N. Mandell. Greenwich, CT: JAI Press.

Alexander, James F. 1973. "Defensive and supportive communication in normal and deviant families." Journal of Consulting and Clinical Psychology 14:223-231.

Allen, Hilary. 1984. "At the mercy of her hormones, premenstrual tension and the law." *m/f* 9:19-44.

Alpert, J. et al. 1967. "A month of illness and health care among low-income families." Public Health Reports 82:705.

Ambert, Anne-Marie. 1990. "The other perspective: children's effect on parents." In Families: Changing Trends in Canada, 2nd ed., ed. by Maureen Baker. Toronto: McGraw-Hill Ryerson.

Ambert, Anne-Marie. 1989. Ex-spouses and New Spouses: A Study of Relationships. Greenwich, CT: JAI Press.

Ambert, Anne-Marie. 1988a. "Relationship between ex-spouses: Individual and dyadic perspectives." Journal of Social and Personal Relationship 5:327-346.

Ambert, Anne-Marie. 1988b. "Relationships with former in-laws after divorce: A research note." Journal of Marriage and the Family 50:679-686.

Ambert, Anne-Marie. 1986. "Sociology of sociology: The place of children in North American sociology." In Sociological Studies of Child Development, ed. by Patricia A. Adler and Peter Adler. Greenwich, CT: JAI Press.

Ambert, Anne-Marie. 1984. "Longitudinal changes in children's behavior toward custodial parents." Journal of Marriage and the Family 46:463-467.

Ambert, Anne-Marie. 1982. "Differences in children's behavior toward custodial mothers and custodial fathers." Journal of Marriage and the Family 44:73-86.

Ambert, Anne-Marie, and Jean-François Saucier. 1984. "Adolescents' academic success and aspirations by parental marital status." Canadian Review of Sociology and Anthropology 21:62-74.

American Psychiatric Association. 1987. Diagnostic and Statistical Manual of Mental Disorders. Third edition revised. Washington, DC: APA.

Anderson, Elaine A., and Mary Martin Lynch. 1984. "A family impact analysis: The deinstitutionalization of the mentally ill." Family Relations 33:41-46.

Anderson, Elaine A., and Graham B. Spanier. 1980. "Treatment of delinquent youth: The influence of the juvenile probation officer's perceptions of self and work." Criminology 17:505-574.

Anderson, E. M., and L. Spain. 1977. The Child with Spina Bifada. London: Methuen.

Anderson, Joan M., and Helen Elfert. 1989. "Managing chronic illness in the family: Women as caretakers." Journal of Advanced Nursing 6:427-434.

Anderson, Joan M. 1981. "The social construction of the illness experience:

Families with a chronically-ill child.'' Journal of Advanced Nursing 6:427-434.

Anderson, Stephen, Candice Russell, and Walter Schumm. 1983. "Perceived marital quality and family life-cycle categories: A further analysis.'' Journal of Marriage and the Family 45:127-139.

Andry, Robert G. 1971. Delinquency and Parental Pathology. Rev. ed. London: Staples.

Andry, Robert G. 1950. ''Faulty paternal and maternal-child relationships, affection and delinquency.'' British Journal of Delinquency 1:34-48.

Arendell, Terry. 1986. Mothers and Divorce. Berkeley, CA: University of California Press.

Arey, Sandra, and George J. Warheit. 1980. ''Psychosocial costs of living with psychologically disturbed family members.'' In The Social Consequences of Psychiatric Illness, ed. by Lee N. Robins, Paula J. Clayton, and John K. Wing. New York: Brunner/Mazel.

Ariès, Philippe. 1962. Centuries of Childhood. New York: Vintage.

Bahr, Stephen J. 1989. Family Interaction. New York: Macmillan Publishing Company.

Baldwin, Sally, and Caroline Glendinning. 1983. "Employment, women and their disabled children.'' In A Labour of Love. Women, Work and Caring, ed. by Janet Finch and Dulcie Groves. London: Routledge and Kegan Paul.

Baldwin, Sally. 1977. Disabled Children: Counting the Costs. London: The Disability Alliance.

Baldwin, Sally. 1976. Some Practical Consequences of Caring for Handicapped Children at Home. University of York, England: Social Policy Research Unit.

Ballinger, Barbara, Dorothy E. Buckley, Graham J. Naylor, and David A. Stansfield. 1979. ''Emotional disturbance following childbirth.'' Psychological Medicine 9:293-300.

Bandura, A., and R. H. Walters. 1959. Adolescent Aggression. New York: Ronald Press.

Baranowski, Marc D. 1978. "Adolescents' attempted influence on parental behaviors.'' Adolescence 13:585-604.

Barkley, Russell A. 1981. "The use of psychopharmacology to study reciprocal influences in parent-child interaction.'' Journal of Abnormal Child Psychology 9:303-310.

Barkley, Russell A., and Charles E. Cunningham. 1979. "The effects of methylphenidate on the mother-child interactions of hyperactive children.'' Archives of General Psychiatry 36:201-208.

Barnett, Larry D., and Richard H. MacDonald. 1976. "A study of the membership of the national organization for non-parents.'' Social Biology 23:297-310.

Barton, William H., and Jeffrey A. Butts. 1990. "Viable options: Intensive supervision programs for juvenile delinquents.'' Crime & Delinquency 36:238-256.

Baruch, Grace K., Rosalind Barnett, and Caryl Rivers. 1983. Lifeprints. New York: McGraw-Hill.

Bates, John E. 1987. "Temperament in infancy." In Handbook of Human Development, 2nd ed., ed. by Jay D. Osofsky. New York: John Wiley & Sons.

Baumrind, Diana. 1980. "New directions in socialization research." American Psychologist 35:639-652.

Baumrind, Diana. 1978. "Reciprocal rights and responsibilities in parent-child relations." Journal of Social Issues 34:179-196.

Beels, C. C. 1974. "Family and social management of schizophrenia." In Family Therapy: Theory and Practice, ed. by Philip Guerin, Jr. New York: Gardner Press.

Beglerter, M. L., W. F. Bury, and D. J. Harris. 1976. "Prevalence of divorce among parents of children with Cystic Fibrosis and other chronic diseases." Social Biology 23:260-264.

Bell, Richard Q. 1974. "Contributions of human infants to caregiving and social interaction." In The Effect of the Infant on Its Caregiver, ed. by Michael Lewis and L. A. Rosenblum. New York: John Wiley.

Bell, Richard Q. 1971. "Stimulus control of parent and caretaker behavior by offspring." Developmental Psychology 4:63-72.

Bell, Richard Q. 1968. "A reinterpretation of the direction of effects in studies of socialization." Psychological Review 75:81-95.

Bell, Richard Q., and Lawrence V. Harper. 1977. Child Effects on Adults. Hillsdale, N.J.: Lawrence Erlbaum Associates.

Belle, Deborah. 1980. "Who uses mental health facilities?" In The Mental Health of Women, ed. by Marcia Guttentag, Susan Salasin and Deborah Belle. New York: Academic Press.

Belsky, Jay. 1985. "The determinants of parenting: A process model." Child Development 56:83-96.

Belsky, Jay. 1980. "Child maltreatment: An ecological integration." American Psychologist 5:320-335.

Belsky, Jay, B. Gilstrap, and M. Rovine. 1984. "The Pennsylvania Infant and Family Development Project, I: Stability and change in mother-infant and father-infant interaction in a family setting at one, three and nine months." Child Development 55:692-705.

Belsky, Jay, M. E. Lang, and M. Rovine. 1985. "Stability and change in marriage across the transition to parenthood: A second study." Journal of Marriage and the Family 47:855-865.

Belsky, Jay, Richard M. Lerner, and Graham B. Spanier. 1984. The Child in the Family. Reading, MA: Addison-Wesley.

Belsky, Jay, Elliot Robins, and Wendy Gamble. 1984. "The determinants of parental competence: Toward a contextual theory. In Beyond the Dyad, ed. by Michael Lewis. New York: Plenum Press.

Belsky, Jay, Graham B. Spanier, and M. Rovine, 1983. "Stability and change in marriage across the transition to parenthood." Journal of Marriage and the Family 45:567-577.

Belson, William A. 1978. Televised Violence and the Adolescent Boy. West Mead, England: Sexon House, Teakfield.

Benedict, Ruth. 1938. "Continuities and discontinuities in cultural conditioning." Psychiatry 1:161-167.

Benin, Mary H., and Joan Agostinelli. 1988. "Husbands' and wives' satisfaction with the division of labor." Journal of Marriage and the Family 50:349-361.

Benin, Mary H., and Debra A. Edwards. 1990. "Adolescents' chores: The difference between dual- and single-earner families." Journal of Marriage and the Family 52:361-373.

Berger, Joseph, Bernard P. Cohen, and Morris Zelditch, Jr. 1972. "Status characteristics and social interaction." American Sociological Review 37:241-255.

Birenbaum, A. 1970. "On managing a courtesy stigma." Journal of Health and Social Behavior 2:196-206.

Blacher, Jan. 1984. Severely Handicapped Young Children and Their Families. New York: Academic Press.

Black, Claudia. 1981. It Will Never Happen to Me. New York: Ballantine Books.

Blake, Judith. 1989. Family Size and Achievement. Berkeley: University of California Press.

Blake, Judith, and Jorge H. del Pinal. 1981. "The childlessness option: Recent American views on nonparenthood." In Predicting Fertility: Demographic Studies of Birth Expectations, ed. by Gerry H. Hendershot and Paul J. Placek. New York: Lexington Books.

Bloom, Allan. 1987. The Closing of the American Mind. New York: Simon and Schuster.

Bloom, Bernard, and K. R. Kindle. 1985. "Demographic factors in the continuing relationship between former spouses." Family Relations 34:375-381.

Bohman, M. 1971. "A comparative study of adopted children, foster children, and children in their biological environment born after undesired pregnancies." Acta Psychiatrica Scandinavica 221:1-38.

Bolton, Mary G. 1983. On Being a Mother. London: Tavistock.

Boocock, Sarane S. 1976. "Children and society." In Rethinking Childhood, ed. by Arlene Skolnick. Boston: Little, Brown.

Bottomley, Gill. 1983. "Feminist and sociological critiques of 'the family.'" In The Family in the Modern World: Australian Perspectives, ed. by Ailsa Burns, G. Bottomley and P. Jools. Sydney: George Allen & Unwin.

Boulding, Elise. 1980. "The nurture of adults by children in family settings." In Research in the Interweave of Social Roles: Women and Men. Vol. 1, ed. by H. Lopata. Greenwich, CT: JAI Press.

Braconnier, A., and D. Marcelli. 1979. "The adolescent and his parents: The parental crisis." Journal of Adolescence 2:325-336.

Bradbury, Thomas N., and Frank D. Fincham. 1990. "Dimensions of marital and family interaction." In Handbook of Family Measurement Techniques, ed. by John Touliatos, Barry Perlmutter, and Murray A. Strauss. New York: Sage.

Bradshaw, J., and D. Lawton. 1978. Tracing the Causes of Stress in Families with Handicapped Children. University of York, England: Social Policy Research Unit.

Brand, Eulalee, W. Glen Clingempeel, and K. Bowen-Woodward. 1988. "Family relationships and children's psychological adjustment in stepmother and stepfather families: Findings and conclusions from the Philadelphia Stepfamily Research Project." In Impact of Divorce, Single Parenting, and Stepparenting on Children, ed. by Mavis E. Hetherington and Josephine D. Arasteh. Hillsdale, NJ: Erlbaum.

Brennan, Tim, David Huizinga, and Delbert S. Elliott. 1978. The Social Psychology of Runaways. Lexington, MA: D. C. Heath.

Brennan, Tim, Fletcher Blanchard, David Huizinga, and Delbert Elliott. 1975. The Incidence and Nature of Runaway Behavior. Boulder, CO: Behavioral Research and Evaluation Corporation.

Breslau, Naomi. 1985. "Psychiatric disorder in children with physical disabilities." Journal of the American Academy of Child Psychiatry 24:87-96.

Breslau, Naomi, K. S. Staruch, and E. A. Mortimer. 1982. "Psychological distress in mothers of disabled children." American Journal of Diseases of Children 136:682-686.

Brett, K. M. 1988. "Sibling response to chronic childhood disorders: Research perspectives and practice implications." Issues in Comprehensive Pediatric Nursing 11:43-57.

Brim, Orville G., Jr. 1968. "Adult socialization." In Socialization and Society, ed. by John A. Clausen. Boston: Little, Brown.

Brim, Orville G., Jr., and Jerome Kagan (eds.). 1980. Constancy and Change in Human Development. Cambridge, MA: Harvard University Press.

Bronfenbrenner, Urie. 1987. "Family support: The quiet revolution." In America's Family Support Programs, ed. by Sharon L. Kagan, D. Powell, B. Weissbourd, and E. Zigler. New Haven: Yale University Press.

Bronfenbrenner, Urie. 1979. The Ecology of Human Development. Cambridge, MA: Harvard University Press.

Bronfenbrenner, Urie. 1977. "Toward an experimental ecology of human development." American Psychologist 32:513-531.

Bronfenbrenner, Urie, and Heather B. Weiss. 1983. "Beyond policies without people: An ecological perspective on child and family policy." In Children, Families, and Government, ed. by Sharon L. Kagan, E. Klugman, and E. Zigler. Cambridge, MA: Cambridge University Press.

Bronfenbrenner, Urie, and A. Crouter. 1982. "Work and family through time and space." In Families that Work: Children in a Changing World, ed. by S. B. Kammerman and C. D. Hayes. Washington, DC: National Academy Press.

Brooks-Gunn, Jeanne, and D. N. Ruble. 1983. "The experience of menarche from a developmental perspective." In Girls at Puberty: Biological and Psychological Perspectives, ed. by Jeanne Brooks-Gunn and A. C. Petersen. New York: Plenum.

Brown, G. R. J., L. T. Birley, and J. K. Winey. 1972. "Influence of family life on the course of schizophrenic disorders: A replication." British Journal of Psychiatry 121:241-258.

Brown, Ronald T., Kathi A. Borden, Stephen R. Clingerman, and Phillippe

Jenkins. 1988. "Depression in attention deficit-disordered and normal children and their parents." Child Psychiatry and Human Development 18:119-132.

Bruner, J. S. 1977. "Early social interaction and language acquisition." In Studies in Mother-Infant Interaction, ed. by H. R. Schaffer. New York: Academic Press.

Brunk, Molly A., and Scott W. Hengeler. 1984. "Child influence on adult controls: An experimental investigation." Developmental Psychology 20:1074-1081.

Buckhault, Joseph A., Robert B. Rutherford, and K. E. Goldberg. 1978. "Verbal and nonverbal interaction of mothers with their Down's syndrome and nonretarded infants." American Journal of Mental Deficiency 82:337-343.

Budoff, Milton. 1975. "Engendering changes in special education practices." Harvard Educational Review 45:507-526.

Buium, Nissan, John Rynders, and J. Turnure. 1974. "Early maternal linguistic environment of normal and Down's syndrome language-learning children." American Journal of Mental Deficiency 79:52-58.

Burr, Barbara H., Bernard Guyer, I. David Todres, Barbara Abrahams, and Thomas Chiodo. 1983. "Home care for children on respirators." New England Journal of Medicine 309:1319-1323.

Burton, Lindy. 1975. The Family Life of Sick Children. London: Routledge and Kegan Paul.

Butler, J. A., P. Budetti, M. McManus, M. Stenmark, and P. Newachek. 1985. "Health care expenditures for children with chronic diseases." In Chronically Ill Children and Their Families, ed. by N. Hobbs, J. Perrin, and H. Ireys. San Francisco: Jossey Bass.

Butler, N., R. Gill, and D. Pomeroy. 1976. Housing Problems of Handicapped People in Bristol. University of Bristol: Child Health Research Unit.

Byles, J. A., and A. Maurice. 1977. The Juvenile Services Project. Final Report for Submission to the Welfare Grants Directorate, Department of Health and Welfare, Ottawa, Canada.

Cadman, David, Michael Boyle, Peter Szatmari, and David Offord. 1987. "Chronic illness, disability, and mental and social well-being: Findings of the Ontario child health study." Pediatrics 79:805-812.

Callahan, D. 1988. "Families as caregivers: The limits of morality." Archives of Physical Medical Rehabilitation 69:13-19.

Callan, Victor J. 1987. "The personal and marital adjustment of mothers and of voluntarily and involuntarily childless wives." Journal of Marriage and the Family 49:847-856.

Camara, Kathleen A., and G. Resnick. 1988. "Interparental conflict and cooperation: Factors moderating post-divorce adjustment." In Impact of Divorce, Single Parenting, and Stepparenting on Children, ed. by E. Mavis Hetherington and Josephine D. Arasteh. Hillsdale, NJ: Lawrence Erlbaum.

Campbell, Angus, Philip E. Converse, and W. L. Rogers. 1976. The Quality of American Life. New York: Russell Sage Foundation.

Campbell, S. 1979. "Mother-infant interaction as a function of maternal ratings of temperament." Child Psychiatry and Human Development 10:67-76.

Canter, Rachelle J. 1982. "Family correlates of male and female delinquency." Criminology 20:149-167.

Caplan, Paula J. 1988. Don't Blame Mother: Mending the Mother-Daughter Relationship. New York: Harper and Row.

Caplan, Paula J., and Ian Hall-McCorquodale. 1985a. "The scapegoating of mothers: A call for change." American Journal of Orthopsychiatry 55:610-613.

Caplan, Paula J., and Ian Hall-McCorquodale. 1985b. "Mother-blaming in major clinical journals." American Journal of Orthopsychiatry 55:345-353.

Carr, Janet. 1988. "Six weeks to twenty-one years old: A longitudinal study of children with Down's syndrome and their families." Journal of Child Psychology and Psychiatry 29:407-431.

Caspi, Avshalom, and Glen H. Elder, Jr. 1988a. "Convergent family patterns: The inter-generational construction of problem behaviour and relationships." In Relationships Within Families: Mutual Influences, ed. by Robert A. Hinde and Joan Stevenson-Hinde. Oxford: Clarendon Press.

Caspi, Avshalom, and Glen H. Elder, Jr. 1988b. "Childhood precursors of the life course: Early personality and life disorganization." In Child Development in Life Span Perspective, ed. by E. M. Hetherington, R. M. Lerner and M. Perlmutter. Hillsdale, NJ: Lawrence Erlbaum.

Caspi, Avshalom, Glenn H. Elder, Jr., and Daryl Bem. 1988. "Moving away from the world: life-course patterns of shy children." Developmental Psychology 24:824-831.

Cernkovich, Stephen A., and Peggy C. Giordano. 1987. "Family relationships and delinquency." Criminology 25:295-321.

Chapman, Christine. 1976. America's Runaways. New York: Morrow.

Charles, Andrew V. 1986. "Physically abused parents." Journal of Family Violence 4:343-355.

Chess, Stella, and A. Thomas. 1982. "Infant bonding: Mystique and reality." American Journal of Orthopsychiatry 52:213-222.

Chodorow, Nancy. 1978. The Reproduction of Mothering: Psychoanalysis and the Sociology of Gender. Berkeley: University of California Press.

Chodorow, Nancy, and Susan Contratto. 1982. "The fantasy of the perfect mother." In Rethinking the Family. Some Feminist Questions, ed. by Barrie Thorne with Marilyn Yalom. New York: Longman.

Christensen, Andrew, and Gayla Margolin. 1988. "Conflict and alliance in distressed and non-distressed families." In Relationships Within Families: Mutual Influences, ed. by Robert A. Hinde and Joan Stevenson-Hinde. Oxford: Clarendon Press.

Cicirelli, Victor G. 1976. "Mother-child and sibling-sibling interactions on a problem-solving task. "Child Development 47:588-596.

Clarke-Stewart, K. Allison. 1978. "And daddy makes three: The father's impact on mother and young child." Child Development 49:466-478.

Clarke-Stewart, K. Allison. 1973. "Interaction between mothers and their young children: Characteristics and consequences." Monographs of the Society for Research in Child Development 153, 38:6-7.

Clausen, John A. 1986. The Life Course. A Sociological Perspective. Englewood Cliffs, NJ: Prentice Hall.

Cleary, Paul D., and David Mechanic. 1983. "Sex differences in psychological distress among married people." Journal of Health and Social Behavior 24:111-121.

Clingempeel, W. Glen, Eulalee Brand, and Sion Segal. 1987. "A multilevel-multivariable developmental perspective for future research on stepfamilies." In Remarriage and Stepparenting, ed. by Kay Pasley and Marilyn Ihinger-Tallman. New York: Guilford Press.

Clingempeel, W. Glen. 1981. "Quasi-kin relationships and marital quality in stepfather families." Journal of Personality and Social Psychology 41:890-901.

Cohen, Elizabeth G. 1982. "Expectation states and inter-racial integration in school settings." Annual Review of Sociology 8:209-235.

Cohen, Susan, and Mary F. Katzenstein. 1988. "The war over the family is not over the family." In Feminism, Children, and the New Families, ed. by S. M. Dornbusch and M. H. Strober. New York: Guilford Press.

Cohen, Elizabeth G., and Susan S. Roper. 1972. "Modification of inter-racial interaction disability: An application of status characteristics theory." American Sociological Review 37:643-647.

Colerick, Elizabeth J., and Linda K. George. 1986. "Predictors of institutionalization among caregivers of patients with Alzheimer's disease." Journal of the American Geriatric Society 34:493-498.

Comer, J. 1989. "Poverty, family and the black experience." In Giving Children a Chance, ed. by George Miller. Washington, DC: Center for National Policy Press.

Contratto, Susan. 1983. "Psychology views mothers and mothering 1897-1980." In Feminist Re-visions: What Has Been and Might Be, ed. by Vivian Patraka and Louise A. Tilly. Ann Arbor, MI: University of Michigan Press.

Cook, Judith A. 1988. "Who 'mothers' the chronically mentally ill?" Family Relations 37:42-49.

Cook, Judith A., and B. Cohler. 1986. "Reciprocal socialization and the care of offspring with cancer and with schizophrenia." In Lifespan Developmental Psychology, ed. by N. Datan, A. Greene and H. Reese. Hillsdale, NJ: Lawrence Erlbaum.

Cornell, Dewey G. 1984. Families of Gifted Children. Ann Arbor, MI: UMI Research Press.

Cowan, P. A., and C. P. Cowan. 1985 (April). "Pregnancy, parenthood, and children at three." Paper presented at the meetings of the Society for Research in Child Development. Toronto.

Cox, Martha J., Margaret T. Owen, Jerry M. Lewis, and V. Kay Henderson.

1989. "Marriage, adult adjustment, and early parenting." Child Development 60:1015-1024.

Crnic, Keith, and Mark Greenberg. 1987. "Maternal stress, social support, and coping: Influences on the early mother-infant relationship." In Research on Support for Parents and Infants in the Postnatal Period, ed. by C. F. Zachariah Boukydis. Norwood, NJ: Ablex Publishing.

Crnic, Keith A., Mark T. Greenberg, A. S. Ragozin, W. M. Robinson and R. Basham. 1983. "Effects of stress and social support on mothers and premature and full-term infants." Child Development 54:209-217.

Crockenberg, Susan B. 1987. "Support for adolescent mothers during the postnatal period: Theory and research." In Research on Support for Parents and Infants in the Postnatal Period, ed. by P. F. Zachariak Boukydis. Norwood, NJ: Ablex Publishing.

Crockenberg, Susan B. 1986. "Are temperamental differences in babies associated with predictable differences in care giving?" In Temperament and Social Interaction in Infants and Children, ed. by Jacqueline V. Lerner and R. M. Lerner. San Francisco: Jossey-Bass Inc.

Crockenberg, Susan B. 1981. "Infant instability, mother responsiveness, and social support influences on the security of infant-mother attachment." Child Development 52:857-865.

Cummings, Jennifer S., David S. Pellegrini, I. Clifford, and E. Mark Cummings. 1989. "Children's responses to angry adult behavior as a function of marital distress and history of interparent hostility." Child Development 60:1035-1043.

Cummings, S. T. 1976. "The impact of the child's deficiency on the father: A study of fathers of mentally retarded and chronically ill children." American Journal of Orthopsychiatry 46:246-255.

Cummings, S. T., H. C. Bayley, and H. E. Rie. 1966. "Effects of the child's deficiency on the mother: A study of mothers of mentally retarded, chronically ill, and neurotic children." American Journal of Orthopsychiatry 36:595-608.

Curtis James E., and William G. Scott. 1979. Social Stratification in Canada, 2nd. ed. Scarborough, Ontario: Prentice-Hall.

Curtis, James E., Edward G. Grabb, L. Neil Guppy and Sid Gilbert (eds.). 1988. Social Inequality Stratification in Canada: Patterns, Problems and Policies. Scarborough, Ontario: Prentice-Hall.

Damrosch, Shirley Petchel, and Lesley A. Perry. 1989. "Self-reported adjustment, chronic sorrow, and coping of parents of children with Down syndrome." Nursing Research 38:25-30.

Daniels, Pamela, and Kathy Weingarten. 1982. Sooner or Later: The Timing of Parenthood in Adult Life. New York: Norton.

Darling, Roslyn B. 1988. "Parental entrepreneurship: A consumerist response to professional dominance." Journal of Social Issues 44:141-158.

Darling, Roslyn B. 1987. "The economic and psychosocial consequences of disability: Family-society relationships." Marriage and Family Review 11:45-61.

Darling, Roslyn B. 1983. "Parent-professional interaction." In The Family With a Handicapped Child: Understanding and Treatment, ed. by Martin Seligman. New York: Grune and Stratton.

Davidson, J. R. 1972. "Postpartum mood change in Jamaican women: A description and discussion of its significance." British Journal of Psychiatry 121:659-663.

Deal, James E., Charles F. Halverson, Jr., and Karen S. Wampler. 1989. "Parental agreement on child-rearing orientations: Relations to parental, marital, family, and child characteristics." Child Development 60:1025-1034.

Deatrick, Janet A., Kathleen A. Knafl, and Michelle Walsh. 1988. "The process of parenting a child with a disability: Normalization through accommodation." Journal of Advanced Nursing 13:15-21.

Deiner, Penny L. 1987. "Systems of care for disabled children and family members: New paradigms and alternatives." Marriage and Family Review 11:193-211.

deMause, Lloyd. 1982. "The evolution of childhood." In The Sociology of Childhood, ed. by Chris Jenks. London: Bat Ford.

deMause, Lloyd. 1974. "The evolution of childhood." In The History of Childhood, ed. by L. deMause. New York: Psychohistory Press.

Demo, David H., and Alan C. Acock. 1988. "The impact of divorce on children." Journal of Marriage and the Family 50:619-648.

Demos, John. 1970. A Little Commonwealth: Family Life in Plymouth Colony. New York: Oxford University Press.

Dickie, Jane R., and Sharon Carnahan Gerber. 1980. "Training in social competence: The effect on mothers, fathers and infants." Child Development 51:1248-1251.

Dinnerstein, Dorothy. 1976. The Mermaid and the Minotaur. New York: Harper & Row.

Dishion, T. J., G. R. Patterson, M. Stoolmiller, and M. L. Skinner. 1991. "Family, school, and behavioral antecedents to early adolescent with antisocial peers." Developmental Psychology 27:172-180.

Doll, William S. 1975. "Home is not sweet anymore." Mental Hygiene 59:2204-2206.

Donzelot, Jacques. 1979. The Policing of Families. New York: Random House.

Dornbusch, Sanford M., and Kathryn D. Gray. 1988. "Single-parent families." In Feminism, Children, and the New Families, ed. by S. M. Dornbusch and M. H. Strober. New York: The Guilford Press.

Dornbusch, Sanford M., P. L. Ritter, P. H. Leiderman, D. F. Roberts, and M. J. Fraleigh. 1987. "The relation of parenting style to adolescent school performance." Child Development 58:1244-1257.

Dornbusch, Sanford M., and Myra H. Strober (eds.). 1988. Feminism, Children and the New Families. New York: The Guilford Press.

Dunn, Judy, and Robert Plomin. 1990. Separate Lives: Why Siblings are so Different. New York: Basic Books.

Dupont, A. 1980. "A study concerning the time-related and other burdens when severely handicapped children are reared at home." In Epidemiological Research as Basis for the Organization of Extramural Psychiatry. Acta Psychiatrica Scandinavica 62, Supplement 285:249-257.

Eagles, J. M., A. Craig, F. Rawlinson, D. B. Restall, J. A. G. Beattie, and J. A. O. Besson. 1987. "The psychological well-being of supporters of the demented elderly." British Journal of Psychiatry 150:293-298.

Eckholm, E. 1986. "Schizophrenia's victims include strained families." The New York Times, March 17, p. 45.

Edginton, Barry. 1989. Health, Disease and Medicine in Canada. A Sociological Perspective. Toronto: Butterworths.

Ehrenreich, Barbara, and Dierdre English. 1986. "The sexual politics of sickness." In The Sociology of Health and Illness: Critical Perspectives, 2nd ed., ed. by Peter Conrad and Rochelle Kern. New York: St. Martin's Press.

Eichler, Margrit. 1988. Families in Canada Today: Recent Changes and Their Policy Consequences, 2nd ed. Toronto: Gage Educational Publishers.

Elder, Glen H. Jr. 1974. Children of the Great Depression. Chicago: University of Chicago Press.

Elder, Glen H. Jr., Jeffrey K. Liker, and Catherine E. Cross. 1984. "Parent-child behavior in the Great Depression: Life course and intergenerational influences." In Life-Span Development and Behavior, Vol. 6, ed. by Paul B. Baltes and Orville G. Brim, Jr. New York: Academic Press.

Elliott, Delbert S., David Huizinga, and Suzanne S. Ageton. 1985. Explaining Delinquency and Drug Use. Beverly Hills, CA: Sage.

Elliott, Glen R., and Carl Eisdorfer (eds.). 1982. Stress and Human Health: Analysis and Implications for Research. New York: Springer.

Ennew, Judith. 1986. The Sexual Exploitation of Children. Cambridge: Polity Press.

Epenshade, T. J. 1980 (September). "Raising a child can now cost $85,000." Intercom, Population Reference Bureau 8:10-13.

Falkman, C. 1977. "Cystic fibrosis: A psychological study of 52 children and their families." Acta Paediatrica Scandinavica, Supplement 269.

Falloon, Ian R. H., and Jean Pederson. 1985. "Family management in the prevention of morbidity of schizophrenia: The adjustment of the family unit." British Journal of Psychiatry 147:156-163.

Farrington, David P. 1986. "Stepping Stones to Adult Criminal Careers." In Development of Antisocial and Prosocial Behavior, ed. by D. Olwens, J. Block, and M. R. Yarrow. New York: Academic Press.

Farrington, David P. 1982. "Longitudinal analyses of criminal violence." In Criminal Violence, ed. by Marvin E. Wolfgang and Neil A. Weiner. Beverly Hills: Sage.

Farrington, David P. 1978. "Family background of aggressive youths." In Aggressive and Anti-social Behavior in Childhood and Adolescence, ed. by Lionel A. Hersov, M. Berger, and David Shaffer. New York: Pergamon Press.

Farrington, David P., G. Gundry, and D. J. West. 1975. "The familial transmission of criminality." Medicine, Science and the Law 15:177-186.

Feagin, Joe R. 1987. "Changing Black Americans to fit a racist system." Journal of Social Issues 43:85-89.

Featherman, David L., and Richard M. Lerner. 1986. "Ontogenesis and sociogenesis: Problematics for theory and research about development and socialization across the life span." American Sociological Review 10:659-676.

Feigelman, William, and Arnold Silverman. 1984. "The long-term effects of transracial adoption." The Social Service Review 58:588-602.

Feinman, Saul, and Michael Lewis. 1984. "Is there social life beyond the dyad?" In Beyond the Dyad, ed. by Michael Lewis. New York: Plenum Press.

Feiring, Candice, and Michael Lewis. 1984. "Changing characteristics of the U.S. family." In Beyond the Dyad, ed. by Michael Lewis. New York: Plenum Press.

Feiring, Candice, and Michael Lewis. 1982. "Early mother-child interaction: Families with only and firstborn children." In The Childbearing Decision, ed. by G. L. Fox. Beverly Hills, CA: Sage.

Feldman, R. A., T. E. Kaplinger, and J. S. Wodarski. 1983. The St. Louis Conundrum: The Effective Treatment of Anti-Social Youths. Englewood Cliffs, NJ: Prentice-Hall.

Feldman, Shirley S., Sharon C. Nash, and Barbara G. Aschenbrenner. 1983. "Antecedents of fathering." Child Development 54:1628-1636.

Felner, Robert D., Janet F. Gillespie, and Rebecca Smith. 1985. "Risk and vulnerability in childhood: A reappraisal." Journal of Clinical Child Psychology 14:2-4.

Ferguson, David M., L. John Horwood, and Michael Lloyd. 1990. "The Effect of preschool children on family stability." Journal of Marriage and the Family 52:531-538.

Ferri, Elsa. 1976. Growing Up in a One-Parent Family: A Long-Term Study of Child Development. London: NFER Publishing Co.

Feshback, Norma D., and Seymour Feshback. 1978. "Toward an historical social, and developmental perspective on children's rights." Journal of Social Issues 34:1-7.

Finch, Janet, and Dulcie Groves (eds.). 1983. A Labour of Love. Women, Work and Caring. London: Routledge & Kegan Paul.

Firestone, Shulamith. 1970. The Dialectic of Sex. The Case for Feminist Revolution. New York: Bantam Books.

Fischer, Claude S. 1982. To Dwell Among Friends. Personal Networks in Town and City. Chicago. The University of Chicago Press.

Fishbein, Diana H. 1990. "Biological perspectives in criminology." Criminology 28:27-57.

Fodden, G. B. 1984. The relatives of patients with depressive disorders: A typology of burden and strategies for coping. M. Phil. thesis, Institute of Psychiatry, London University.

Foster, Martha A., and Michael Berger. 1985. "Research with handicapped children: A multilevel systemic perspective." In The Handbook of Family Psychology and Therapy, ed. by Luciano L'Abate. Homewood, IL: The Dorsey Press.

Foster, S., and D. Hoskins. 1981. "Home care of the child with a tracheotomy tube." Pediatric Clinics of North America 28:855-857.

Fraser, Nancy. 1987. "Women, welfare and the politics of need interpretation." Hypatia 2:103-121.

Frates, Ralph, Jr., Mark Splaingard, E. O. Smith, and Gunyon M. Harrison. 1985. "Outcome of home mechanical ventilation in children." The Journal of Pediatrics 106:850-856.

Freedman, Ronald. 1968. "Norms for family size in underdeveloped areas." Reprinted in Readings on Population, ed. by D. M. Heer. Englewood Cliffs, NJ: Prentice-Hall.

Friday, Nancy. 1977. My Mother/My Self. New York: Delacorte.

Fried, S., and P. Holt. 1980. "Parent education: One strategy for the prevention of child abuse." In Handbook on Parent Education, ed. by Marvin J. Fine. New York: Academic Press.

Furstenberg, Frank F., Jr. 1988. "Child care after divorce and remarriage." In Impact of Divorce, Single Parenting, and Stepparenting on Children, ed. by E. Mavis Hetherington and J. D. Arasteh. Hillsdale, NJ: Lawrence Erlbaum.

Furstenberg, Frank F., Jr. 1987. "The new extended family: The experience of parents and children after remarriage." In Remarriage and Stepparenting, ed. by Kay Pasley and Marilyn Ihinger-Tallman. New York: Guilford Press.

Furstenberg, Frank F., Jr. 1985. "Sociological ventures in child development." Child Development 56:281-288.

Furstenberg, Frank F., Jr., S. Philip Morgan, and Paul D. Allison. 1987. "Paternal participation and children's well-being after marital dissolution." American Sociological Review 52:695-701.

Galambos, Nancy L., and Jacqueline V. Lerner. 1987. "Child characteristics and the employment of mothers with young children: A longitudinal study." Journal of Child Psychology and Psychiatry 28:87-98.

Gallagher, James John, P. Beckman, and A. H. Cross. 1983. "Families of handicapped children: Sources of stress and its amelioration." Exceptional Children 50:10-19.

Ganong, Lawrence H., and Marilyn Coleman. 1987a. "Effects of children on parental sex-role orientation." Journal of Family Issues 8:278-290.

Ganong, Lawrence H., and Marilyn Coleman. 1987b. "Effects of parental remarriage on children: An updated comparison of theories, methods, and findings from clinical and empirical research." In Remarriage and Stepparenting, ed. by Kay Pasley and Marilyn Ihinger-Tallman. New York: Guilford Press.

Garbarino, James. 1982. Children and Families in the Social Environment. New York: Aldine.

Gard, Gary C., and Kenneth K. Berry. 1986. "Oppositional children: Taming tyrants." Journal of Clinical Child Psychology 15:148-158.

Gath, Ann, and Dianne Gumley. 1986. "Family background of children with

Down's syndrome and of children with a similar degree of mental retardation.'' British Journal of Psychiatry 149:161-171.

Gath, Ann. 1978. Down's Syndrome and the Family: The Early Years. London: Academic Press.

Gath, Ann. 1977. ''The impact of an abnormal child upon the parents.'' British Journal of Psychology 130:405-410.

Gayton, W. F., S. B. Friedman, J. F. Tavoramina and F. Tucker. 1977. ''Children with Cystic Fibrosis: 1. Psychological test findings of patients, parents and siblings.'' Pediatrics 59:888-894.

Geisman, Ludwig L., and Katherine M. Wood. 1986. Family and Delinquency. Resocializing the young offender. New York: Human Sciences Press.

Gelles, Richard J. 1989. ''Child abuse and violence in single-parent families: Parent absence and economic deprivation.'' American Journal of Orthopsychiatry 59:492-501.

Gelles, Richard J., and Claire P. Cornell. 1985. Intimate Violence in Families. Beverly Hills, CA: Sage.

Gilleard, C. J. 1984. ''Problems posed by supporting relatives of geriatric and psychogeriatric day patients.'' Acta Psychiatrica Scandinavica 70:198-208.

Gilleard, C. J., H. Belford, E. Gilleard, J. E. Whittick, and K. Gledhill. 1984. ''Emotional distress amongst the supporters of the elderly mentally infirm.'' British Journal of Psychiatry 145:172-177.

Gilleard, C. J., E. Gilleard, and J. E. Whittick, 1984. ''Impact of psychogeriatric day hospital care on the patient's family.'' British Journal of Psychiatry 145:487-492.

Gillis, John R. 1981. Youth and History. Tradition and Change in European Age Relations, 1770-Present. New York: Academic Press.

Giordano, Peggy C., Stephen A. Cernkovich, and M. D. Pugh. 1985. ''Friendships and delinquency.'' American Journal of Sociology 91:1170-1202.

Giovannoni, R. 1984. ''Chronic ventilator care: From hospital to home.'' Respiratory Therapy 29:29-33.

Glascoe, Frances P., and William E. MacLean. 1990. ''How parents appraise their child's development.'' Family Relations 39:280-283.

Glaser, Kristin. 1987. ''A comparative study of social support for new mothers of twins.'' In Research on Support for Parents and Infants in the Postnatal Period, ed. by C. F. Zachariah Boukydis. Norwood, NJ: Ablex Publishing.

Glendinning, Caroline. 1983. Unshared Care. London: Routledge and Kegan Paul.

Glenn, Norval D., and Sara McLanahan. 1982. ''Children and marital happiness: A further specification of the relationship.'' Journal of Marriage and the Family 44:63-72.

Glenn, Norval D., and Charles N. Weaver. 1979. ''A note on family situation and global happiness.'' Social Forces 57:269-282.

Goetting, Ann. 1980. ''Former spouse-current spouse relationship.'' Journal of Family Issues 1:350-378.

Goldscheider, Calvin. 1971. Population, Modernization and Social Structure. Boston: Little, Brown.

Goldstein, H. S. 1984. "Parental composition, supervision, and conduct problems in youth 12 to 17 years old." Journal of the American Academy of Child Psychiatry 23:679-684.

Goode, David. 1986. "Kids, culture and innocents." Human Studies 9:83-106.

Goodman, C. 1986. "Research on the informal carer: A selected literature review." Journal of Advanced Nursing 11:705-712.

Gosher-Gottstein, E. R. 1979. "Family of twins: A longitudinal study of coping." Twins: Newsletter of the International Society for Twin Studies 2:4-5.

Gottlieb, Benjamin H. 1989. "A contextual perspective on stress in family care of the elderly." Canadian Psychology 30:596-607.

Gove, Walter R., and Robert D. Crutchfield. 1982. "The family and juvenile delinquency." The Sociological Quarterly 23:301-319.

Government of Canada. 1984. "Summary of sexual offences against children in Canada"; report of the Committee on Sexual Offences against Children and Youths.

Grad, Jacqueline, and Peter Sainsbury. 1963. "Mental illness in the family." Lancet 1:544-547.

Graham, Hilary. 1985. "Providers, negotiators, and mediators: Women as the hidden carers." In Women, Health, and Healing, ed. by Ellen Lewin and Virginia Olesen. London: Tavistock.

Graham, Hilary. 1983. "Social policy: Psychology subordinated to economics." In A Labour of Love: Women, Work and Caring, ed. by Janet Finch and Dulcie Groves. London: Routledge and Kegan Paul.

Grant, Linda, Layne A. Simpson, Xue Rong, and Holly Peters-Golden. 1990. "Gender, parenthood, and work hours of physicians." Journal of Marriage and the Family 52:39-49.

Gregory, S. 1976. The Deaf Child and His Family. London: George Allan & Unwin.

Greif, Esther B., and Kathleen J. Ulman. 1982. "The psychological impact of menarche on early adolescent females: A review of the literature." Child Development 53:1413-1430.

Greif, Geoffrey, L. 1985. Single Fathers. Lexington, MA: Lexington Books.

Grotevant, Harold, Ruth G. McRoy and Vivian Y. Jenkins. 1988. "Emotionally disturbed, adopted adolescents: Early patterns of family adaptation." Family Process 27:439-457.

Grow, Lucille J., and Deborah Shapiro. 1974. Black Children-White Parents: A Study of Transracial Adoption. New York: Child Welfare League of America.

Gubman, Gayle D., and Richard C. Tessler. 1987. "The impact of mental illness on families." Journal of Family Issues 8:226-245.

Haines, Michael R. 1985. "The life cycle, savings, and demographic adaptation: Some historical evidence for the United States and Europe." In Gender and the Life Course, ed. by Alice S. Rossi. New York: Aldine.

Hall, G. Stanley. 1904. Adolescence: Its Psychology and Its Relation to Physiology, Anthropology, Sociology, Sex Crime, Religion and Education. New York: Appleton.

Hallinan, Maureen. 1982. "Classroom racial composition and children's friendships." Social Forces 61:56-72.

Halpern, Robert. 1990. "Poverty and early childhood parenting: Toward a framework for intervention." American Journal of Orthopsychiatry 60:6-18.

Hardman, Michael L., C. J. Drew, and M. W. Egan. 1987. Human Exceptionality: Society, School and Family, 2nd ed. Boston: Allyn and Bacon.

Hareven, Tamara K. 1977. "Family and work patterns of immigrant laborers in a planned industrial town, 1900-1930." In Immigrants in Industrial America, ed. by Richard L. Ehrlich. Charlottesville: University Press of Virginia.

Harper, Lawrence V. 1975. "The scope of offspring effects: From caregiver to culture." Psychological Bulletin 82:784-801.

Hartup, Willard W. 1982. "Symmetries and asymmetries in children's relationships." In Perspectives in Child Study, ed. by Jan de Wit and Arthur L. Benton. Amsterdam: Lisse.

Haskell, Martin R., and Lewis Yablonsky. 1982. Juvenile Delinquency, 3rd edition. Boston: Houghton Mifflin Co.

Hatfield, Agnes B. 1979. "The family as a partner in the treatment of mental illness." Hospital and Community Psychiatry 30:338-340.

Hatfield, Agnes B. 1978. "Psychological costs of schizophrenia to the family." Social Work 355-359.

Hawkins, R. P., and P. Meadowcroft. 1984. "Practical program evaluation in a family-based treatment program for disturbing and disturbed youngsters." Unpublished manuscript. Morganstown: West Virginia University, Department of Psychology.

Heffner, Elaine. 1978. The Emotional Experience of Motherhood after Freud and Feminism. New York: Doubleday.

Herbert, Martin. 1987. Conduct Disorders of Childhood and Adolescence. 2nd ed. Chichester, U.K.: John Wiley & Sons.

Herz, Marvin I., Jean Endicott, and M. Gibbon. 1979. "Brief hospitalization: Two-year follow-up." Archives of General Psychiatry 36:701-705.

Hetherington, E. Mavis. 1989. "Coping with family transitions: Winners, losers, and survivors." Child Development 60:1-14.

Hetherington, E. Mavis. 1987. "Family relations six years after divorce." In Remarriage and Stepparenting, ed. by Kay Pasley and Marilyn Ihinger-Tallman. New York: Guilford Press.

Hetherington, E. Mavis, and Paul B. Baltes. 1988. "Child psychology and life-span development." In Child Development in Life-Span Perspective, ed. by E. M. Hetherington, R. M. Lerner, and M. Perlmutter. Hillsdale, NJ: Lawrence Erlbaum.

Hetherington, E. Mavis, Kathleen A. Camara, and David L. Featherman. 1983. "Achievement and intellectual functioning of children in one-parent households." In Achievement and Achievement Motives: Psychological and Sociological Approaches, ed. by Janet T. Spence. San Francisco: W. H. Freeman.

Hetherington, E. Mavis, E. M. Cox, and R. Cox. 1982. "Effects of divorce on parents and children." In Nontraditional Families: Parenting and Child Development, ed. by Michael E. Lamb. Hillsdale, NJ: Lawrence Erlbaum.

Hewitt, S. 1976. "Research on families with handicapped children: An aid or impediment to understanding?" Birth Defects 12:35-46.

Hill, John P., and G. N. Holmbeck. 1987. "Familial adaptation to biological change during adolescence." In Biological-psychological Interactions in Early Adolescence: A Life-span Perspective, ed. by Richard M. Lerner and T. Foch. Hillsdale, NJ: Lawrence Erlbaum.

Hill, John P. 1980. "The family." In Toward Adolescence: The Middle School Years, ed. by M. Johnson. Chicago: University of Chicago Press.

Hill, John P., G. N. Holmbeck, L. Marlow, T. M. Green, and M. E. Lynch. 1985. "Menarcheal status and parent-child relations in families of seventh-grade girls." Journal of Youth and Adolescence 14:301-316.

Hirschi, Travis. 1969. Causes of Delinquency. Berkeley, CA: University of California Press.

Hobart, Charles. 1988. "The family system in remarriage: An exploratory study." Journal of Marriage and the Family 50:649-662.

Hochschild, Arlie. 1983. The Managed Heart. Berkeley: The University of California Press.

Hoffman, Lois W. 1984. "Maternal employment and the young child." In Minnesota Symposium in Child Psychology, ed. by M. Perlmutter. Hillsdale, NJ: Lawrence Erlbaum.

Hoffman, Lois, W. 1978. "Influences of children on marital interaction and parental satisfactions and dissatisfactions." In Child Influences on Marital and Family Interactions, ed. by R. Lerner and G. B. Spanier. New York: Academic Press.

Hoffman, Lois W. 1975. "The value of children to parents and the decrease in family size." Proceedings of the American Philosophical Society 119:430-438.

Hoffman, Lois W., and J. D. Manis. 1979. "The value of childcare in the United States: A new approach to the study of fertility." Journal of Marriage and the Family 41:583-596.

Hogan, Dennis P., Ling-Xin Hao, and William L. Parish. 1990. "Race, kin networks, and assistance to mother-headed families." Social Forces 68:797-812.

Holden, George W. 1990. "Parenthood." In Handbook of Family Measurement Techniques, ed. by John Touliatos, Barry F. Perlmutter, and Murray A. Strauss. New York: Sage.

Hollingshead, August B., and Frederich C. Redlich. 1958. Social Class and Mental Illness. A Community Study. New York: John Wiley.

Holroyd, Jean. 1976. "Mental retardation and stress on the parents: A contrast between Down's syndrome and childhood autism." American Journal of Mental Deficiency 80:431-436.

Holroyd, Jean. 1975. "Stress in families of institutionalized and non-institutionalized autistic children." Journal of Community Psychiatry 2:26-31.

Holroyd, Jean. 1974. "The questionnaire on resources and stress: An instrument to measure family response to a handicapped family member." Journal of Community Psychiatry 2:92-94.

Howes, Paul, and Howard J. Markham. 1989. "Marital quality and child functioning: A longitudinal investigation." Child Development 60:1044-1051.

Huesmann, L. Rowell, Leonard D. Eron, Monroe M. Lefkowitz, and Leopold O. Walder. 1984. "The stability of aggression over time and generations." Developmental Psychology 20:1120-1134.

Hughes, Michael, and David M. Demo. 1989. "Self-perception of Black Americans: Self-esteem and personal efficacy." American Journal of Sociology 95:132-159.

Humphrey, Michael. 1977. "Sex differences in attitude to parenthood." Human Relations 30:737-749.

Ishii-Kuntz, Masako, and Karen Seccombe. 1989. "The impact of children upon social support networks throughout the life course." Journal of Marriage and the Family 51:777-790.

Jeffries, Vincent, and H. Edward Ransford. 1980. Social Stratification: A Multiple Hierarchy Approach. Boston: Allyn and Bacon.

Jensen, Gary J., and Raymond Eve. 1975. "Sex differences in delinquency." Criminology 13:427-448.

Jensen, Larry, C. 1985. Adolescence. Theories, Research, Applications. New York: West Publishing Co.

Johnson, Richard E. 1985. "Family structure and delinquency: General patterns and gender differences." Criminology 24:65-80.

Kagan, Sharon L., and A. Shelley. 1987. "The promise and problems of family support programs." In America's Family Support Programs, ed. by Sharon L. Kagan, D. R. Powell, B. Weissbourd and E. Zigler. New Haven: Yale University Press.

Kahn, Robert, and Toni Antonucci. 1980. "Convoys over the life course: Attachment, roles and social support." In Life-span Development and Behavior, vol. 3, ed. by Paul B. Baltes and O.G. Brim. New York: Academic Press.

Kanter, J., H. R. Lamb, and C. Loeper. 1987. "Expressed emotion in families: A critical review." Hospital and Community Psychiatry 38:374-380.

Kazak, Anne E. 1987. "Professional helpers and families with disabled children: A social network perspective." Marriage and Family Review 11:177-191.

Kazak, Anne E., and A. Clark. 1986. "Stress in families of children with myleomeningocele." Developmental Medicine and Child Neurology 28:220-228.

Kazak, Anne E., and Robert S. Marvin. 1984. "Differences, difficulties and adaptation: Stress and social networks in families with a handicapped child." Family Relations 33:66-77.

Keith, Verna M., and Barbara Finley. 1988. "The impact of parental divorce on children's educational attainment, marital timing, and likelihood of divorce." Journal of Marriage and the Family 50:797-810.

Kelley, Penelope. 1976. "The relation of infant's temperament and mother's psychopathology to interactions in early infancy." In The Developing Individual in a Changing World (vol. II), ed. by Klaus F. Riegel and John A. Meacham. Chicago: Aldine.

Kendrick, C., and J. Dunn. 1980. "Caring for a second baby: Effects on interaction between mother and first born." Developmental Psychology 16:303-311.

Kert, Bernice. 1983. The Hemingway Women. New York: W. W. Norton.

Kessler, Ronald, and James McRae, Jr. 1982. "The effects of wives' employment on the mental health of married men and women." American Sociological Review 47:216-227.

Kett, Joseph F. 1977. Rites of Passage: Adolescence in America 1790 to the Present. New York: Basic Books.

Kew, Stephen. 1975. Handicap and Family Crisis. London: Pitman.

Kidwell, Jeanne S. 1981. "Number of siblings, sibling spacing, sex, and birth order: Their effects on perceived parent-adolescent relationships." Journal of Marriage and the Family 43:315-332.

Kinney, Jennifer M., and Mary Ann Parris Stephens. 1989. "Caregiving hassles scale: Assessing the daily hassles of caring for a family member with dementia." The Gerontologist 29:328-332.

Klaus, Marshall H., and John H. Kennell. 1976. Mother-infant Bonding: The Impact of Early Separation or Loss on Family Development. St. Louis: Mosby.

Klein, S. 1976. "Measuring the outcome of the impact of chronic childhood illness on the family." In Chronic Childhood Illness: Assessment of Outcome, ed. by G. Grave and I. Pless. Washington, DC: U.S. Department of Health, Education and Welfare, No. 76-877.

Koch, Helen L. 1955. "The relation of certain family constellation characteristics and the attitudes of children toward adults." Child Development 26:13-40.

Kochanska, Grazyna, Leon Kuczynski, and Marian Radke-Yarrow. 1989. "Correspondence between mothers' self-reported and observed child-rearing practices." Child Development 60:56-63.

Koeske, Gary F., and Randi D. Koeske. 1990. "The buffering effect of social support on parental stress." American Journal of Orthopsychiatry 60:440-451.

Koller, Marvin R. 1974. Families. A Multigenerational Approach. New York: McGraw-Hill.

Konstantareas, M. et al. 1983. "Mothers of autistic children: Are they the 'unacknowledged victims?'" Paper presented to the Canadian Psychological Association. Winnipeg.

Korner, A. F. 1971. "Individual differences at birth: Implications for early experience and later development." American Journal of Orthopsychiatry 41:608-619.

Krantz, Susan E. 1988. "Divorce and children." In Feminism, Children, and the New Families, ed. by Sanford M. Dornbusch and Myra H. Strober. New York: Guilford Press.

Krause, Neal. 1983. "The racial context of Black self-esteem." Social Psychology Quarterly 46:98-107.

Kreisman, Dolores E., S. J. Simmens, and Virginia D. Joy. 1979. "Deinstitutionalization and the family's well-being." Paper presented at the meeting of the American Psychological Association, New York.

Kurdek, Lawrence. 1990. "Effects of child age on the marital quality and psychological distress of newly married mothers and stepfathers." Journal of Marriage and the Family 52:81-85.

Kurdek, Lawrence A., and D. Blisk. 1983. "Dimensions and correlates of mothers' divorce experiences." Journal of Divorce 6:1-24.

Lamb, Michael (ed.). 1987. The Father's Role: Cross-cultural Perspectives. Hillsdale, NJ: Lawrence Erlbaum.

Lamb, Michael. 1983. "Fathers of exceptional children." In The Family with a Handicapped Child: Understanding and Treatment, ed. by Martin Seligman. New York: Grune and Stratton.

Lamb, Michael E., and A. B. Elster. 1985. "Adolescent mother-infant-father relationships." Developmental Psychology 21:760-773.

Lamb, Michael E., and Kathleen E. Gilbride. 1985. "Compatibility in parent-infant relationships: Origins and processes." In Compatibility and Incompatible Relationships, ed. by William Ickes. New York: Springer-Verlag.

Lamb, Michael E., J. H. Pleck, and J. A. Levine. 1985. "The role of the father in child development: The effects of increased paternal involvement." In Advances in Clinical Child Psychology, vol. 8, ed. by B.S. Lakey and A.E. Kazdin. New York: Plenum.

Land, Hilary. 1978. "Who cares for the family?" Journal of Social Policy 7:13-35.

Land, Hilary. 1977. "Inequalities in large families—more of the same or different?" In Equalities and Inequalities in Family Life, ed. by Robert Chester and John Peel. London: Academic Press.

LaRossa, Ralph, and M. LaRossa. 1981. Transition to Parenthood: How Infants Change Families. Beverly Hills, CA: Sage.

Leff, Julian, Liz Kuipers, Ruth Berkowitz, Rosemarie Eberlein-Vries, and David Sturgeon. 1982. "A controlled trial of social intervention in the families of schizophrenic patients." British Journal of Psychiatry 141:121-124.

Lefkowitz, Monroe M., Leonard D. Eron, Leopold O. Walder, and L. Rowel Huesman. 1977. Growing Up to Be Violent: A Longitudinal Study of the Development of Aggression. New York: Pergamon.

Leigh, Geoffrey K. 1982. "Kinship interaction over the family life span." Journal of Marriage and the Family 44:197-208.

Lein, L. 1979. "Male participation in home life: Impact of social supports and breadwinner responsibility on the allocation of tasks." Family Coordinator 28:489-495.

Lempers, Jacques D., Dania Clark-Lempers, and Ronald L. Simons. 1989. "Economic hardship, parenting, and distress in adolescence." Child Development 60:25-39.

Lerner, Jacqueline V., and Nancy L. Galambos. 1986a. "The child's development and family change: The influences of maternal employment." In Advances in Infancy Research, vol. 4, ed. by L. P. Lipsitt. Hillsdale, NJ: Ablex.

Lerner, Jacqueline V., and Nancy L. Galambos. 1986b. "Temperament and maternal employment." In Temperament and Social Interaction in Infants and Children, ed. by J. V. Lerner and Richard M. Lerner. San Francisco: Jossey-Bass.

Lerner, Jacqueline V., Christopher Hertzog, Karen A. Hooker, Makin Hassibi, and Alexander Thomas. 1988. "A longitudinal study of negative emotional states and adjustment from early childhood through adolescence." Child Development 59:356-366.

Lerner, Jacqueline V., and Richard M. Lerner (eds.). 1986. Temperament and Social Interaction in Infants and Children. San Francisco: Jossey-Bass Inc.

Lerner, Jacqueline V., and R. M. Lerner. 1983. "Temperament and adaptation across life: Theoretical and empirical issues." In Life-Span Development and Behavior, vol. 5, ed. by P. B. Baltes and O. G. Brim, Jr. New York: Academic Press.

Lerner, Richard M. 1991. "Changing organism-context relations as the basic process of development: A developmental contextual perspective." Developmental Psychology 27:27-32.

Lerner, Richard M. 1988. "Personality development: A Life-span perspective." In Child Development in Life-Span Perspective, ed. by E. M. Hetherington, R. M. Lerner, and M. Perlmutter. Hillsdale, NJ: Lawrence Erlbaum.

Lerner, Richard M. 1986. Concepts and Theories of Human Development. 2nd ed. New York: Random House.

Lerner, Richard M. 1984. On the Nature of Human Plasticity. Cambridge: Cambridge University Press.

Lerner, Richard M. 1982. "Children and adolescents as producers of their own development." Developmental Review 2:342-370.

Lerner, Richard M., and Jacqueline V. Lerner. 1987. "Children in their contexts: A goodness-of-fit model." In Parenting Across the Life Span, ed. by Jane B. Lancaster, Jeanne Altman, Alice S. Rossi, and Lennie R. Sherrod. New York: Aldine de Gruyter.

Lerner, Richard M., and N. Busch-Rossnagel (eds.). 1981. Individuals as Producers of their Own Development: A Life-span Perspective. New York: Academic Press.

Lerner, Richard M., and Graham B. Spanier (eds.). 1978. Child Influences on Marital Quality: A Life-Span Perspective. New York: Academic Press.

Levine, Sarah, and Robert A. Levine. 1985. "Age, gender, and the demographic transition: The life course in agrarian societies." In Gender and the Life Course, ed. by Alice S. Rossi. New York: Aldine.

Lewis, Michael. 1984. "Social influences on development." In Beyond the Dyad, ed. by Michael Lewis. New York: Plenum Press.

Lewis, Michael, Candice Feiring, and M. Kotsonis. 1984. "The social network of the young child." In Beyond The Dyad, ed. by Michael Lewis. New York: Plenum Press.

Lewis, Michael, and S. Lee-Painter. 1974. "An interactional approach to the mother-infant dyad." In The Effect of the Infant on Its Caregiver, ed. by M. Lewis and L. A. Rosenblum. New York: Wiley.

Lewis, Michael, and Leonard A. Rosenblum. 1974. The Effect of the Infant on Its Caregiver. New York: John Wiley.

Leyton, Elliott. 1979. The Myth of Delinquency: An Anatomy of Juvenile Nihilism. Toronto: McClelland and Stewart.

Liem, Joan H. 1974. "Effects of verbal communications of parents and children: A comparison of normal and schizophrenic families." Journal of Consulting and Clinical Psychology 42:438-450.

Lifshitz, Michaela, Ronnie Baum, Irith Balgur, and Chauna Cohen. 1975. "The impact of the social milieu upon the nature of the adoptees' emotional difficulties." Journal of Marriage and the Family 37:221-228.

Linden, Eric, and James C. Hackler. 1973. "Affective ties and delinquency" Pacific Sociological Review 16:27-46.

Lipton, Wendy L., and M. Dwayne Smith. 1983. "Explaining delinquent involvement: a consideration of the suppressor effects." Journal of Research in Crime and Delinquency 30:199-213.

Litman, Theodor. 1974. "The family as a basic unit in health and medical care: A social behavioral overview." Social Science and Medicine 8:495-519.

Litman, Theodor. 1971. "Health care and the family: A three-generation analysis." Medical Care 9:67-81.

Loeber, Rolf. 1982. "The stability of antisocial and delinquent child behavior: A review." Child Development 53:1431-1446.

Loeber, Rolf, and Magda Stouthamer-Loeber. 1986. "Family factors as correlates and predictors of juvenile conduct problems and delinquency." In Crime and Justice, vol. 7, ed. by Michael Tonry and Norval Morris. Chicago: University of Chicago Press.

Loeber, Rolf, W. Weismann, and J. B. Reid. 1983. "Family interaction of assaultive adolescents, stealers, and nondelinquents." Journal of Abnormal Child Psychology 11:1-14.

Long, Theodore E., and Jeffrey K. Hadden. 1985. "A recognition of socialization." Sociological Theory 3:39-49.

Lopez, F. G. 1986. "Family structure and depression: Implications for the counselling of depressed college students." Journal of Counseling and Development 64:508-511.

Luepnitz, Deborah. 1982. Child Custody. Lexington, MA: D. C. Heath & Co.

Luiselli, James K., Tracy P. Evans, Delma A. Boyce. 1985. "Contingency management of food sensitivity and oppositional eating in a multiply handicapped child." Journal of Clinical Child Psychology 14:153-156.

Lynn, Kenneth S. 1987. Hemingway. New York: Simon and Schuster.

Lytton, Hugh. 1980. Parent-child Interaction: The Socialization Process Observed in Twin and Singleton Families. New York: Plenum.

Lytton, Hugh. 1979. "Disciplinary encounters between young boys and their mothers and fathers. Is there a contingency system?" Developmental Psychology 15:256-268.

Lytton, Hugh. 1977. "Do parents create, or respond to, differences in twins?" Developmental Psychology 13:456-459.

Maccoby, Eleanor E., Charlene E. Depner, and Robert H. Mnookin. 1990. "Co-parenting in the second year after divorce." Journal of Marriage and the Family 52:141-155.

Maccoby, Eleanor E., and J. A. Martin. 1983. "Socialization in the context of the family: Parent-child interaction." In Handbook of Child Psychology, vol. 4, 4th ed., ed. by E. Mavis Hetherington. New York: Wiley.

MacDermid, Shelley M., Ted L. Huston, and Susan M. McHale. 1990. "Changes in marriage associated with the transition to parenthood: Individual differences as a function of sex-role attitudes and changes in the division of household labor." Journal of Marriage and the Family 52:475-486.

Mack, Judith E., and C. D. Webster, 1980. "The family phenomenon." In Autism, ed. by Christopher D. Webster, M. Mary Konstantareas, Joel Oxman, and Judith E. Mack. New York: Pergamon Press.

Madden, Denis J., and Henry T. Harbin. 1983. "Family structures of assaultive adolescents." Journal of Marital and Family Therapy 9:311-316.

Madiros, M. 1982. "Mothers of disabled children: A study of parental stress." Nursing Papers 14:47-56.

Mandell, Nancy. 1988. "The child question: Links between women and children in the family." In Reconstructing the Canadian Family: Feminist Perspectives, ed. by Nancy Mandell and Ann Duffy. Toronto: Butterworths.

Mannheim, Karl. 1952. "The problem of generations." In Essays in the Sociology of Knowledge, ed. by K. Mannheim. London: Routledge & Kegan Paul.

Martin, P. 1975. "Marital breakdown in families with Spina Bifida Cystica." Developmental Medicine and Child Neurology 17:757-764.

Matthiasson, Carolyn (ed.). 1974. Many Sisters: Women in Cross-Cultural Perspective. New York: The Free Press.

McAndrew, I. 1976. "Children with a handicap and their families." Child: Care, Health and Development 2:213-237.

McCord, Joan. 1990. "Crime in moral and social contexts—The American Society of Criminology, 1989 Presidential Address." Criminology 28:1-26.

McCord, Joan. 1982. "A longitudinal view of the relationship between paternal absence and crime." In Abnormal Offenders, Delinquency, and the Criminal Justice System, ed. by John Gunn and David P. Farrington. New York: John Wiley.

McCubbin, Hamilton, and J. M. Patterson. 1983. "Family stress and adaptation to crisis: A double ABCX model of family behavior." Family Studies Review Yearbook 1:87-97.

McKeever, Patricia T. 1982. "Siblings of chronically-ill children, a literature review with implications for research and practice." American Journal of Orthopsychiatry 53:209-218.

McLanahan, Sara. 1985. "Family structure and the reproduction of poverty." American Journal of Sociology 90:873-901.

McLanahan, Sara, and Julia A. Davis. 1989. "The effects of children on adults' psychological well-being: 1957-1976." Social Forces 68:124-146.

McMichael, Joan K. 1971. Handicap: A Study of Physically Handicapped Children and their Families. London: Staples Press.

McRobbie, H. 1982. "The politics of feminist research: Between talk, text and action." Feminist Review 12:46-57.

Mead, Margaret. 1928. Coming of Age in Samoa. New York: William Morrow.

Mendes, Helen A. 1976. "Single fatherhood." Social Work 21:308-312.

Meyer, Hans-Jürgen. 1988. "Marital and mother-child relationships: Developmental history, parent personality, and child difficultness." In Relationships Within Families: Mutual Influences, ed. by Robert A. Hinde and Joan Stevenson-Hinde. Oxford: Clarendon Press.

Meyer, John W. 1988. "The social construction of the psychology of childhood: Some contemporary processes." In Child Development in Life-Span Perspective, ed. by E. M. Hetherington, R. M. Lerner, and M. Perlmutter. Hillsdale, NJ: Lawrence Erlbaum.

Meyer, John W., F. O. Ramirez, H. A. Walker, N. Langton, and S. M. O'Connor. 1988. "The state and the institutionalization of the relations between women and children." In Feminism, Children and the New Families, ed. by S. M. Dornbusch and M. H. Strober. New York: Guilford Press.

Meyer, Philippe. 1977. L'Enfant et la Raison d'Etat. Paris: Editions de la Maison des Sciences de L'Homme.

Miller, Brent C. 1987. "Marriage, family, and fertility." In Handbook of Marriage and the Family, ed. by M. B. Sussman and S. Steinmetz. New York: Plenum Press.

Miller, Brent C., and J. Myers-Walls. 1983. "Stresses of parenting." In Stress and the Family, ed. by H. McCubbin and C. Figley. New York: Brunner-Mazel.

Miller, Brent C., and D. L. Sollie. 1980. "Normal stresses during the transition to parenthood." Family Relations 29:29-35.

Mink, Iris, and Kazuo Nihira. 1986. "Family life-styles and child behaviors: A study of direction of effects." Developmental Psychology 22:610-616.

Minton, C., J. Kagan, and J. Levine. 1971. "Maternal control and obedience in the two-year-old." Child Development 42:1873-1894.

Minturn, Leigh, and William W. Lambert. 1964. Mothers of Six Cultures: Antecedents of Child Rearing. New York: John Wiley & Sons.

Minuchin, Salvatore. 1974. Families and Family Therapy. Cambridge, MA: Harvard University Press.

Minuchin, Salvatore, Bernice L. Rosman, and Lester Baker. 1978. Psychosomatic Families: Anorexia Nervosa in Context. Cambridge: Harvard University Press.

Mishler, Elliot G., and Nancy E. Waxler. 1966. "Family interaction and schizophrenia: An approach to the experimental study of family interaction and schizophrenia." Archives of General Psychiatry 15:64-74.

Moen, Phyllis, and Donna I. Dempster-McClain. 1987. "Employed parents: Role strain, work time, and preference for working less." Journal of Marriage and the Family 49:579-590.

Montemayor, Raymond. 1986. "Family variation in parent-adolescent storm and stress." Journal of Adolescent Research 1:15-31.

Montemayor, Raymond. 1983. "Parents and adolescents in conflict: All families some of the time and some families most of the time." Journal of Early Adolescence 3:83-103.

Montemayor, Raymond, and Eric A. Hanson. 1985. "A naturalistic view of conflict between adolescents and their parents and siblings." Journal of Early Adolescence 5:83-103.

Moroney, Robert M. 1981. "Mental disability: The role of the family." In Changes in Government Policies for the Mentally Disabled, ed. by Joseph J. Bevilacqua. Cambridge, MA.: Ballinger Publ.

Moss, P., and O. Silver. 1972. Mentally handicapped school children and their families. University of Birmingham, England: Clearing House for Local Authority Social Services Research.

Mumford, Emily. 1983. Medical Sociology. Patients, Providers, and Politics. New York: Random House.

Munroe, Ruth H., Robert L. Munroe, and Beatrice Whiting. 1981. Handbook of Cross-Cultural Human Development. New York: Garland Press.

Musgrove, Frank. 1964. Youth and the Social Order. Bloomington: Indiana University Press.

Nasow, David. 1985. Children of the City: At Work and Play. Garden City, NY: Anchor Press.

Nett, Emily, 1981. "Canadian families in social-historical perspective." Canadian Journal of Sociology 6:239-260.

Newman, J. 1983. "Handicapped persons and their families: Philosophical, historical and legislative perspectives." In The Family with a Handicapped Child: Understanding and Treatment, ed. by Martin Seligman. New York: Grune and Stratton.

Nolan, T., and I. B. Pless. 1986. "Emotional correlates and consequences of birth defects." The Journal of Pediatrics 109:201-216.

Nye, F. Ivan. 1980. "A theoretical perspective on running away." Journal of Family Issues 1:274-299.

Nye, F. Ivan. 1958. Family Relationships and Delinquent Behavior. Westport, CT: Greenwood Press.

Nylander, I. 1979. "A 20-year prospective follow-up study of 2164 cases at the child guidance clinics in Stockholm." Acta Paediatrica Scandinavica 276:1-45.

O'Donnell, Lydia. 1982. "The social world of parents." Marriage and Family Review 5:9-36.

Offord, David R. 1982. "Family backgrounds of male and female delinquents." In Abnormal Offenders, Delinquency and the Criminal Justice System, ed. by John Gunn and David P. Farrington. New York: John Wiley.

Offord, David, R., N. Allen, and N. Abrams. 1978. "Parental psychiatric illness, broken homes and delinquency." Journal of the American Academy of Child Psychiatry 17:224-238.

Ogbu, John. 1987. "Cultural influence on plasticity in human development." In The Malleability of Children, ed. by James J. Gallagher and Craig T. Ramey. Baltimore: Paul H. Brookes.

Ogbu, John. 1985. "A cultural ecology of competence among inner-city blacks." In Beginnings: The Social and Affective Development of Black Children, ed. by Margaret B. Spencer, Geraldine Kerse-Brookins, and Walter R. Allen. Hillsdale, NJ: Lawrence Erlbaum.

O'Hara, Michael W., Ellen M. Zekoski, Laurie H. Phillipps, and Ellen J. Wright. 1990. "Controlled prospective study of postpartum mood disorders: Comparison of childbearing and nonchildbearing women." Journal of Abnormal Psychology 99:3-15.

Okamura, Jonathan Y. 1981. "Situational ethnicity." Ethnic and Racial Studies 4:452-465.

Opie, I., and P. Opie. 1959. The Lore and Language of School Children. London: Oxford University Press.

Osofsky, J. D. 1986. "Perspectives on infant mental health." In A Decade of Progress in Primary Prevention, ed. by Marc Kessler and Stephen E. Goldston. Hanover, NH: University Press of New England.

Owen, Margaret T., Jerry M. Lewis, and V. Kay Henderson. 1989. "Marriage, adult adjustment, and early parenting." Child Development 60:1015-1024.

Packard, Vince. 1983. Our Endangered Children. Boston: Little, Brown.

Pahl, J., and L. Quine. 1984. "Families with mentally handicapped children: A study of stress and of service response." Report Health Research Unit, University of Kent.

Palmer, Sushma, and Sue Horn. 1978. "Feeding Problems in Children." In Pediatric Nutrition in Developmental Disorder, ed. by Sushma Palmer and Shirley Ekvall. Springfield, IL: Thomas.

Parke, Ross D. 1986. "Fathers, families, and support systems." In Families of Handicapped Persons: Research, Programs, and Policy Issues, ed. by James John Gallagher and Peter M. Vietze. Baltimore: P. H. Brookes Publishing Company.

Parke, Ross D., and Barbara J. Tinsley. 1987a. "Fathers as agents and recipients of support in the postnatal period." In Research on Support for Parents and Infants in the Postnatal Period, ed. by C. F. Zachariah Boukydis. Norwood, NJ: Ablex Publishing.

Parke, Ross D., and Barbara J. Tinsley. 1987b. "Family interaction in infancy." In Handbook of Infant Development, 2nd ed., ed. by Jay D. Osofsky. New York: John Wiley & Sons.

Parr, Joy. 1980. Labouring Children. London: Croom Helm.

Parsons, Talcott. 1951. The Social System. New York: Free Press.

Parsons, Talcott, and Robert F. Bales. 1955. Socialization and Interaction Process. New York: Free Press.

Patterson, Gerald R. 1982. Coercive Family Process. Eugene, OR: Castalia.

Patterson, Gerald R. 1980. Mothers: The Unacknowledged Victims. Monographs of the Society for Research in Child Development, serial no. 186.

Patterson, Gerald R. 1976. Families of Antisocial Children: An Interactional Approach. Eugene, OR: Castalia.

Patterson, Gerald R., and Magda Stouthamer-Loeber. 1984. "The correlation of family management practices and delinquency." Child Development 55:1299-1307.

Pedersen, F. A. 1982. "Mother, father, and infant as an interactive system." In the Beginning, ed. by Jay Belsky. New York: Columbia University Press.

Peters, John F. 1988. "Gender, youth possessions, college costs, and parental assistance." Youth & Society 20:148-158.

Peters, John F. 1985. "Adolescents as socialization agents to parents." Adolescence 20:921-933.

Peterson, Gary W., and Boyd C. Rollins. 1987. "Parent-child socialization." In Handbook of Marriage and the Family, ed. by Marvin B. Sussman and Susanne K. Steinmetz. New York: Plenum Press.

Peterson, Evan T., and Phillip R. Kunz. 1975. "Parental control over adolescents according to family size." Adolescence 10:419-427.

Philp, Mark, and Derek Duckworth. 1982. Children with Disabilities and their Families. A Review of Research. Windsor, England: NFER-Nelson.

Pillemer, Karl, and David Finkelhor. 1989. "Cause of elder abuse: Caregiver stress versus problem relatives." American Journal of Orthopsychiatry 59:179-187.

Pirie, Marion. 1988. The promotion of PMS: a sociological investigation of women and the illness role. Toronto, Canada: Doctoral Dissertation, Department of Sociology, York University.

Pless, I.B., and P. Pinkerton. 1975. Chronic Childhood Disorder: Promoting Patterns of Adjustment. London: Henry Kimpton.

Postman, Neil. 1982. The Disappearance of Childhood. New York: Delacorte.

Powell, Brian, and Lola C. Steelman. 1990. "Beyond sibship size: sibling density, sex composition, and educational outcome." Social Forces 69:181-206.

Procaccini, Joseph, and Mark W. Kiefaber. 1983. Parent Burnout. Garden City, NY: Doubleday.

Purrington, Beverly T. 1980. Effects of Children on Their Parents: Parents' Perceptions. Ph.D. Dissertation. Michigan State University.

Qvortrup, Jens. 1985. "Placing children in the division of labour." In Family and Economics in Modern Society, ed. by Paul Close and Rosemary Collins. London: The Macmillan Press.

Radin, N., and R. Goldsmith. 1985. "Caregiving fathers of preschoolers: Four years later." Merrill-Palmer Quarterly 31:375-383.

Radin, N., and G. Russell. 1983. "Increased father participation and child development outcomes." In Fatherhood and Family Policy, ed. by Michael E. Lamb and A. Sage. Hillsdale, NJ: Lawrence Erlbaum.

Rankin, Joseph H. 1983. "The family context of delinquency." Social Problems 30:466-479.

Rankin, Joseph H., and L. Edward Wells. 1990. "The effect of parental attachments and direct controls on delinquency." Journal of Research in Crime and Delinquency 27:149-165.

Rausch, Jeffrey L., and David S. Janowsky. 1983. "Premenstrual tension: etiology." In Behavior and the Menstrual Cycle, ed. by Richard C. Friedman. New York: Marcel Dekker, Inc.

Raymond, Margaret E., Andrew E. Slaby, and Julian Lieb. 1975. "Familial responses to mental illness." Social Casework 56:492-498.

Reece, Shirley A., and Barbara Levin. 1968. "Psychiatric disturbances in adopted children." Social Work 13:101-111.

Reynolds, Michael. 1986. The Young Hemingway. New York: B. Blackwell.

Ricci, Carol. 1970. "Analysis of child-rearing attitudes of mothers of retarded, emotionally disturbed, and normal children." American Journal of Mental Deficiency 74:756-761.

Rich, Adrienne. 1976. Of Woman Born: Motherhood as Experience and Institution. New York: W.W. Norton.

Richards, Pamela. 1979. "Middle class vandalism and age-status conflict." Social Problems 26:482-497.

Richards, Martin P. M. 1982. "Post-divorce arrangements for children: A psychological perspective." Journal of Social Welfare Law 133-151.

Richardson, Rhonda A., R. H. Abramovitz, E. E. Asp, and A. C. Petersen. 1986. "Parent-child relationships in early adolescence: Effects of family structure." Journal of Marriage and the Family 48:805-811.

Rittenhaus, Joan D., and Judith D. Miller. 1984. "Social learning and teenage drug use — an analysis of family dyads." Health Psychology 3:329-346.

Robins, Lee N., and Kathryn Ratcliffe. 1980. "Childhood conduct disorders and later arrest." In The Social Consequences of Psychiatric Illness, ed. by Lee N. Robins, Paula J. Clayton, and John K. Wing. New York: Brunner/Mazel.

Robins, Lee N., and Kathryn S. Ratcliffe. 1979. "Risk factors in the continuation of childhood antisocial behavior into adulthood." International Journal of Mental Health 7:96-111.

Robins, Lee N. 1974. "Anti-social behavior disturbances in childhood." In The Child in His Family: Children at Psychiatric Risk, ed. by Evelyn J. Anthony and Cyrille Koupernik. London: Wiley.

Robins, Peter V., Nancy L. Mace, Mary J. Lucas. 1982. "The impact of dementia on the family." Journal of the American Medical Association 248:333-335.

Rodman, Hyman, and P. Graves. 1967. "Juvenile delinquency and the family: A review and discussion." In Juvenile Delinquency and Youth Crime, President's Commission on Law Enforcement and Administration of Justice. Task Force Report. Washington, DC: U.S. Government Printing Office.

Rogers, Carl M., and Lawrence S. Wrightsman. 1978. "Attitudes toward children's rights: Nurturance or self-determination?" Journal of Social Issues 34:59-68.

Romans-Clarkson, S. E., J. E. Clarkson, I. Dittmer, R. Flett, C. Linsell, P. E.

Mullen, and B. Mullen. 1987. "Impact of a handicapped child on the mental health of parents." British Medical Journal 293:1395-1397.

Rosen, Lawrence. 1985. "Family and delinquency: structure or function?" Criminology 23:553-573.

Rosen, Lawrence, and Kathleen Neilson. 1982. "Broken homes." In Contemporary Criminology, ed. by Leonard D. Savitz and Norman Johnston. New York: Wiley.

Rosenberg, Harriet. 1987. "Motherwork, stress, and depression: The costs of privatized social reproduction." In Feminism and Political Economy. Women's Work, Women's Struggles, ed. by H. J. Maroney and M. Luxton. Toronto: Methuen.

Rosenberg, Morris, and Leonard Pearlin. 1978. "Social class and self-esteem among children and adults." American Journal of Sociology 84:55-77.

Rosenberg, Morris, and Roberta G. Simmons. 1971. Black and White Self-Esteem: The Urban School Child. Washington, DC, American Sociological Association.

Rosenthal, K. M., and H. F. Keshet. 1981. Fathers Without Partners. Totowa, NJ: Rowman and Littlefield.

Roskies, Ethel. 1972. Abnormality and Normality. The Mothering of Thalidomide Children. Ithaca, NY: Cornell University Press.

Ross, Catherine E., John Mirowcky, and Joan Huber. 1983. "Marriage patterns and depression." American Sociological Review 48:312-317.

Ross, Helgola G., and Joel I. Milgram. 1982. "Important variables in adult sibling relationships: A qualitative study." In Sibling Relationships: Their Nature and Significance Across the Lifespan, ed. by M. E. Lamb. Hillsdale, NJ: Lawrence Erlbaum.

Rubin, Stefi, and Noreen Quinn-Curan. 1983. "Lost, then found: Parents' journey through the community service maze." In The Family with a Handicapped Child; Understanding and Treatment, ed. by Milton Seligman. New York: Grune and Stratton.

Rubin, Zick, and Jane Sloman. 1984. "How parents influence their children's friendships." In Beyond the Dyad, ed. by Michael Lewis. New York: Plenum Press.

Ruble, Diane. 1977. "Premenstrual symptoms: A reinterpretation." Science 197:291-292.

Ruddick, Sara. 1989. Maternal Thinking: Toward a Politics of Peace. Boston: Beacon Press.

Rutter, Michael. 1988. "Functions and consequences of relationships: Some psychological considerations." In Relationships Within Families: Mutual Influences, ed. by Robert A. Hinde and Joan Stevenson-Hinde. Oxford: Clarendon Press.

Rutter, Michael. 1987a. "Continuities and discontinuities from infancy." In Handbook of Infant Development, 2nd ed., ed. by Jay D. Osofsky. New York: John Wiley & Sons.

Rutter, Michael. 1987b. "Psychosocial resilience and protective mechanisms." American Journal of Orthopsychiatry 57:316-331.

Rutter, Michael. 1985. "Family and school influences on behavioural development." Journal of Child Psychology and Psychiatry 26:349-368.

Rutter, Michael. 1982. "Temperament: Concepts, issues and problems." In Temperamental Differences in Infants and Young Children. A Ciba Foundation Symposium 89, London: Pitman.

Rutter, Michael. 1981. Maternal Deprivation Reassessed, 2nd ed. Harmondsworth, England: Penguin.

Rutter, Michael. 1978. "Family, area and school influences in the genesis of conduct disorder." In Aggression and Anti-social Behaviour in Childhood and Adolescence, ed. by L. A. Hersov et al. Oxford: Pergamon.

Rutter, Michael, and H. Giller. 1983. Juvenile Delinquency: Trends and Perspectives. Harmondsworth, England: Penguin.

Rutter, Michael, D. Quinton, and C. Liddle. 1983. "Parenting in two generations: looking backwards and looking forwards." In Families at Risk, ed. by N. Madge. London: Heinemann Educational.

Rutter, Michael, J. Tizard, and K. Whitmore. 1970. Education, Health and Behaviour. London: Longmans.

Sabbeth, Barbara F., and John M. Leventhal. 1984. "Marital adjustment to chronic illness: A critique of the literature." Pediatrics 73:762-768.

Samenow, Stanton E. 1984. Inside the Criminal Mind. New York: Time Books.

Sameroff, Arnold. 1975. "Transactional models of early social relations." Human Development 18:65-79.

Sanford, Marcelline H. 1961. At the Hemingways: A Family Portrait. London: Putnam.

Saraceno, Chiara. 1984. "The social construction of childhood: Child care and education policies in Italy and the United States." Social Problems 31:351-363.

Satir, Virginia. 1983. Conjoint Family Therapy: A Guide to Theory and Technique. Palo Alto: Science and Behavior Books.

Scarr, Sandra, and Kathleen McCartney. 1983. "How people make their own environments: A theory of genotype-environment correlations." Child Development 54:424-435.

Scheck, D. C., and R. Emerick. 1976. "The young male adolescent's perception of early childrearing behavior: The differential effects of socioeconomic status and family size." Sociometry 39:39-52.

Schilling, Robert F., Steven Paul Schinke, and Maura A. Kirkham. 1985. "Coping with a handicapped child: Differences between mothers and fathers." Social Science and Medicine 21:857-863.

Schneider, Barry H. 1987. The Gifted Child in Peer Group Perspective. New York: Springer-Verlag.

Schopler, Eric, and Julie Loftin. 1969. "Thought disorders in parents of psychotic children." Archives of General Psychiatry 20:174-181.

Schorr, Lisbeth B. 1988. Within Our Reach. New York: Anchor-Doubleday.

Schreiner, Mark S., Mary E. Donar, and Robert G. Kettrick. 1987. "Pediatric home mechanical ventilation." Pediatric Clinics of North America 34:47-60.

Segal, Julius, and Herbert Yahraes. 1978. "Bringing up Mother." Psychology Today, November, 90-96.

Seitz, Victoria, Laurie K. Rosenbaum, and Nancy H. Apfel. 1985. "Effects of family support intervention: A ten-year follow-up." Child Development 56:376-391.

Seligman, Martin. 1987. "Adaptation of children to a chronically ill or mentally handicapped sibling." Canadian Medical Association Journal 136:1249-1252.

Seltzer, Judith A., Nora C. Schaeffer, and Judith S. Wallerstein. 1989. "Family ties after divorce: The relationship between visiting and paying child support." Journal of Marriage and the Family 51:1013-1032.

Senior, Neil, and Elaine Himadi. 1985. "Emotionally disturbed, adopted, in-patient adolescents." Child Psychiatry and Human Development 15:189-197.

Seywert, F. 1984. "Some critical thoughts on expressed emotion." Psychopathology 7:233-243.

Sidel, Ruth. 1986. Women and Children Last: The Plight of Poor Women in Affluent America. New York: Viking.

Siegal, Michael. 1985. Children, Parenthood, and Social Welfare in the Context of Developmental Psychology. Oxford: Clarendon Press.

Sigel, Irving E. 1983. "The ethics of intervention." In Changing Families, ed. by Irving E. Sigel. New York: Plenum.

Silbert, A. R., J. W. Newberger, and D. C. Fyler. 1982. "Marital stability and congenital heart disease." Pediatrics 69:747-750.

Silverberg, Susan B. and Laurence Steinberg. 1987. "Adolescent autonomy, parent-adolescent conflict, and parental well-being." Journal of Youth and Adolescence 16:293-312.

Simeonsson, R. J., and S. M. McHale. 1981. "Review: research on handicapped children: Sibling relationships." Child Care, Health and Development 7:153-171.

Simon, Rita J., and Howard Altstein. 1981. Transracial Adoption: A Follow-Up. Lexington, MA: D. C. Heath.

Simons, Ronald L., Les B. Whitebeck, Rand D. Conger, and Janet N. Melby. 1990. "Husband and wife differences in determinants of parenting: A social learning and exchange model of parental behavior." Journal of Marriage and the Family 52:375-392.

Skolnick, Arlene. 1980. "Children's rights, children's development." In Children's Rights and Juvenile Justice, ed. by L. T. Empey. Charlottesville: University of Virginia Press.

Skolnick, Arlene. 1978. The Intimate Environment. Boston: Little, Brown.

Smetana, Judith G. 1989. "Adolescents' and parents' reasoning about actual family conflict." Child Development 60:1052-1067.

Snow, Catherine E. 1972. "Mothers' speech to children learning language." Child Development 43:549-565.

Snyder, James J. 1977. "A reinforcement analysis of interaction in problem and nonproblem children." Journal of Abnormal Psychology 86:528-535.

Sokoloff, N. J. 1980. Between Money and Love: The Dialectics of Women's Home and Market Work. New York: Praeger.

Solnit, Albert. 1983. "Foreword." In Working with Disadvantaged Parents and their Children, ed. by Sally Provence and Audrey Naylor. New Haven: Yale University Press.

Sommerville, Charles J. 1982. The Rise and Fall of Childhood. Beverly Hills, CA: Sage Publications.

Spaniol, LeRoy, Anthony Zippie, and Stefanie Fitzgerald. 1984. "How professionals can share power with families: Practical approaches to working with families of the mentally ill." Psychosocial Rehabilitation Journal 8:77-84.

Speed, Fred, and David Appleyard. 1985. The Bright and the Gifted. Toronto: University of Toronto Guidance Centre.

Spiegel, David. 1982. "Mothering, fathering, and mental illness." In Rethinking the Family. Some Feminist Questions, ed. by Barrie Thorne and Marilyn Yalom. New York: Longman.

Spillane-Grieco, Eileen. 1984. "Feelings and perceptions of parents of runaways." Child Welfare 63:159-166.

Spinetta, J., and P. Deasy-Spinetta (eds.). 1981. Living with Childhood Cancer. St. Louis: C. V. Mosby.

Sprey, Jetse. 1979. "Conflict theory and the study of marriage and the family." In Contemporary Theories About the Family, ed. by W. R. Burr, R. Hill, T. E. Nye and I. L. Reiss. New York: MacMillan.

Spurgen, Deborah. 1984. And I Don't Want to Live This Life. New York: Fawcett Crest.

Sroufe, L. Alan. 1985. "Attachment classification from the perspective of infant-caregiver relationships and infant temperament." Child Development 56:1-14.

Stacey, M. 1985. "Women and health: The United States and the United Kingdom compared." In Women, Health and Healing: Toward a New Perspective, ed. by E. Lewis and V. Olesen. London: Tavistock.

Steinberg, Laurence D. 1988. "Reciprocal relations between parent-child distance and pubertal maturation." Developmental Psychology 24:122-128.

Steinberg, Laurence D. 1985. Adolescence. New York: Alfred A. Knopf.

Steinberg, Laurence D. 1981. "Transformations in family relations at puberty." Developmental Psychology 17:833-840.

Steinglass, Peter. 1987. The Alcoholic Family. New York: Basic Books.

Steinmetz, Suzanne K. 1981. "A cross-cultural comparison of sibling violence." International Journal of Family Psychiatry 2:337-351.

Stern, Daniel. 1977. The First Relationship: Infant and Mother. Cambridge: Harvard University Press.

Stevenson-Hinde, J., and A. E. Simpson. 1982. "Temperament and relationships." In Temperamental Differences in Infants and Young Children. Ciba Foundation Symposium 89. London: Pitman.

Stier, Serena. 1978. "Children's rights and society's duties." Journal of Social Issues 34:46-58.

Stone, Lawrence. 1977. The Family, Sex and Marriage in England 1500-1800. New York: Harper & Row.

Stott, D. H. 1966. Studies of Troublesome Children. London: Tavistock.

Stouthamer-Loeber, Magda, K. B. Schmaling, and Rolf Loeber. 1984. "The relationship of single parent family status and marital discord to antisocial child behavior." Unpublished manuscript. Pittsburgh: University of Pittsburgh, Department of Psychiatry.

Strauss, Murray, R. J. Gelles, and S. K. Steinmetz. 1980. Behind Closed Doors: Violence in the American Family. Garden City, NJ: Doubleday, Anchor Press.

Strickland, B. 1982. Perceptions of Parents and School Representatives Regarding Their Relationship Before, During, and After the Due Process Hearing. Doctoral Dissertation, University of North Carolina, Chapel Hill.

Strober, Myra H., and Sanford M. Dornbusch. 1988. "Public policy alternatives." In Feminism, Children, and New Families, ed. by S. M. Dornbusch and M. H. Strober. New York: The Guilford Press.

Strong, P. M. 1979. The Ceremonial Order of the Clinic: Parents, Doctors and Medical Bureaucracies. London: Routledge and Kegan Paul.

Super, C. M., and S. Harkness. 1981. "Figure, ground, and Gestalt: The cultural context of the active individual." In Individuals as Producers of their Development: A Life-span Perspective, ed. by R. M. Lerner and N. A. Busch-Rossnagel. New York: Academic Press.

Takanishi, Ruby. 1978. "Childhood as a social issue: Historical roots of contemporary child advocacy movements." Journal of Social Issues 34:8-28.

Tarver-Behring, Shari, and Russell A. Barkley. 1985. "The mother-child interactions of hyperactive boys and their normal siblings." American Journal of Orthopsychiatry 55:202-209.

Tavormina, J. B., J. T. Boll, N. J. Dunn, R. L. Luscomb, and J. R. Taylor. 1981. "Psychosocial effects of raising a physically handicapped child." Journal of Abnormal Child Psychology 9:121-131.

Telleen, Sharon, Allen Herzog, Teresa L. Kilbane. 1989. "Impact of a family support program on mothers' social support and parenting stress." American Journal of Orthopsychiatry 59:410-419.

Terkelsen, Kenneth G. 1983. "Schizophrenia and the family: II. Adverse effects of family therapy." Family Process 22:191-200.

Test, Mary Ann, and Leonard I. Stein. 1980. "Alternative to mental hospital treatment. III. Social cost." Archives of General Psychiatry 37:409-412.

Teyber, Edward. 1983. "Structural family relations: Primary dyadic alliances and adolescent adjustment." Journal of Marital and Family Therapy 9:89-99.

Thaxton, Lynn. 1985. "Wife abuse." In The Handbook of Family Psychology and Therapy, ed. by Luciano L'Abate. Homewood, NJ: The Dorsey Press.

Thomas, Alexander, and Stella Chess. 1981. "The role of temperament in the contributions of individuals to their development." In Individuals as Producers of their Development. A Life-Span Perspective, ed. by Richard M. Lerner and Nancy A. Busch-Rossnagel. New York: Academic Press.

Thomas, Alexander, and Stella Chess. 1980. The Dynamics of Psychosocial Development. New York: Brunner/Mazel.

Thomas, Alexander, and Stella Chess. 1977. Temperament and Development. New York: Brunner/Mazel.

Thomas, Robin B. 1986. Ventilator Dependency: Consequences for Child and Family. Unpublished Ph.D. Dissertation, University of Washington.

Thompson, Edward H., Jr., and William Doll. 1982. "The burden of families coping with the mentally ill: An invisible crisis." Family Relations 31:379-388.

Thorne, Barrie. 1987. "Revisioning women and social change: Where are the children?" Gender and Society 1:85-109.

Thorne, Barrie. 1982. "Feminist rethinking of the family: An overview." In Rethinking the Family: Some Feminist Questions, ed. by Barrie Thorne. New York: Longman.

Thurnher, Majda. 1976. "Midlife marriage: Sex differences in evolution and perspective." International Journal of Aging and Human Development 7:129-135.

Tims, Albert R., and Jonathan D. Masland. 1985. "Measurement of family communication patterns." Communication Research 12:35-58.

Tinkleman, D. G., J. Brice, G. N. Yoshida, and J. E. Sadler, Jr. 1976. "The impact of chronic asthma on the developing child: Observations made in a group setting." Annals of Allergy 37:174-179.

Tinsley, Barbara R., and Ross D. Parke. 1984. "Grandparents as support and socialization agents." In Beyond the Dyad, ed. by Michael Lewis. New York: Plenum Press.

Tolan, Patrick. 1988. "Socioeconomic, family and social stress correlates of adolescent antisocial and delinquent behavior." Journal of Abnormal Child Psychology 16:317-331.

Traughber, B., K. E. Erwin, T. R. Risley, J. F. Schnelle. 1983. "Behavioral nutrition: An evaluation of a simple system for measuring food and nutrient consumption." Behavioral Assessment 5:263-280.

Travis, G. 1976. Chronic Illness in Children, Its Impact on Child and Family. Stanford: Stanford University Press.

Trojanowicz, Robert C., and Merry Morash. 1987. Juvenile Delinquency: Concepts and Control. 4th ed. Englewood Cliffs, NJ: Prentice-Hall.

Tyler, Nancy B., and Kate L. Kogan. 1977. "Reduction of stress between mothers and their handicapped children." American Journal of Occupational Therapy 31:151-155.

Umberson, Debra. 1989. "Relationships with children: Explaining parents' psychological well-being." Journal of Marriage and the Family 51:999-1012.

Umberson, Debra, and Walter R. Gove. 1989. "Parenthood and psychological well-being: Theory, measurement, and stage in the family life course." Journal of Family Issues 10:440-462.

Vaillant, George E., and Caroline O. Vaillant. 1990. "Natural history of male psychological health, XII: A 45-year study of predictors of successful aging at age 65." American Journal of Psychiatry 149:31-37.

Vaughn, C. E., and J. P. Leff. 1976. "The influence of family and social factors on the course of psychiatric illness: A comparison of schizophrenic and depressed neurotic patients." British Journal of Psychiatry 129:125-137.

Veroff, Joseph, Richard A. Kulka, and Elizabeth Douvan. 1981. Mental Health in America: Patterns of Help-seeking from 1957 to 1976. New York: Basic Books.

Vinokur-Kaplan, D. 1977. "Family planning decision making: A comparison and analysis of parents' considerations." Journal of Comparative Family Studies 8:79-98.

Voysey, Margaret. 1975. A Constant Burden: The Reconstitution of Family Life. London: Routledge and Kegan Paul.

Waggener, Ellen L. 1980. Social and psychological influences on premenstrual tension. Cincinatti, Ohio: Doctoral Dissertation, Department of Nursing, University of Cincinatti.

Wahler, Robert. 1975. "Some structural effects of deviant child behavior." Journal of Applied Behavior Analysis 8:27-49.

Wallerstein, Judith S., and Sandra Blakeslee. 1989. Second Chances. New York: Ticknor & Fields.

Wallerstein, Judith S., S. B. Corbin, and J. M. Lewis. 1988. "Children of divorce: A ten-year study." In Impact of Divorce, Single-Parenting, and Stepparenting on Children, ed. by E. Mavis Hetherington and Josephine D. Arasteh. Hillsdale NJ: Lawrence Erlbaum.

Wallman, Sandra. 1979. Ethnicity at Work. London: Macmillan.

Walters, James, and Lynda H. Walters. 1980. "Parent-child relationships: A review, 1970-1979." Journal of Marriage and the Family 42:807-827.

Walters, James, and N. Sinnett. 1971. "Parent-child relationships: A decade review of research." Journal of Marriage and the Family 33:70-111.

Wateska, L. P., L. L. Sattler, and E. Steiger. 1980. "Cost of a home parenteral nutrition program." Journal of the American Medical Association 244:2303-2304.

Waxler, N. E. 1974. "Parent and child effects on cognitive performance: An experimental approach to the etiological and responsive theories of schizophrenia." Family Process 13:1-22.

Webster-Stratton C., and S. Eyberg. 1982. "Child temperament: Relationship with child behavior problems and parent-child interaction." Journal of Clinical Child Psychiatry 11:123-129.

Weiner, J. P., and P. Boss. 1985. "Exploring gender bias against women: Ethics for marriage and family therapy." Counselling and Values 30:9-23.

Weis, Joseph G., and John Sederstrom. 1981. The Prevention of Serious Delinquency: What to Do? Washington, DC: U.S. Government Printing Office.

Weisner, Thomas S. 1984. "The social economy of childhood. A cross-cultural view." In Beyond the Dyad, ed. by Michael Lewis. New York: Plenum Press.

Weisner, Thomas S., R. Gallimore, and R. Tharp. 1982. "Concordance between ethnographer and folk perspectives: Observed performance and self-ascription of sibling caretaking roles." Human Organization 41:237-244.

Weiss, Heather B. 1989. "State family support and education programs: Lessons from the Pioneers." American Journal of Orthopsychiatry 59:32-48.

Weissbourd, Bernice, and Sharon L. Kagan. 1989. "Family support programs: Catalysts for change." American Journal of Orthopsychiatry 59:20-31.

Weissbourd, Bernice. 1983. "The family support movement: Greater than the sum of its parts." Zero to Three 4:8-10.

Weitzman, Lenore J. 1988. "Women and children last: The social and economic consequences of divorce law reforms." In Feminism, Children, and the New Families, ed. by Sanford M. Dornbusch and Myra H. Strober. New York: Guilford Press.

Weitzman, Lenore J. 1985. The Divorce Revolution: The Unexpected Social and Economic Consequences for Women and Children in America. New York: The Free Press.

Wentworth, William M. 1980. Context and Understanding: An Inquiry Into Socialization Theory. New York: Elsevier.

Werner, Emmy E. 1989. "High-risk children in young adulthood: A longitudinal study from birth to 32 years." American Journal of Orthopsychiatry 59:72-81.

West, Donald J. 1982. Delinquency: Its Roots, Careers and Prospects. London: Heinemann Educational.

West, Donald J., and D. P. Farrington. 1977. The Delinquent Way of Life. New York: Crane Russak.

Whalen, Carol K., and Barbara Henker. 1980. "The social ecology of psychostimulant treatment: A model for conceptual and empirical analysis." In Hyperactive Children. The Social Ecology of Identification and Treatment, ed. by C. K. Whalen and B. Henker. New York: Academic Press.

White, Burton L. 1975. The First Three Years of Life. Englewood Cliffs, NJ: Prentice-Hall.

White, Lynn K., Alan Booth, and John N. Edwards. 1986. "Children and marital happiness: Why the negative correlation?" Journal of Family Issues 7:131-147.

White, Lynn K., and Alan Booth. 1985. "The quality and stability of remarriages: The role of stepchildren." American Sociological Review 50:689-698.

White, Lynn K., and David B. Brinkerhoff. 1981. "Children's work in the family: Its significance and meaning." Journal of Marriage and the Family 43:789-800.

Wikler, Lynn. 1983. "Chronic stresses of families of mentally retarded children." Family Studies Review Yearbook 1:143-150.

Wikler, Lynn. 1981. "Chronic stresses of families of mentally retarded children." Family Relations 30:281-288.

Wilkin, D. 1981. "A task oriented approach to the assessment of the distribution of the burden of care, levels of support and felt needs in the family." In Assessing the Handicaps and Needs of Mentally Retarded Children, ed. by B. Cooper. London: Academic Press.

Wilkinson, Doris. 1987. "Ethnicity." In Handbook of Marriage and the Family, ed. by M. B. Sussman and S. K. Steinmetz. New York: Plenum Press.

Wilkinson, Karen, B., Grant Stitt, and Maynard L. Erickson. 1982. "Siblings and delinquent behavior." Criminology 20:223-240.

Wilson, Anne. 1984. "'Mixed race' children in British Society: Some theoretical considerations." British Journal of Sociology 35:42-61.

Wilson, Anne. 1981a. "Mixed race children: An explanatory study of racial categorization." New Community 9:36-43.

Wilson, Anne. 1981b. "In-between: The mother in the inter-racial family." New Community 9:208-215.

Windle, M., and R. M. Lerner. 1986. "The 'goodness of fit' model of temperament-content relations: Interaction or correlation?" In Temperament and Social Interaction in Infants and Children: New Directions for Child Development, ed. by R. Porter and G. M. Collins. San Francisco: Jossey-Bass.

Wineberg, Howard. 1990. "Childbearing after remarriage." Journal of Marriage and the Family 52:31-38.

Witt, Reni L., and Jeannine Masterson-Michael. 1983. What Every Woman Should Know About Premenstrual Tension. New York: Stein and Day.

Wolking, S. N., and W. De Salis. 1982. "Infant temperament, maternal mental state and child behaviour problems." In Temperamental Differences in Infants and Young Children. Ciba Foundation Symposium 89. London: Pitman.

Work, Henry H., and Hans Anderson. 1971. "Studies in adoption requests for psychiatric treatment." American Journal of Psychiatry 127:948-950.

Yoshida, Roland, Kathleen Fenton, Martin J. Kaufman, and James P. Maxwell. 1978. "Parental involvement in the special education pupil planning process: The school's perspective." Exceptional Children 44:531-533.

Youniss, James, and Jacqueline Smollar. 1985. Adolescent Relations with Mothers, Fathers, and Friends. Chicago: University of Chicago Press.

Zelizer, Viviana A.R. 1985. Pricing the Priceless Child: The Changing Social Value of Children. New York: Basic Books.

Zigler, Edward, and W. Berman. 1983. "Discerning the future of early childhood intervention." American Psychologist 38:894-906.

Zigler, Edward, and Kathryn B. Black. 1989. "America's family support movement: Strengths and limitations." American Journal of Orthopsychiatry 59:6-19.

Zigler, Edward, and Heather B. Weiss. 1985. "Family support system: An ecological approach to child development." In Children, Youth, and Families: The Action-Research Relationship, ed. by R. Rapoport. Cambridge: Cambridge University Press.

Zill, Nicholas. 1988. "Behavior, achievement, and health problems among children in stepfamilies: Findings from a national survey of child health." In Impact of Divorce, Single-parenting, and Stepparenting on Children, ed. by E. Mavis Hetherington and Josephine D. Arasteh. Hillsdale, NJ: Lawrence Erlbaum.

Subject Index

Author Index